Table of Contents

Preface

For many years, grantseekers using Foundation Center libraries, our web site, and print and electronic directories have been asking us for help beyond research into potential funders for their work. They need assistance in writing the proposal and advice on the proper way to submit it, given the widely differing policies and preferences among foundations and corporate grantmakers. To respond to this demand, in 1993 we commissioned Jane C. Geever and Patricia McNeill of the firm J. C. Geever, Inc., to write a guide for us, based on their many years of fundraising experience and knowledge of a great variety of grantmakers. Several editions followed, and the *Guide* as well as seminars we offer based on the advice herein have proven very popular with our audiences. This fifth edition includes responses to a series of interview questions by 40 grantmakers and excerpts from actual proposals to illustrate the text.

We hope this guide to proposal writing proves useful to all of you who are seeking grants, and we would welcome your comments and reactions to it.

We wish to thank the following grantmakers who participated in the interviews for their time and the valuable insights they provided:

Karen Topakian, Executive Director
Agape Foundation
San Francisco, CA

Karen L. Rosa, Vice President and
    Executive Director
Altman Foundation
New York, NY

Michele Pritchard, Grants Administrator
The Peyton Anderson Foundation, Inc.
Macon, GA

Carol Kurzig, Vice President and
    Executive Director
Avon Foundation
New York, NY

Julie Brooks, Grants Administrator
Anne Corriston, Program Director
John Williams, Program Director
John S. and James L. Knight Foundation
Miami, FL

Christine Park, President
Lucent Technologies Foundation
Murray Hill, NJ

Bruce Esterline, Vice President, Grants
The Meadows Foundation, Inc.
Dallas, TX

Rick Moyers, Program Officer
Eugene and Agnes E. Meyer
   Foundation
Washington, DC

Maria Mottola, Executive Director
New York Foundation
New York, NY

Nancy Wiltsek, Executive Director
The Pottruck Family Foundation
San Francisco, CA

Rene Deida, Program Officer
The Prudential Foundation
Newark, NJ

Marilyn Hennessy, President
The Retirement Research Foundation
Chicago, IL

David Ford, Executive Director
Richard and Susan Smith Family Foundation
Chestnut Hill, MA

Danah Craft, First Vice President,
Community/Government Affairs
SunTrust Bank, Atlanta Foundation
Atlanta, GA

Vincent Stehle, Program Officer
Jonathan Goldberg, Grants Administrator and
   Manager of Information Systems
Surdna Foundation, Inc.
New York, NY

E. Belvin Williams, Trustee
Turrell Fund
Montclair, NJ

We also wish to thank the following nonprofit organizations whose leaders graciously permitted us to use excerpts from their proposals to illustrate the text:

The Ali Forney Center
New York, NY
Carl Siciliano, Executive Director

Arts & Business Council of Miami
Miami Beach, FL
Laura Bruney, Executive Director

Careers Through Culinary Arts
New York, NY
Michael Osso, Executive Director

Center for Alternative Sentencing and
   Employment Services
New York, NY
Joel Copperman, CEO/President

Center for Black Women's Wellness
Atlanta, GA
Jamea Smith, Chief Executive Officer

The Children's Institute
Verona, NJ
Bruce Ettinger, Executive Director

Common Ground
New York, NY
Roseanne Haggerty, President

Dress For Success Atlanta
Atlanta, GA
Elizabeth Kelly, Executive Director

East Side House
Bronx, NY
John Sanchez, Co-founder and
    Executive Director

Groundwork
Brooklyn, NY
Richard R. Buery, Executive Director

Highbridge
Bronx, NY
Brother Edward Phelan, Executive Director

King Manor Association of Long Island
Jamaica, NY
Mary Anne Mrozinski, Executive Director

National Industries for the Blind
Alexandria, VA
Karen Pal, Director, Business Leaders
    Program

Neighbors Together
Brooklyn, NY
Ed Fowler, Executive Director

Next Generation
San Anselmo, CA
Roni Krouzman, Founding Executive
    Director

Operation Exodus Inner City
New York, NY
Mathew Mahoney, Director

Ronald McDonald House of New York City
New York, NY
William Sullivan, President and CEO

St. Ann School
Flushing, NY
Robert DiNardo, Principal

Sponsors for Educational Opportunity
New York, NY
William Goodloe, President

South Asian Youth Action
Elmhurst, NY
Annetta Seecharran, Executive Director

WomensLaw.org
Brooklyn, NY
Elizabeth Martin, Executive Director

Youth Ensemble Atlanta
Atlanta, GA
Deborah Barber, Executive Director

From the Author

Proposal writing is essential to the fundraising process, but it can be intimidating for the novice. There is nothing worse than staring at a blank piece of paper or computer screen with the sinking feeling that so much is riding on the prose you must create. Yet, if you follow the step-by-step process described in this book, you can create a proposal with a minimum of anxiety.

Take the steps one at a time. You will be successful in writing exciting and compelling proposals, proposals that will capture the interest of foundations and corporations, proposals that will generate grant support for your nonprofit organization.

In preparing this book, I interviewed a cross section of foundation and corporate representatives to find out their current thoughts on what should go into a proposal. While this material reinforces the steps I describe for writing a proposal, it also presents some notable insights into how grantmakers do their work, the challenges facing funders today, and how they are responding. These insights are a distinguishing feature of this book: They show the reality of the fundraising process from the funder's side of the proposal.

The 40 funding representatives interviewed include a geographic mix of local and national grantmakers, as well as representatives of independent, corporate, and community foundations and grantmaking public charities. Some of the funders represented have been in existence for many years. Others are fairly new. One foundation does not have paid staff; some have at least one person on staff; others employ many people.

While the grantmakers interviewed reflect a relatively broad spectrum, it is important to remember that there are close to 68,000 grantmaking private and community foundations in the United States. The majority of these have no staff and in fact are so small that the few local grants they award each year can be handled by trustees, lawyers, or family members. Therefore, the comments made here do not necessarily apply to all funders, but they do provide an indication of how some of the larger funders operate and how they evaluate the proposals they receive.

A series of questions was designed for the interview sessions in order to elicit views not only on proposal writing but also on the entire funding process and particularly on the impact of the economy on this process. Interviews were conducted via the telephone, following a questionnaire format. Questions were posed as to desired proposal contents, layout, length, and presentation. Funders were asked how proposals captured and kept their attention, what the characteristics of a successful proposal are, and what red flags are raised when they read proposals. Discussion ensued about their due diligence and the proposal review process. They weighed in on follow-up strategies once an agency receives a grant and whether, and how, to resubmit a rejected proposal. They were also asked to describe trends they perceived in the current funding climate.

Information and quotes gleaned from these interviews are used throughout the text. Chapter 14, "What the Funders Have to Say," reflects the substance of the interviews. Here, the reader will find specific questions asked of each grantmaking representative with some of their responses. The goal in presenting this information is distinctly not to help the reader learn about particular funders but rather to provide a more general sense of grantmakers' perspectives on proposal writing. The funders interviewed have spoken frankly. They have all granted permission to the Foundation Center to use their quotes.

Acknowledgments

I would like to express appreciation to the staff of J. C. Geever, Inc., particularly to Cheryl Austin, who helped prepare the manuscript, and to Judith Margolin, Heather O'Neil, Elizabeth Chiappa, Jimmy Tom, and Christine Johnson of the Foundation Center who saw this guide through production.

Introduction

If you are reading this book, you probably have already decided that foundations should be part of your fundraising strategy. You should be aware that, together, foundations and corporations provide only 16.8 percent of private gift support to nonprofit institutions [*Giving USA 2006*, published by the Giving USA Foundation]. Their support, however, can be extremely important in augmenting other forms of income, in permitting major new initiatives, or simply in promoting the mission of your agency.

Since the early 1990s, the number of foundations has more than doubled, while their assets and giving have more than tripled. In 2004, foundations held combined assets of over \$510 billion. For 2005, their estimated giving totaled close to \$34 billion. Over the next several years, foundations will likely experience continued growth in their resources, although gains will be far more modest than those seen during the boom years of the late 1990s.

Unfortunately, competition for these grant dollars has also increased. Many nonprofits were created to respond to new or heightened social needs during the 1990s. In the early 21st century some of these nonprofit organizations have fallen by the wayside or merged with other similar organizations. Cutbacks in government funding for nonprofit services and activities have meant that many groups that previously relied primarily on government funds are now turning to private sources to support their work. Meanwhile, private foundations have experienced significant reductions in their own assets due to stock market losses. In comparison with the figures for foundation giving, according to the Giving USA Foundation, giving by living individuals was \$199.07 billion in 2005, more than six times that of foundations. (Bequests totaled an additional \$17.44 billion.) What you need to attract donors to your agency is a comprehensive fundraising strategy that includes a variety of sources and approaches. This book focuses on how to create proposals to win foundation and corporate support. You will want to tell your story clearly, keeping the interests of those you are approaching in mind. You need to recognize the potential for partnership with those you are approaching.

The Proposal Is Part of a Process

The subject of this book is proposal writing. But the proposal does not stand alone. It must be part of a process of planning and of research on, outreach to, and cultivation of potential foundation and corporate donors.

This process is grounded in the conviction that a partnership should develop between the nonprofit and the donor. When you spend a great deal of your time seeking money, it is hard to remember that it can also be difficult to give money away. In fact, the dollars contributed by a foundation or corporation have no value until they are attached to solid programs in the nonprofit sector.

This truly *is* an ideal partnership. The nonprofits have the ideas and the capacity to solve problems, but no dollars with which to implement them. The foundations and corporations may have the financial resources but not necessarily the other resources needed to create programs. Bring the two together effectively, and the result is a dynamic collaboration. Frequently, the donor is transformed into a stakeholder in the grantee organization, becoming deeply interested and involved in what transpires.

Karen Topakian of the Agape Foundation says: "We're not your parents. I'm not going to yell at you if you don't do something. I'm not going to be disappointed in you. We're your colleagues and your peers. We'll treat you in a professional manner and expect the same in return. We're definitely in this together." E. Belvin Williams of the Turrell Fund adds: "This is a relationship of trust. Nonprofits should come across honestly and candidly. Don't pull the wool over our eyes. Be honest about what you are saying. Don't embellish or gloss over it. Don't tell us what you think we want to hear. Be convinced about the worthiness of your work. All we are doing is giving the money."

You need to follow a step-by-step process in the search for private dollars. As Nancy Wiltsek of the Pottruck Family Foundation admonished us in the past, "Abide by the process!" It takes time and persistence to succeed. After you have written a proposal, it could take a year or more to obtain the funds needed to carry it out. And even a perfectly written proposal submitted to the right prospect might be rejected for any number of reasons.

Raising funds is an investment in the future. Your aim should be to build a network of foundation and corporate funders, many of which give small gifts on a fairly steady basis, and a few of which give large, periodic grants. By doggedly pursuing the various steps of the process, each year you can retain most of your regular supporters and strike a balance with the comings and goings of larger donors. The distinctions between support for basic, ongoing operations and special projects are discussed elsewhere in this book. For now, keep in mind that corporate givers and small family foundations tend to be better prospects for annual support than the larger, national foundations.

The recommended process is not a formula to be rigidly adhered to. It is a suggested approach that can be adapted to fit the needs of any nonprofit and the peculiarities of each situation. Fundraising is an art, not a science. You must bring your own creativity to it and remain flexible.

An example might help. It is recommended that you attempt to speak with the potential funder prior to submitting your proposal. The purpose of your call is to test your hypothesis gleaned from your research about the potential match between your nonprofit organization and the funder. Board member assistance, if you are fortunate enough to have such contacts, ordinarily would not come into play until a much later stage. But what do you do if a board member indicates that his law partner is chairman of the board of a foundation you plan to approach? He offers to submit the proposal directly to his partner. You could refuse the offer and plod through the next steps, or you could be flexible in this instance, recognizing that your agency's likelihood of being funded by this foundation might have just risen dramatically. Don't be afraid to take the risk.

Recognizing the importance of the process to the success of your agency's quest for funds, let's take a look at each step.

Step One: Setting Funding Priorities

In the planning phase, you need to map out all of your agency's priorities, whether or not you will seek foundation or corporate grants for them. Ideally these priorities are determined in an annual planning session. The result of the meeting should be a solid consensus on the funding priorities of your organization for the coming year. Before seeking significant private sector support, you need to decide which of your organization's funding priorities will translate into good proposals. These plans or projects are then developed into funding proposals, and they form the basis of your foundation and corporate donor research.

Step Two: Drafting the Basic Proposal

You should have at least a rough draft of your proposal in hand before you proceed, so that you can be really clear about what you'll be asking funders to support. In order to develop this core proposal, you will need to assemble detailed background information on the project, select the proposal writer, and write the actual components of the document, including the executive summary, statement of need, project description, budget, and organizational information.

Step Three: Packaging the Proposal

At this juncture you have laid the groundwork for your application. You have selected the projects that will further the goals of your organization. You have written the basic proposal, usually a "special project" proposal, or a variation, such as one for a capital campaign or endowment fund.

Before you can actually put the document together and get it ready to go out the door, you will need to tailor your basic proposal to the specific funder's priorities. When you have taken that step, you will need to add a cover letter and, where appropriate, an appendix, paying careful attention to the components of the package and how they are put together.

Step Four: Researching Potential Funders

You are now ready to identify those sources that are most likely to support your proposal. You will use various criteria for developing your list, including the funders' geographic focus and their demonstrated interest in the type of project for which you are seeking funds. This research process will enable you to prepare different finished proposal packages based on the guidelines of specific funders.

Step Five: Contacting and Cultivating Potential Funders

This step saves you unnecessary or untimely submissions. Taking the time to speak with a funder about your organization and your planned proposal submission sets the tone for a potentially supportive future relationship, *if* they show even a glimmer of interest in your project. This step includes judicious use of phone and/or e-mail communication, face-to-face meetings, board contacts, and written updates and progress reports. Each form of cultivation is extremely important and has its own place in the fundraising process. Your goal in undertaking this cultivation is to build a relationship with the potential donor and to communicate important information while your request is pending. Persistent cultivation keeps your agency's name in front of the foundation or corporation. By helping the funder learn more about your group and its programs, you make it easier for them to come to a positive response on your proposal—or, failing that, to work with you in the future.

Step Six: Responding to the Result

No matter what the decision from the foundation or corporation, you must assume responsibility for taking the next step. If the response is positive, good follow-up is critical to turning a mere grant into a true partnership.

Unfortunately, even after you have followed all of the steps in the process, statistically the odds are that you will learn via the mail or a phone call that your request was denied. Follow-up is important here, too, either to find out if you might try again at another time or with another proposal or to learn how to improve your chances of getting your proposal funded by others.

1

Getting Started: Establishing a Presence and Setting Funding Priorities

Every nonprofit organization needs to raise money. That is a given. Yet some nonprofits believe that their group must look special or be doing something unique before they are in a position to approach foundations and corporate grantmakers for financial support. This assumption is mistaken. If your organization is meeting a valid need, you are more than likely ready to seek foundation or corporate support.

But three elements should already be in place. First, your agency should have a written mission statement. Second, your organization should have completed the process of officially acquiring nonprofit status, or you need to have identified an appropriate fiscal agent to receive the funds on your behalf. Finally, you should have credible program or service achievements or plans in support of your mission.

Mission Statement

When your agency was created, the founders had a vision of what the organization would accomplish. The mission statement is the written summary of that vision. It is the global statement from which all of your nonprofit's programs and services flow. Such a statement enables you to convey the excitement of the purpose of your nonprofit, especially to a potential funder who has not previously heard of your work. Of course, for you to procure a grant, the foundation or corporation must agree that the needs being addressed are important ones.

1

Acquiring Nonprofit Status

The agency should be incorporated in the state in which you do business. In most states this means that you create bylaws and have a board of directors. It is easy to create a board by asking your close friends and family members to serve. A more effective board, though, will consist of individuals who care about the cause and are willing to work to help your organization achieve its goals. They will attend board meetings, using their best decision-making skills to build for success. They will actively serve on committees. They will support your agency financially and help to raise funds on its behalf. Potential funders will look for this kind of board involvement.

In the process of establishing your nonprofit agency, you will need to obtain a designation from the federal Internal Revenue Service that allows your organization to receive tax-deductible gifts. This designation is known as 501(c)(3) status. A lawyer normally handles this filing for you. Legal counsel can be expensive. However, some lawyers are willing to provide free help or assistance at minimal cost to organizations seeking 501(c)(3) status from the IRS.

Once your nonprofit has gone through the filing process, you can accept tax-deductible gifts. If you do not have 501(c)(3) status and are not planning to file for it in the near future, you can still raise funds. You will need to find another nonprofit with the appropriate IRS designation willing to act as a fiscal agent for grants received by your agency. How does this work? Primary contact will be between your organization and the funder. The second agency, however, agrees to be responsible for handling the funds and providing financial reports. The funder will require a formal written statement from the agency serving as fiscal agent. Usually the fiscal agent will charge your organization a fee for this service.

Credible Programs

Potential funders will want to know about programs already in operation. They will invest in your agency's future based on your past achievements. You will use the proposal to inform the funder of your accomplishments, which should also be demonstrable if an on-site visit occurs.

If your organization is brand new or the idea you are proposing is unproven, the course you plan to take must be clear and unambiguous. Your plan must be achievable and compelling. The expertise of those involved must be relevant. Factors such as these must take the place of a track record when one does not yet exist. Funders are often willing to take a risk on a new idea, but be certain that you can document the importance of the idea and the strength of the plan.

Like people, foundations have different levels of tolerance for risk. Some will invest in an unknown organization because the proposed project looks particularly innovative. Most, however, want assurance that their money is going to an agency with strong leaders who have proven themselves capable of implementing the project described in the proposal.

What really makes the difference to the potential funder is that your nonprofit organization has a sense of direction and is implementing, or has concrete plans to implement, programs that matter in our society. You have to be able to visualize exciting programs and to articulate them via your proposal. Once you've got these three elements in place, you're ready to raise money from foundations and corporations!

Setting Funding Priorities

Once your organization has established a presence, the first step of the proposal process is determining the priorities of your organization. Only after you do that can you select the right project or goals to turn into a proposal.

Your Priorities

There is one rule in this process: You must start with your organization's needs and then seek funders that will want to help with them. Don't start with a foundation's priorities and try to craft a project to fit them. Chasing the grant dollar makes little sense from the perspectives of fundraising, program design, or agency development.

When you develop a program tailored to suit a donor, you end up with a project that is critically flawed. First, in all likelihood the project will be funded only partially by the grant you receive. Your organization is faced with the dilemma of how to fund the rest of it. Further, it will likely be hard to manage the project as part of your total program without distorting your other activities. Scarce staff time and scarcer operating funds might have to be diverted from the priorities you have already established. At worst, the project might conflict with your mission statement.

Start with a Planning Session

A planning session is an excellent way to identify the priorities for which you will seek foundation grants and to obtain agencywide consensus on them. Key board members, volunteers, and critical staff, if your agency has staff, should come together for a several-hour discussion. Such a meeting will normally occur when the budget for the coming fiscal year is being developed. In any case, it cannot be undertaken until the overall plan and priorities for your organization are established.

The agenda for the planning session is simple. With your organization's needs and program directions clearly established, determine which programs, needs, or activities can be developed in proposal form for submission to potential funders.

Apply Fundability Criteria

Before moving ahead with the design of project proposals, test them against a few key criteria:

1. *The money cannot be needed too quickly.* It takes time for funders to make a decision about awarding a grant. If the foundation or corporate grantmaker does not know your agency, a cultivation period will probably be necessary.

   A new program can take several years to be fully funded, unless specific donors have already shown an interest in it. If your new program needs to begin immediately, foundation and corporate donors might not be logical sources to pursue. You should begin with other funding, from individuals, churches, or civic groups, from earned income, or from your own operating budget, or else you should delay the start-up until funding is secured from a foundation or corporate grantmaker.

   A project that is already in operation and has received foundation and corporate support stands a better chance of attracting additional funders within a few months of application. Your track record will provide a new funder with an easy way to determine that your nonprofit can deliver results.

2. *Specific projects tend to be of greater interest to most foundation and corporate funders than are general operating requests.* This fundraising fact of life can be very frustrating for nonprofits that need dollars to keep their doors open and their basic programs and services intact. There is no doubt, though, that it is easier for the foundation or corporate funder to make a grant when the trustees will be able to see precisely where the money is going, and the success of their investment can be more readily assessed.

Keep in mind the concerns of the foundation and corporate funders about this question when you are considering how to develop your proposals for them. You may have to interpret the work of your organization according to its specific functions. For example, one nonprofit agency uses volunteers to advocate in the courts on behalf of children in the foster care system. Its goal is to bring about permanent solutions to the children's situations. When this agency first secured grants from foundations and corporations, it did so for general support of its program. Finding supporters reluctant to continue providing general support once the program was launched, the staff began to write proposals for specific aspects of the agency's work, such as volunteer recruitment, volunteer training, and advocacy, thus making it easier for donors to continue to fund ongoing, core activities.

Some foundations do give general operating support. You will use the print and electronic directories, web sites, annual reports, the foundations' own 990-PFs, and other resources described elsewhere in this book to target those that are true candidates for operating and annual support requests, if you find that your funding priorities cannot be packaged into projects. Alternatively, your general operating dollars *might* have to come from non-foundation sources.

3. ***Support from individual donors and/or government agencies might be better sources for some of the priorities you are seeking to fund.*** Moreover, having a diverse base of funding support is beneficial to the financial well-being of your nonprofit agency and is important to foundation and corporate prospects. They look for the sustainability of organizations beyond receipt of their own gifts. Foundation and corporation support usually will not take the place of support from individuals in the form of personal gifts raised via face-to-face solicitation, special events, direct mail, and/or by earned income in the form of fees or dues.

You know the priorities of your organization. You have determined which ones should be developed for submission to foundations and corporations in the form of a proposal. You are now ready to move on to the proposal-writing step.

2

Developing the Proposal: Preparation, Tips on Writing, Overview of Components

One advantage of preparing your proposal before you approach any funders is that all of the details will have been worked out. You will have the answers to just about any question posed to you about this project.

You can then take steps to customize your basic proposal with a personalized cover letter and revisions or adjustments to the document to reflect the overlapping interests of each particular grantmaker and your nonprofit. If a prospective funder requires a separate application form, it will be much easier to respond to the questions once you have your basic proposal all worked out.

Gathering Background Information

The first thing you will need to do in writing your proposal is to gather the documentation for it. You will require background documentation in three areas: concept, program, and expenses.

If all of this information is not readily available to you, determine who will help you gather each type of information. If you are part of a small nonprofit with no staff, a knowledgeable board member will be the logical choice. If you are in a larger agency, there should be program and financial support staff who can help you. Once you know with whom to talk, identify the questions to ask.

This data-gathering process makes the actual writing much easier. And by involving other stakeholders in the process, it also helps key people within your agency seriously consider the project's value to the organization.

CONCEPT

It is important that you have a good sense of how the project fits into the philosophy and mission of your agency. The need that the proposal is addressing must also be documented. These concepts must be well articulated in the proposal. Funders want to know that a project reinforces the overall direction of an organization, and they might need to be convinced that the case for the project is compelling. You should collect background data on your organization and on the need to be addressed so that your arguments are well documented.

PROGRAM

Here is a checklist of the program information you require:

- the nature of the project and how it will be conducted;
- the timetable for the project;
- the anticipated outcomes and how best to evaluate the results; and
- staffing and volunteer needs, including deployment of existing staff and new hires.

EXPENSES

You will not be able to pin down all of the expenses associated with the project until the program details and timing have been worked out. Thus, the main financial data gathering takes place after the narrative part of the proposal has been written. However, at this stage you do need to sketch out the broad outlines of the budget to be sure that the costs are in reasonable proportion to the outcomes you anticipate. If it appears that the costs will be prohibitive, even anticipating a foundation grant, you should then scale back your plans or adjust them to remove the least cost-effective expenditures.

Deciding Who Will Write the Proposal

While gathering data, you can make the decision about who will actually write the document. You might decide to ask someone else to draft it for you. This is a tough decision. If the obvious staff member you identify to write the first draft will have to put aside some other major task, it might not be cost-effective for the agency, and you might consider whether someone else on staff is a skilled writer or a willing learner and could be freed up from routine assignments.

If you lack a staff member with the skills and time to take on the task, a volunteer or board member might be an excellent alternative. You will need to identify someone who knows the agency and writes well. You will spend substantial time with this person, helping to describe the kind of document you want. In the long run, this can be time well spent, because you now have identified a willing and skilled volunteer proposal writer.

If you have found your writer on staff or among your volunteer ranks, you are all set. The information for the proposal has been gathered, and work can commence. Should you fail to find someone this way, then an outsider will be needed. Bear in mind, before you choose this option, that the most successful proposals are often "homegrown," even if they aren't perfect. A too-slick proposal obviously written by an outsider can be a real turnoff to funders.

On the other hand, while someone inside your agency will always know your organization better than a consultant, an outsider can bring objectivity to the process and may write more easily, especially with the data gathering already complete. Once the decision is made to use a consultant, you will need to make a list of prospective consultants, interview the leading candidates, check references, and make your selection.

You and the consultant will develop a contract that adequately reflects the proposed relationship. This document should include:

- details on the tasks to be performed by the consultant;

- the date when the contract becomes effective and the date of its expiration;

- a cancellation clause that can be exercised by either party within a specific number of days' notice, usually not less than 30 or more than 90 days;

- a statement that the agency owns the resulting proposal;

- information on the fee that the consultant will be paid and when it is to be paid (perhaps tying it to delivery of the product or completion of specified tasks);

- details on reimbursement of out-of-pocket expenses or on an expense advance on which the consultant may draw; and

- a provision for the contract to be signed both by the consultant and by an officer of the nonprofit.

If possible, your nonprofit organization should use legal counsel in developing the contract. At a minimum, an attorney should review the document to see that the agency's interests are protected. Seek out pro bono legal assistance, if need be. Do not consider oral agreements to be binding on either side. Put everything in writing.

Tips on Writing the Proposal

Regardless of who writes the proposal, grant requests are unique documents. They are unlike any other kind of writing assignment.

For many grantseekers, the proposal is the only opportunity to communicate with a foundation or corporate donor. The written document is the one thing that remains with a funder after all the meetings and telephone calls have taken place. It must be self-explanatory. It must reflect the agency's overall image. Your proposal will educate the funder about your project and agency. It should motivate the potential funder to make a gift.

You do need to put as much care into preparing your proposal as you have put into designing the project and as you are planning to put into operating it. You have spent a fair amount of time determining priorities for raising funds and gathering the appropriate information for the proposal. The information you have collected should be thoroughly woven into an integrated whole that dramatically depicts your agency's project for the funder.

There are some basic rules that apply to all writing and a few that are unique to proposals to foundations and corporations. Here are some tips for the proposal writer:

GET YOUR THOUGHTS SORTED OUT

A proposal must deliver critical ideas quickly and easily. Your writing must be clear if you want others to understand your project and become excited by it. It will be hard to accomplish this if you have not clarified your thoughts in advance.

This means identifying the central point of your proposal. All of your subsequent points should flow easily from it. Once you have clearly thought through the broad concepts of the proposal, you are ready to prepare an outline.

OUTLINE WHAT YOU WANT TO SAY

You understand the need for the program. You have already gathered the facts about how it will unfold, if funded. You have identified the benchmarks of success and the financial requirements. With this information in hand, outline what should be said and in what order. If you take the time to create this outline, the process of writing will be much easier, and the resulting proposal will be stronger. Rushing to write a document without an outline only leads to frustration, confusion, and a poorly articulated proposal.

AVOID JARGON

Jargon confuses the reader and hampers his or her ability to comprehend your meaning. It impedes your style. It may be viewed as pretentious. With so much at stake in writing a proposal, it makes sense to avoid words (and acronyms) that are not generally known and to select words for their precision.

BE COMPELLING, BUT DON'T OVERSTATE YOUR CASE

People give to people. While your proposal has to present the facts, it must let the human element shine through. Personify the issue. Tell your story with examples. Illuminate your vision so that the funder can share it with you. Don't be afraid to humanize the materials once the facts are in place. But never assume that your writing is so compelling that programmatic details are unnecessary. A number of the grantmakers interviewed for this guide indicated a preference for real-life examples to enhance the text of a proposal. Nancy Wiltsek of Pottruck Family Foundation says: "Tell your story and back it up with data. I want the proposal to be personalized, but brief." And Matthew Klein of Blue Ridge Foundation New York explains: "The best proposals describe a very specific problem as well as solution that is uniquely tailored to address the particular elements of that problem. The reader should get the sense that if the grantseeker does what they describe, they are likely to have an impact. Many proposals make the mistake of being too general in describing the issues they are confronting, and as a result their proposed solutions are less plausible."

Try to be realistic in presenting your case. Take care that in your enthusiasm you do not overstate the need, the projected outcomes, or the basic facts about your organization. It is dangerous to promise more than you can deliver. The proposal reviewer is sure to raise questions, and the result could be damaged credibility with the funder. Worse, if the proposal is funded, and the results do not live up to the exaggerated expectations, future support is jeopardized.

KEEP IT SIMPLE

In the old days, fundraisers believed that the longer the document and the more detail it had, the better it was and the more money could be requested. Today, foundation and corporate funders look for concisely presented ideas. Eliminate wordiness. Simply present the key thoughts.

KEEP IT GENERIC

As you progress through the fundraising process, you may well approach a number of different potential funders with the same or a similar proposal. Thus, it makes sense to develop a basic proposal that, with certain customizing touches, can be submitted to a number of sources. Some funders today are even beginning to accept proposals submitted online.

In some areas of the country, groups of foundations have agreed to adopt a common application form. It makes sense to inquire as to whether one exists in your geographic area and whether the funder you are applying to accepts proposals in this form. The very same careful research that goes into identifying appropriate funders pertains to contacting those that accept common application forms. Examples of common application forms can be found at the Foundation Center's web site at foundationcenter.org.

Components of a Proposal

Executive Summary:	statement of your case and summary of the entire proposal	1 page

Statement of Need:	why this project is necessary	2 pages

Project Description:	nuts and bolts of how the project will be implemented and evaluated	3 pages

Budget:	financial description of the project plus explanatory notes	1 page

Organization Information:	history and governing structure of the nonprofit; its primary activities, its audiences, and its services	1 page

Conclusion:	summary of the proposal's main points	2 paragraphs

REVISE AND EDIT

Once you have completed the proposal, put it away temporarily. Then in a day or two, reread it with detachment and objectivity, if possible. Look for the logic of your arguments. Are there any holes? Move on to analyzing word choices and examining the grammar. Victoria Kovar of the Cooper Foundation reminds us: "Details matter in the document. Take a break. Get someone else to look at the document. Let it rest as long as you can and let someone else check it. Check the spelling and the grammar. Check the numbers: Do they add up? Do they match your supporting documentation?" And Lita Ugarte of The Community Foundation for Greater Atlanta adds: "Have someone else read your application. Be sure that it makes sense and uses proper grammar." As the grantmakers suggest, give the document to someone else to read. Select someone with well-honed communication skills who can point out areas that remain unclear and raise unanswered questions. Ask for a critical review of the case and of the narrative flow. This last step will be most helpful in closing any gaps, in eliminating jargon, and in heightening the overall impact of the document.

A well-crafted document should result from all these hours of gathering, thinking and sifting, and writing and rewriting. Carol Robinson, former executive director of the Isaac H. Tuttle Fund, provided us with an ideal to strive for that is still very telling today: "To me a proposal is a story. You speak to the reader and tell the reader a story, something you want him/her to visualize, hear, feel. It should have dimension, shape and rhythm and, yes, it should 'sing.'" (private letter, December 30, 1985)

The following chapters include many examples to assist you in better understanding the points being made. All are excerpts from actual proposals and are reprinted with permission from the issuing agency. Please note that to keep the design of the book as straightforward as possible, we did not always reproduce these examples in their original formats.

No two proposals are precisely the same in their execution, and no single proposal is absolutely perfect. In fact, some of the examples presented here have flaws. These examples are used to underscore a specific point, but together they illustrate the more general one that flexibility on the part of the proposal writer is essential. In a winning proposal, often the nature of the issues being addressed overrides rules about format.

A full sample proposal appears in Appendix A.

3

Developing the Proposal: The Executive Summary

This first page of the proposal is the most important section of the entire document. Here you will provide the reader with a snapshot of what is to follow. Specifically, it summarizes all of the key information and is a sales document designed to convince the reader that this project should be considered for support. Be certain to include:

Problem—a brief statement of the problem or need your agency has recognized and is prepared to address (one or two paragraphs);

Solution—a short description of the project, including what will take place and how many people will benefit from the program, how and where it will operate, for how long, and who will staff it (one or two paragraphs);

Funding requirements—an explanation of the amount of grant money required for the project and what your plans are for funding it in the future (one paragraph); and

Organization and its expertise—a brief statement of the name, history, purpose, and activities of your agency and its capacity to carry out this proposal (one paragraph).

How will the executive summary be used? First, in the initial review of your request, it will enable the funder to determine that the proposal is within its guidelines. Then it is often forwarded to other staff or board members to assist in their general review of the request. If you don't provide a summary, someone at the funder's office may well do it for you and emphasize the wrong points.

Here's a tip: It is easier to write the executive summary *last*. You will have your arguments and key points well in mind. It should be concise. Ideally, the summary should be no longer than one page or 300 words.

Here is an example of an executive summary, taken from a proposal submitted by East Side House to the Altman Foundation. The summary immediately identifies the financial request. It explains clearly why improved evaluation is necessary, what the consultant will do, and it talks about the organization.

EXECUTIVE SUMMARY

East Side House requests a $75,000 grant from the Altman Foundation to hire an Evaluation Consultant, who will create a formalized evaluation model to be used throughout East Side House's programs. To best serve our constituents, East Side House seeks to create a systematic method of evaluation across the entire organization, designed to meet the specific needs of our diverse student population and programs. An outside consultant will:

- Bring proven expertise in evaluation of multi-tiered youth service agencies in New York, and
- Provide an efficient and effective evaluative approach for East Side House's many educational programs, which serve thousands of individuals

This evaluation system will improve the overall efficacy of all our programs, our ability to report on our participants' successes, and ultimately our ability to leverage funding from additional sources.

Founded in 1891, East Side House Settlement is one of New York City's oldest and most prestigious not-for-profit community service organizations. Supported by a dedicated Board of Managers and a creative professional staff team, East Side House has the experience and stability to develop, implement, evaluate and sustain innovative programs that break from cookie-cutter models and are based on the unique needs of the Mott Haven community in the South Bronx. East Side House serves over 8,000 children, teens, adults and seniors each year from 16 program sites. We have always been committed to improving quality of life for constituents, rooting our efforts in educational attainment in accordance with our mission statement:

"East Side House is a community resource in the South Bronx. We believe education is the key that enables all people to create economic and civic opportunities for themselves, their families and their communities. Our focus is on critical development periods—early childhood and adolescence—and critical junctures—points at which people are determined to become economically independent. We enrich, supplement and enhance the public school system and place college within reach of motivated students. We provide services to families in order that other family members may pursue their educational goals. We provide technology and career readiness training to enable students to improve their economic status and lead more fulfilling lives."

Mott Haven is located in the heart of our nation's poorest congressional district. It is a community filled with people who wake each day to the challenges of urban life - poverty, unemployment, poor school performance, drugs and gangs. It is also a community of promise with vibrant and proud Latino and African-American cultures, parents who dream of a better future for their children, and children who want to live up to their promise.

A more cohesive evaluation system will allow East Side House to track participants' improvements and identify any modifications that need to be made to each program's curriculum to better meet our participants' needs. A stronger evaluation model will help ensure that each of our participants is receiving the educational and other support services that they need in order to reap the full benefits of our programs and to combat the destructive cycle of poverty that marks so many lives in Mott Haven.

This second example was submitted to The Frances L. & Edwin L. Cummings Memorial Fund by Groundwork. Once again, the request to the grantmaker is prominent. There is a straightforward explanation of the project, the reason for the request, and information about the applicant.

Executive Summary

In December of 2004, the Cummings Memorial Fund made a $30,000 grant to Groundwork to hire an additional full-time counselor (social worker). With this funding Groundwork has been able to hire Ms. Jamali Moses as the full-time Support Services Coordinator. Groundwork now employs two full-time counselors who supervise six MSW, counseling and/or psychology student interns, all of whom provide supportive services to Groundwork children and families. Groundwork is seeking a renewal grant from The Frances L. & Edwin L. Cummings Memorial Fund in the amount of $40,000 to underwrite the salary of the Support Services Coordinator for one additional year.

Founded in early 2002, Groundwork's mission is to help young people living in high-poverty, urban communities develop their strengths, skills, talents and competencies through effective experiential learning and work programs. Our vision is that young people who grow up in the neighborhoods we serve should have the same chance of a good life as young people who did not grow up in an under-resourced neighborhood. For us, a good life means that as an adult, you can answer "yes" to three questions:

- "Are you happy?"
- "Do you feel financially and physically secure?"
- "Have you been able to make real choices about the course of your life?"

Groundwork is based in East New York, a physically isolated community in eastern Brooklyn where over 70 percent of children are born into poverty. We take a geographically focused approach to working with youth and their families: we identify ten to fifteen block areas with high rates of young people living in poverty (typically public housing developments or similar communities) and develop programs to serve a significant percentage of the families who reside in those areas. We believe that this approach allows us to maximize the impact of our services; by reaching many children in a small, well-defined area, Groundwork can impact the youth culture of that entire community.

Children growing up in East New York face numerous obstacles to their personal development. Poverty and violence rates are significantly higher than other New York City neighborhoods. The health disparities facing this neighborhood are numerous and include high rates of AIDS, childhood obesity and mental illness. Groundwork estimates that 70 to 80 percent of Groundwork's participants have experienced childhood trauma such as parental separation, loss, abuse and neglect. Without intervention, these children will fall into the devastating cycle of their environment.

Groundwork's Family Resource Center, formerly called the Support Services Program, assists children and families by offering individual, group and family counseling, play therapy, classroom management support and crisis intervention. Over the past year, Ms. Moses has enabled Groundwork to begin offering family counseling as a formal component of the program, increase the total percentage of children served through the Family Resource Center, increase outreach efforts, implement new initiatives such as Fresh Start, and strengthen relationships with the public schools Groundwork students attend. We hope to continue this record of achievement with renewed funding from the Cummings Memorial Fund.

Neither example contains every element of the ideal executive summary, but both persuasively make the case for reading further.

4

Developing the Proposal: The Statement of Need

If the funder reads beyond the executive summary, you have successfully piqued his or her interest. Your next task is to build on this initial interest in your project by enabling the funder to understand the problem that the project will remedy.

The statement of need enables the reader to learn more about the issues. It presents the facts and evidence that support the need for the project and establishes that your nonprofit understands the problems and therefore can reasonably address them. The information used to support the case can come from authorities in the field, as well as from your agency's own experience.

You want the need section to be succinct, yet persuasive. Like a good debater, you must assemble all the arguments and then present them in a logical sequence that will readily convince the reader of their importance. As you marshal your arguments, consider the following six points:

First, decide which facts or statistics best support the project. Be sure the data you present are accurate. There are few things more embarrassing than to have the funder tell you that your information is out of date or incorrect. Information that is too generic or broad will not help you develop a winning argument for your project. Information that does not relate to your organization or the project you are presenting will cause the funder to question the entire proposal. There should be a balance between the information presented and the scale of the program. Here is a list of possible sources to call upon when compiling facts, figures, and statistics to back up your case:

- needs assessments conducted by objective outside parties or by your own agency

- surveys—local or regional or national, conducted by your organization or by others

- focus groups with representatives of key audiences

- interviews with stakeholders

- usage statistics

- media coverage of the problem or lack of service

- reports from government agencies or other nonprofits

- demographic studies

- projections for the future, suggesting how bad things will get if this problem is not addressed, and/or how good things will be if it is.

These should all derive from authorities with impeccable credentials and be as up-to-date as possible.

An example might be helpful here. Your nonprofit organization plans to initiate a program for battered women, for which you will seek support from foundations and corporations in your community. You have impressive national statistics on hand. You can also point to an increasing number of local women and their children seeking help. However, local data is limited. Given the scope of the project and the base of potential supporters, you should probably use the more limited local information only. It is far more relevant to the interests of funders close to home. If you were to seek support from more nationally oriented funders, then the broader information would be helpful, supplemented by details based on local experience.

Second, give the reader hope. The picture you paint should not be so grim that the situation appears hopeless. The funder will wonder whether an investment in a solution will be worthwhile. Here's an example of a solid statement of need: "Breast cancer kills. But statistics prove that regular check-ups catch most breast cancer in the early stages, reducing the likelihood of death. Hence, a program to encourage preventive checkups will reduce the risk of death due to breast cancer." Avoid overstatement and overly emotional appeals.

Third, decide if you want to put your project forward as a model. This could expand the base of potential funders, but serving as a model works only for certain types of projects. Don't try to make this argument if it doesn't really fit. Funders may well expect your agency to follow through with a replication plan if you present your project as a model.

If the decision about a model is affirmative, you should document how the problem you are addressing occurs in other communities. Be sure to explain how your solution could be a solution for others as well.

Fourth, determine whether it is reasonable to portray the need as acute. You are asking the funder to pay attention to your proposal because either the problem you address is worse than others or the solution you propose makes more sense than others. Here is an example of a balanced but weighty statement: "Drug abuse is a national problem. Each day, children all over the country die from drug overdose. In the South Bronx the problem is worse. More children die here than any place else. It is an epidemic. Hence, our drug prevention program is needed more in the South Bronx than in any other part of the city."

Fifth, decide whether you can demonstrate that your program addresses the need differently or better than other projects that preceded it. It is often difficult to describe the need for your project without being critical of the competition. But you must be careful not to do so. Being critical of other nonprofits will not be well received by the funder. It may cause the funder to look more carefully at your own project to see why you felt you had to build your case by demeaning others. The funder may have invested in these other projects or may begin to consider them, now that you have brought them to its attention.

If possible, you should make it clear that you are cognizant of, and on good terms with, others doing work in your field. Keep in mind that today's funders are very interested in collaboration. They may even ask why you are not collaborating with those you view as key competitors. So at the least you need to describe how your work complements, but does not duplicate, the work of others.

Sixth, avoid circular reasoning. In circular reasoning, you present the absence of your solution as the actual problem. Then your solution is offered as the way to solve the problem. For example, the circular reasoning for building a community swimming pool might go like this: "The problem is that we have no pool in our community. Building a pool will solve the problem." A more persuasive case would cite what a pool has meant to a neighboring community, permitting it to offer recreation, exercise, and physical therapy programs. The statement might refer to a survey that underscores the target audience's planned usage of the facility and conclude with the connection between the proposed usage and potential benefits to enhance life in the community.

To make your need statement compelling, you'll want to put a human face on the problem. There are a number of ways you might do this:

- use anecdotes, succinctly related

- provide real-life examples (with fictitious names if need be) to make those you serve come alive

- supply actual quotes from those who have benefited or will benefit from your services

- emphasize the needs of those you serve, not your own

- always make the funder feel that there is hope that the problem will be solved.

The statement of need does not have to be long and involved. Short, concise information captures the reader's attention. This is the case in the following example from the Center for Black Women's Wellness proposal to The Community Foundation for Greater Atlanta, Inc.

Statement of Need

Since 1988, the Center's collaborative efforts and community-centered approach have uniquely positioned it to effectively deliver holistic health services. In doing so, the Center has had extraordinary success in utilizing cultural values, beliefs and attitudes as assets to positively influence lifestyle changes, independent of socioeconomic status. However, diverse challenges within the community and the nation, including issues of increasing health disparities, welfare reform, gentrification, and decreases in many agency budgets have created additional needs. Furthermore, despite the availability of numerous providers in and near our target area, awareness about services, distrust of the health professionals, and competing priorities are challenging to clients' accessing care. Strengthening organizational structure is pivotal to address these growing needs.

The Center is at a point of critical growth and change, making the need for organizational development and fund development more pressing. There have been staff and board changes that have occurred recently. For example, Jamea Smith, former Program Coordinator and Vice President of the organization, transitioned into the role of CEO of the Center in May 2005. Additionally, in the past months there has been the addition of board members. Due to these changes in staff and board structure, additional staff and board development will aid in ensuring organizational success during this transition. Secondly, in May 2005, the Center was awarded an additional four years of the Healthy Start grant. However, because this grant comprises 57% of the Center's total operating budget, a fund development plan is needed to ensure the sustainability of programs beyond the funding period. Lastly, access to appropriate technology is essential to the effective delivery of services. The ongoing development of software, technology and systems upgrades, and technology and database training for staff and community workers will increase efficiency and data quality, build skill sets, and enhance documentation efforts needed to attract additional resources.

The next example comes from a proposal to the Blue Ridge Foundation New York from WomensLaw.org. Note the use of footnotes.

Nearly one third (31%) of American women report being physically or sexually abused by a husband or boyfriend at some point in their lives.[1] Abuse and violence, in the place where you sleep, eat, and live, is nothing short of terrifying for many women and their children. Fortunately, every state in the United States provides a way for women to seek a court order requiring an abuser to stay away and to stop abusive behavior. These restraining order laws are designed so that victims can go to court and request an order without the assistance of a lawyer. In reality, the laws can be intimidating and confusing. Procedurally, the experience can be a nightmare.

For women throughout the country, information about restraining order laws and procedures is often hard to find. Usually it requires a trip to the courthouse, to legal aid, or to a domestic violence agency. This is difficult for women who are afraid that their abuser will discover their activities and retaliate, for women with no childcare, for women with little or no money, or for women who work full-time jobs. For rural women the obstacles can be prohibitive. For domestic violence advocates, it is also difficult to find legal information for states other than their own. Often, women living with domestic violence also need clear legal information about divorce, custody, immigration, tribal courts, housing, or their rights within the military.

The Internet provides us with a unique tool to address these problems. The rate of growth of Internet use in the U.S. is currently two million new Internet users per month, and more than half of the nation is online. Rural and low-income households are among the fastest growing groups of new Internet users.[2] Through its website, WomensLaw.org can provide plain-language legal information and step-by-step procedural information directly to unlimited numbers of people, at a low cost. Through the Internet, we provide an intermediate step that allows women to access up-to-date information anonymously, safely, and easily.

1. The Commonwealth Fund, Health Concerns Across A Woman's Lifespan: The Commonwealth Fund 1998 Survey of Women's Health, May 1999.

2. A Nation Online: How Americans Are Expanding Their Use of the Internet, U.S. Dept. of Commerce, Economics and Statistics Administration, National Telecommunications and Information Administration, February 2002.

A final example was submitted to The Community Foundation for Greater Atlanta, Inc., by the Youth Ensemble of Atlanta. It describes the difficulties the Youth Ensemble has been facing without permanent rehearsal and performance space.

Need

A lack of performance and rehearsal space has YEA busting at the seams of the facilities currently available to us, and we are often unable to secure enough appropriate performance space for our productions. Our current three-year strategic plan calls for increased performances of our Tippy Toes Arts Series and our GRIP Program, as well as continuing to expand our mainstage programming. A lack of space is inhibiting our greatest ability to raise revenue - ticket sales. This move will not only mean that we can perform in the timeframe and with the run time most appropriate for our productions, we will also be able to plan our season in advance, free of the many hurdles we usually face.

For 15 years, YEA has been a nomadic company performing in more than eight venues in just the past three years. These venues increase our costs for productions (many times, the technical costs will exceed $12,000 a week) and only provide us with a single week of performance time, which limits our ability to get reviewed in the major papers and earn the money at the door we need to increase our earned revenue. All of these venues also fail to give our ensemble members the kind of grounding they desire. YEA is about more than performances and arts training; we are a company determined to change our world through empowered youth.

These space problems are limiting YEA's organizational capacity. Without proper space for our programs, we will not be able to continue our expansion and reach toward our goal of owning our own theatre space and becoming an institution in the Atlanta arts landscape.

As you can see from all three examples, the need statement begins the process whereby the organization builds its case and tells its story. This process continues in the next section of the proposal, which describes how the project will address the need.

5

Developing the Proposal: The Project Description

In this section, describe the nuts and bolts of the project in a way that gets the reader excited about it, while making a compelling case for the approach you have adopted. It is worth stating right up front that your plan is not written in stone. It might change based on feedback on your proposal and the experience you gain through implementation. It is not worth putting your organization in a defensive position in negotiating with grantmakers, and you certainly don't want to surprise a funder if in the project's final report you state that you changed your approach.

This section of your proposal should have five subsections: objectives, methods, staffing/administration, evaluation, and sustainability. Together, objectives and methods dictate staffing and administrative requirements. They then become the focus of the evaluation to assess the results of the project. The project's sustainability flows directly from its success, hence its ability to attract other support. The five subsections present an interlocking picture of the total project.

Objectives

Objectives are the measurable outcomes of the program. They help delineate your methods. Your objectives must be tangible, specific, concrete, measurable, and achievable in a specified time period. Grantseekers often confuse objectives with goals, which are conceptual and more abstract. For the purpose of illustration, here is the goal of a project with a subsidiary objective:

> Goal: Our afterschool program will help children read better.
>
> Objective: Our afterschool remedial education program will assist 50 children in improving their reading scores by one grade level as demonstrated on standardized reading tests administered after participating in the program for six months.

The goal in this case is abstract: improving reading, while the objective is much more specific. It is achievable in the short term (six months) and measurable (improving 50 children's reading scores by one grade level).

With competition for dollars so great, well-articulated objectives are increasingly critical to a proposal's success.

Calling upon a different example, there are at least four types of objectives:

1. Behavioral—A human action is anticipated.
   Example: Fifty of the 70 children participating will learn to swim.

2. Performance—A specific time frame within which a behavior will occur, at an expected proficiency level, is anticipated.
   Example: Fifty of the 70 children will learn to swim within six months and will pass a basic swimming proficiency test administered by a Red Cross-certified lifeguard.

3. Process—The manner in which something occurs is an end in itself.
   Example: We will document the teaching methods utilized, identifying those with the greatest success.

4. Product—A tangible item will result.
   Example: A manual will be created to be used in teaching swimming to this age and proficiency group in the future.

In any given proposal, you will find yourself setting forth one or more of these types of objectives, depending on the nature of your project. Be certain to present the objectives very clearly. Make sure that they do not become lost in verbiage and that they stand out on the page. You might, for example, use numbers, bullets, or indentations to denote the objectives in the text. Above all, be realistic in setting objectives. Don't promise what you can't deliver. Remember, the funder will want to be told in the final report that the project actually accomplished these objectives.

The example that follows is excerpted from a proposal to the Dade Community Foundation submitted by the Arts & Business Council of Miami, Inc. It states the project's objectives succinctly. These are numbered for the grantmaker's review.

Objectives:

Amplifying Arts Audiences will:

1. Empower arts groups to drive new traffic to their programs and will build significant new audiences for the arts in South Florida, especially in underserved communities.
2. Help arts groups use technology to eliminate their current marketing mistakes, which result in poor attendance or stagnant audiences.
3. Provide the arts community with tools to effectively and collectively market themselves to current patrons and new patrons.
4. Work with a team of computer experts and marketing professionals to educate arts executives about efficient and cost-effective use of technology and on-line promotion.
5. Use technology and analysts to develop a blueprint to maximize the marketing efforts of participating groups by identifying buying patterns, multi-buyers and patrons, and targeting prospects for upgrades.
6. Work with facilities managers in 25 arts facilities to map their seats and provide this resource to the arts groups that perform in their space.
7. Provide arts marketers from local groups with access to experts in the private sector on how to maximize web and on-line marketing.

Methods

By means of the objectives, you have explained to the funder what will be achieved by the project. The methods section describes the specific activities that will take place to achieve the objectives. It might be helpful to divide our discussion of methods into the following: how, when, and why.

How: This is the detailed description of what will occur from the time the project begins until it is completed. Your methods should match the previously stated objectives. In our example about teaching 50 children to swim, appropriate methods would describe 1) how the youngsters will be recruited, 2) how they will be taught to enhance their skills, and 3) how their swimming skills will be measured. There would be no reason to describe an extraneous activity like helping the parents learn to enjoy swimming with their children, because using swimming to bring the family together in wholesome exercise is not a stated objective of the project.

In the next example from Common Ground's proposal to The Frances L. & Edwin L. Cummings Memorial Fund, we learn how the agency will implement its S2Hi program.

S2Hi seeks support from the Fund to continue providing the chronic homeless of West Midtown the support and services needed to secure and maintain housing. By doing so, we will reach our goal of reducing the West Midtown street homeless population by two-thirds and provide the follow-up support needed to ensure our clients' housing stability. S2Hi's successes have proven that, with individualized outreach, coordinated case management and expedited housing placement, chronically homeless individuals can successfully make the transition from homelessness directly into stable housing. As we come closer to achieving our initial goals for the program, we are developing an exit strategy, which will include an after-care initiative for clients placed in housing and a new focus on assisting other organizations that are interested in replicating the model. In the coming year we will focus on the following key activities:

- Housing the remaining chronically homeless population of West Midtown
- Implementing an Aftercare Initiative
- Advocating Project Homeless Connect
- Assisting other organizations in replicating the S2Hi model

A) HOUSING PLACEMENT

Our initial estimates, based on our semi-annual "counts" of the street homeless in West Midtown, had indicated a baseline of 416 homeless individuals in the neighborhood. However, these counts did not differentiate between the long-term homeless and those who have been on the streets for less than a year. As we continued to refine our efforts and collect more reliable data on this population, we began identifying the chronically homeless by name.

Over the summer, in collaboration with the Times Square Alliance and the Fashion Business Improvement District (BID), we have created a registry of the 75 most vulnerable homeless individuals remaining in the area and will actively target this group over the coming year. Once we have housed these individuals, we will focus on the Port Authority bus station and Penn Station, where an additional 80 chronically homeless live.

Since the program's inception, we have housed 75 individuals, and have close to 100 in the placement process. Between these clients and our focus population described above, we believe we can house a total of 277 individuals (or two-thirds of our baseline number) by the end of 2006.

B) AFTERCARE INITIATIVE

The S2Hi program has successfully placed chronically homeless individuals directly into permanent housing. As we have come to find, however, housing maintenance and post-placement support is as crucial as the initial placement. As we approach our goal, we have begun a targeted effort to address the needs of those we have already placed in housing. S2Hi's clients have been on the streets an average of ten years, which can make re-integration with society and the responsibilities of maintaining stable housing daunting. Throughout the program's development, we have maintained contact with our clients after their housing placement, helping to enhance our good reputation among housing providers throughout New York City. Indeed, in recent months housing providers have been contacting *us* for client referrals to fill upcoming vacancies.

As more and more S2Hi clients are placed into housing, we have begun developing a formalized component of the S2Hi program to engage clients in "Aftercare." Although our staff maintains regular contact with past clients, we will dedicate a new position to housing maintenance and post-replacement support. Our Aftercare Specialist will work with our clients' new case managers at their respective supportive housing sites, helping our clients to maintain their housing and adjust to their new lives.

C) PROJECT HOMELESS CONNECT

This past September 13th, Common Ground Community with the Times Square Alliance launched New York City's first Project Homeless Connect. A one-day event modeled after San Francisco's successful initiative, Homeless Connect brought together a wide range of services – from housing to medical care to benefits counseling – under one roof, all with the ultimate goal of housing Times Square's homeless. Outreach teams blanketed the Times Square neighborhood and brought homeless individuals to the Homeless Connect site, where each individual was evaluated by a caseworker and connected to needed services.

This event was a great success, bringing together over 200 volunteers from Common Ground staff, S2Hi's partner organizations, and the community at large. In just one day, we:

- Engaged 124 homeless clients
- Assisted 77 people with their benefits, including Medicaid, Food Stamps, Public Assistance, and legal aid
- Provided medical and/or dental care to 54 people
- Helped 4 people enter drug treatment
- Gave emergency medical treatment to 2 people
- Provided individualized housing advice and consultations with S2Hi staff to 67 people
- Referred 25 people to shelters or drop-in centers
- Placed 13 people in temporary housing for 10 days while we worked to secure appropriate permanent housing.

Project Homeless Connect has already expanded the impact of the S2Hi program through a single day of mass mobilization. By using volunteers to supplement the work of S2Hi staff, we reached far more homeless individuals than we could on our own. In addition, by providing a "hands-on" demonstration of the initial steps of the S2Hi housing process, we have illustrated the first steps toward replicating our program model for other organizations. Based on our initial success, we are encouraging the City of New York to adopt this program, joining other Project Connect cities around the country, as a permanent component of the City's commitment to solving homelessness.

D) TECHNICAL ASSISTANCE

A fundamental goal of the S2Hi program is to spread this successful model to other in-need communities, thereby shifting service providers' response to homelessness away from emergency measures to permanent solutions and permanent housing. As S2Hi has continued to place chronic homeless individuals into housing, proving that these individuals are indeed housing-ready, the program's reputation has spread among government agencies, community stakeholders, and supportive housing providers. Two organizations, one on the Upper East Side and one in the Bronx, have begun implementing our program model, hiring housing specialists and working with S2Hi staff to develop their program. In addition, six other New York City neighborhoods have expressed interest in replicating the S2Hi program. Finally, the U.S. Department of Housing and Urban Development has pledged support for a variation of our program that will target that subset of the chronically homeless who are also chronic inebriates.

In the coming year, we will work to develop a replication curriculum that will then be offered to interested organizations in the following year. The development of this curriculum will be informed by our work with the two organizations we are currently assisting. Our replication program will engage interested organizations in a series of seminars consisting of lectures, field visits to program sites, and trainings on outreach methods, basic psycho-social evaluations, and benefits counseling, as well as the steps for expediting the housing application and placement process. We will dedicate a full-time staff position to working with these organizations, ensuring that our proven "best practices" are adopted by start-up programs. As the S2Hi program model continues to spread, we are confident it will provide a long-term, cost-effective solution to chronic homelessness in urban communities throughout the City.

Next Generation, in its proposal for its Youth Peace Campaign, described to the Agape Foundation a series of very clear activities aimed at accomplishing its objectives.

Next Generation is applying for $2,000 to fund our Youth Peace Campaign, which helps young people to learn about U.S. foreign policy and military spending, gain activist skills, organize at the grassroots, and work for peace. Our vision is a planet with peaceful, non-violent conflict resolution and sustainable lifestyles, businesses, and governments prioritizing social and environmental needs over corporate profits and band-aid solutions, through the empowerment of local communities collaborating for peace and sustainability.

Our youth are currently organizing to create a youth movement that can help end the war in Iraq and prevent future wars. Next Generation works to accomplish our goals through six elements of organizing. The goals and activities of each element are outlined below:

- *Education:* Increase the knowledge of 1000 students in Marin County about topics related to peace through workshops, assemblies, and classroom presentations about the root causes of war and peace, U.S. foreign policy, how the government spends our tax dollars/national budget, media bias, sustainability, civil liberties, and more. Last year, our workshops and assemblies reached 500 young people at 6 schools, and several hundred more through our events.
- *Training and Leadership Development:* Increase the leadership and organizing skills of 100 youth throughout Marin County through trainings and conferences teaching effective leadership, grassroots

organizing, building membership, public speaking, event and action planning, fundraising, publicity, etc. Last year, we trained 50 young peace and justice activists through workshops, conferences, and retreats at local schools and through our Action Team.

- *Grassroots Organizing:* Support the organizing and activism work of 50-100 youth in Marin through working closely with leaders of student clubs, individual student activities, and members of Next Generation's Student Action Team to mobilize and engage more participants in their peace and sustainability efforts. The Student Action Team is a countrywide coalition of 20 students from diverse schools and backgrounds that meets weekly to run collaborative campaigns and support specific projects and clubs in their individual schools.

- *Community Events:* Increase awareness and understanding about issues related to peace, and connections between people, of 1,000 residents (youth and adults) through events including conferences, speakers, awards ceremonies, and festivals. Past events have included our annual Iraq War forum, Youth Activism Awards Ceremony, and our gala event, Turn the Tide. Past speakers have included Julia Butterfly Hill, Randy Hayes, Helen Caldicott, and Van Jones, among others.

- *Grassroots Actions and Campaigns:*
  This year, our Youth Peace Campaign goals include:
    - Creating a vibrant, diverse youth-led peace movement.
    - Increasing the visibility of peace issues in the County through youth-led vigils, marches, rallies, media events, etc., involving 500 youth and 200 adults.
    - Supporting local, county and state legislation that promotes an end to the war. We are currently leading the local campaign to persuade the California State Assembly to pass a resolution condemning the war in Iraq and calling for a withdrawal of our National Guardsmen and Guardswomen.

- *Collaboration:* Bringing together community-based groups, non-profits, local governments, schools, and individual residents through the activities of the campaign, especially our education, community events, and grassroots actions elements. Past and present collaborators include the Marin Peace and Justice Coalition, the Marin County Board of Supervisors, the Marin County Youth Commission, Code Pink, the Environmental Education Council of Marin, the Marin County Bicycle Coalition, many students, teachers, schools, individuals, and community members.

Think about how you can most readily construct a logical sequence from each objective to its relevant method. This can be accomplished in a number of ways, some relating simply to visual placement on the page.

One means of organizing this section is to write out each objective and to list beneath it the method(s) that will make the objective possible. For example, it might look like this:

Objective: to recruit 70 children

Methods:

- Put up signs in the Y.

- Go to each school and address classes on the fun of swimming.

- Put ads in the local paper.

- Enclose a flyer about the program with the next mailer sent out to each family in the community.

The methods should match the magnitude of the objectives. Once you are sure that each objective has related methods that describe how the objective will be achieved, you should check that the emphasis given each method matches the importance of the related objective. In our swimming example, recruitment of 70 children is probably the least important objective; demonstrating that 50 of them can pass the Red Cross test is more critical. To match the magnitude of the objectives with appropriate detail about the project, more emphasis should be placed on the testing than on recruiting. (This refining and highlighting of information will enable the reader to understand the project and to have confidence in your agency.)

The methods should appear doable; otherwise, you lose credibility. For example, if the swimming course is to be taught by an Olympic swimmer who remains anonymous, the reader might question whether the organization can deliver what it has promised. However, if the Olympic star is identified by name and has already agreed to run the program, the reader will likely be convinced.

When: The methods section should present the order and timing for the various tasks. It might make sense to provide a timetable so that the reader does not have to map out the sequencing on his or her own. The timetable could look like this one, excerpted from the Arts & Business Council of Miami's proposal. Note, the anticipated number of months to undertake each task is provided in parentheses.

Project Timeline

1. Work directly with arts groups to reach over 100,000 patrons, donors, sponsors and arts participants by applying new ticketing solutions to venues throughout the tri-county. This will not require any additional investment on the part of the venue and will help support cultural activity by making it easier for performing groups to present at a variety of venues in the region. (*12 months*)

2. Leverage existing infrastructure to reduce total regional spending on ticketing operations throughout the cultural sector. (*12 months*)

3. Reach over 100 arts executives and broaden arts managers' understanding of customer service and audience development through a variety of training events offered through the Arts & Business Council. (*6 to 9 months*)

4. Enhance service levels for patrons of the arts by providing 24/7 Internet ticketing and a fully functioning call center open 7 days per week. (*Final 3 months*)

5. Encourage collaboration among 100 arts groups to help reach new audiences and attract new sources of funding via the web site. (*Final 3 months*)

6. Develop an Amplifying Arts Audiences task force made up of arts executives, arts board members, business executives and partners from local chambers, arts councils and related nonprofits. (*Final 3 months of project*)

Another presentation of a solid work plan comes from a proposal submitted to the Flinn Foundation by the Hualapai Tribal Health Department for the prior edition of this *Guide.* The time line depicts a one-year project.

Time Line

	2000			2001								
	Oct	Nov	Dec	Jan	Feb	Mar	Apr	May	Jun	July	Aug	Sept
Planning for Diabetes Conference	⊢——⊣											
Schedule Work Site/School Site Screening	⊢———⊣											
Implement Diabetes Conference		⊦										
Conduct Monthly Work Site/ School Site Screenings			⊢————————————————⊣									
Expand Individual Care Form				⊢——⊣								
Place Expanded Form into Practice				⊢——————————————⊣								
Develop Data Entry System			⊢——⊣									
Staff Training for Data Entry					⊢——⊣							
Data Entry					⊦———————————⊣							
Data Analysis								⊢———⊣				
Final Report											⊦	

The current staff member who works half time will be hired to work full time. No additional time is needed for hiring or training.

The timetable tells the reader "when" and provides another summary of the project that supports the rest of the methods section.

Why: You need to defend your chosen methods, especially if they are new or unorthodox. Why will the planned work lead to the outcomes you anticipate? You can answer this question in a number of ways, including using examples of other projects that work and expert testimony.

The methods section enables the reader to visualize the implementation of the project. It should convince the reader that your agency knows what it is doing, thereby establishing credibility.

Staffing/Administration

In describing the methods, you will have mentioned staffing for the project. You now need to devote a few sentences to discussing the number of staff, their qualifications, and specific assignments. Details about individual staff members involved in the project can be included either as part of this section or in the appendix, depending on the length and importance of this information.

"Staffing" can refer to volunteers or to consultants, as well as to paid staff. Most proposal writers do not develop staffing sections for projects that are primarily volunteer-run. Describing tasks that volunteers will undertake, however, can be most helpful to the proposal reader. Such information underscores the value added by the volunteers and the cost-effectiveness of the project.

For a project with paid staff, be certain to describe which staff will work full time and which will work part time on the project. Identify staff already employed by your nonprofit and those to be recruited specifically for the project. How will you free up the time of an already fully deployed individual?

Salary and project costs are affected by the qualifications of the staff. Delineate the practical experience you require for key staff, as well as level of expertise and educational background. If an individual has already been selected to direct the program, summarize his or her credentials and include a brief biographical sketch in the appendix. A strong project director can help influence a grant decision.

Explain anything unusual about the proposed staffing for the project. It is better to include such information in the proposal narrative than to have the funder raise questions once the proposal review begins.

Three samples of staffing sections follow. The first is part of a proposal from National Industries for the Blind.

Staffing

Karen Pal is the Program Manager for National Industries for the Blind's Business Leaders Program and is responsible for the development, implementation and management of this new and exciting initiative. With over 15 years of experience in leadership development, program management, communications and human resources, she most recently held the position of Manager, Communications and Implementation at the American Red Cross, where she directed its national leadership program implementation and led the strategic communications function in a 30-person division with a $1 million budget. Ms. Pal holds a Master of Public Health degree in Social Marketing and Health Promotion from George Washington University and an undergraduate degree from the University of Washington in Seattle. In addition, she holds a Senior Professional in Human Resources (SPHR) accreditation from the Human Resources Certification Institute.

Sandra Smith is the program's Training and Developing Specialist. With an M.S.W. from the University of Tennessee and Bachelor's Degree in Social Work from Cedar Crest College, Ms. Smith brings over two decades of experience in social work and social work supervision to the Business Leaders Program. She has worked for both Associated Services for the Blind and Center for the Blind in Philadelphia as well as in private industry. As a field instructor, she provided various training to groups of graduate students and medical professionals.

NIB's very active and fully independent Board of Directors contributes its combined experience and talent to this project. An *ad hoc* committee of the Board, together with Jim Gibbons, President and CEO and the first individual who is blind to graduate from the Harvard Graduate School of Business Administration with an MBA, initially identified a need for this program. That committee oversaw program development and ensured that the program is meeting its goals.

The staffing section excerpted from a proposal of Operation Exodus Inner City describes the work of staff as well as volunteers.

Staff

Exodus' programming is supervised by Matthew Mahoney, Executive Director. Mr. Mahoney is a Princeton graduate, former New York City teacher and Washington Heights community member. His responsibilities include, but are not limited to: curriculum development; coordination of on-going staff training; and evaluation of the program and staff.

Our staff also includes paid and trained tutors who work with the children and allow us to maintain a 1:10 adult-to-student ratio. A low adult-to-student ratio is critical in that individualized tutoring sessions often act as informal counseling sessions allowing staff to better pinpoint areas of trouble for our students both in and out of the school environment. Our teachers participate in weekly in-house training workshops on curriculum, and regularly attend workshops at PASE (Partnership for After School Education).

Exodus' staff and volunteers are remarkably committed to the program: the average tenure for a tutor is 2-3 years, and several tutors have been with the program since 2001. The low staff turnover helps us to maintain consistent, high quality academic programming and form strong relationships with both students and their families.

Finally, here is a simple, straightforward staffing section from a proposal for the Ali Forney Center.

Ali Forney Center was founded by Executive Director Carl Siciliano, who has worked with homeless people for the past twenty years. Since 1994, he has focused on providing services to homeless adolescents and has created programs which have received national recognition for their quality and innovation. Joining Mr. Siciliano are 29 full-time and 8 part-time AFC staff members including the Mental Health Specialist, the Housing Director, the Vocational Coordinator, the Coordinator of Policy and Training, and a number of youth counselors. AFC also has a group of over 50 dedicated volunteers, who are managed by AFC's Volunteer Coordinator.

Describe for the reader your plans for administering the project. This is especially important in a large operation, if more than one agency is collaborating on the project, or if you are using a fiscal agent. It needs to be crystal clear who is responsible for financial management, project outcomes, and reporting.

Evaluation

A key aspect of most project descriptions is the evaluation component of the grant proposal. This section of the proposal describes how you and the funder will know if the proposed project succeeds or not. In recent years this component of your proposal has become important enough to warrant a separate discussion in this *Guide* (see Chapter 6).

Sustainability

A clear message from grantmakers today is that grantseekers will be expected to demonstrate in very concrete ways the long-term financial viability of the project to be funded and of the nonprofit organization itself. Most of the grantmakers we interviewed indicated that they look for lists of current and prospective donors among the attachments to a proposal. This is high on the list of items they expect grantseekers to provide.

It stands to reason that most grantmakers will not want to take on a permanent funding commitment to a particular agency. David Egner of Hudson Webber Foundation identified this as a "risk area" for his foundation when delineating a list of items he looks for during the grant review process: "Is there an exit strategy for the foundation? Since we can't fund anything in perpetuity is there an immediate way out or one that we know is going to take a decade?" Funders will want you to prove either that your project is finite (with start-up and ending dates); or that it is capacity-building (that it will contribute to the future self-sufficiency of your agency and/or enable it to expand services that might be revenue generating); or that it will make your organization attractive to other funders in the future. With the trend toward adopting some of the investment principles of venture capital groups to the practice of philanthropy, evidence of fiscal sustainability becomes a highly sought-after characteristic of the successful grant proposal. Think of what you are presenting as the plan to make your project sustainable. The details will fall into place as the project and your fundraising efforts unfold. Should your project be a one-time thing, a pilot, or one that will soon be self-sustaining, hence does not require future support, be sure to explain that to the funder.

The two sustainability samples that follow were both excerpted from proposals submitted to The Community Foundation for Greater Atlanta, Inc. The first is from a proposal for Dress for Success Atlanta.

> Our annual fundraising plan for the next three years projects an 8% increase in revenues per year. These increases will come primarily from individual and organizational donors who make contributions on an annual basis (in 2005, we raised over $20,000 from these sources) and from income from quarterly sales of excess inventory (this is a new effort for 2006 but, based on the experiences of other Dress for Success affiliates, we are optimistic about results). If we receive a grant from the Community Foundation for this cycle, we plan to be in the position to provide funds to replace the Foundation's grant from our regular fundraising efforts by June of 2007.

And here is a sustainability plan for Youth Ensemble Atlanta.

> This grant will enable Youth Ensemble Atlanta to expand our community programming and productions, while increasing the opportunities for YEA to support itself through ticket sales and rental income for years to come. In fact, following this initial campaign for our original expenses, we expect the space to be able to pay for itself without further support from the funding community. Over the past four years, YEA has made huge strides in becoming financially stable and preparing to occupy a space of our own. We have operated with a surplus since our founding and have been able to increase earned and contributed revenue by more than 20% a year for the past five years.
>
> We are projecting an annual operating expense increase of $60,000-90,000 including increased program, production, staff and facility expenses. These expenses will easily be covered by the estimated annual addition of $100,000 in ticket sales. We currently average $10,000-15,000 a week in sales in a 200-seat venue. We will be adding at least 10 more weeks of performances in a 600-seat venue, which will comfortably meet these initial projections. Surpluses will be set aside as cash reserves to help us purchase a space of our own in the future.

It behooves you to be very specific about current and projected funding streams, both earned income and fundraised, and about the base of financial support for your nonprofit. Here is an area where it is important to have backup figures and prognostications at the ready, in case a prospective funder asks for these. Some grantmakers, of course, will want to know who else will be receiving a copy of this same proposal. You should not be shy about sharing this information with the funder.

6

Developing the Proposal:
The Evaluation

Introduction

Evaluation of the effectiveness of programs and strategies is a growing trend among today's foundations and other nonprofit organizations, and one to which the proposal writer should pay special attention. The well-constructed evaluation component of a grant proposal is an increasingly important vehicle for describing how both the grant applicant and the potential funder will be able to tell how well the organization succeeds at what it proposes to do.

Viewed in this context, evaluation is far more than accountability for how grant funds will be used. Rather it is a mechanism for organizational capacity building that will enable your nonprofit to excel at whatever it sets out to do. If done well, evaluation answers the following questions: Did the desired outcomes occur? Did they result from the organization's intervention? Were the strategies adopted the correct ones, or were there approaches that would have been more effective? Is the impact on the nonprofit's audience discernable and will it last? The evaluation component you construct as part of the project description for your proposal should respond to as many of these questions as possible.

Evaluation is most effective when it is conducted as a partnership between the funder and the nonprofit, with all stakeholders, including board members and those who will benefit from the grant project, engaged in its design. The best evaluation plans entail gathering both objective and subjective data that will contribute to learning by everyone involved with the grant project. Evaluation as an activity should be ongoing, not something you think about once and then never revisit.

Evaluation in the context of grantmaking derives from the social sciences. As such it has a specific vocabulary associated with it. Nonprofit grantseekers applying to U.S. foundations in the 21st century, especially the larger ones and those with staff, will encounter a variety of terminology related to evaluation in guidelines these funders set forth for their grant applicants. For complete definitions and an in-depth discussion of these various terms as they are commonly used by grantmakers, refer to *A Funder's Guide to Evaluation* by Peter York, 2006.

The Evaluation Plan and the Grant Report

Among the grantmakers we interviewed for this *Guide,* evaluation was often discussed, and in several different contexts. All seemed in agreement that it is essential for the nonprofit grantseeker to have a plan to evaluate its programs and strategies, and that a succinct description of that evaluation plan was a necessary ingredient of the successful proposal. Several funders when asked about evaluation referred immediately to grantee reports as the primary mechanisms for determining success. Indeed the "evaluative report" seems to be on many funders' minds.

It stands to reason that having a solid evaluation plan in place will greatly facilitate the report on the use of funds that you will need to compile at the end of the grant project and may well lay the groundwork for future funding. For these reasons evaluation is not something that can be treated as an "add-on" at the end of the process of constructing the grant proposal. It needs to be built into the conceptual design of the grant project from the outset. To quote Laura Gilbertson of the William Bingham Foundation: "We want to see that an organization has internal mechanisms in place to evaluate programs. How do they decide if the program was a success? They need to learn to keep track for their own use. In a report on the grant we ask the grantee to address the objectives set forth in the proposal."

For more about grant reporting see Chapter 12.

The Rationale for Evaluation

Most of the funders we interviewed for this *Guide* indicated that they expect to see at least one or two paragraphs describing a well thought-out evaluation plan and some projected indicators of success, either qualitative, quantitative or both, laid out in the body of the proposal. In point of fact more and more grantmakers, specifically prescribe what the evaluation component of your proposal should contain, and they will not consider applications that are missing this key element. For a number of the larger foundations whose leadership advocates for more rigorous evaluation on the part of nonprofits, the instructions for composing this section of the grant proposal can be quite extensive. Here is an excerpt from the Evaluation Toolkit posted at the W. K. Kellogg Foundation's web site to assist grant applicants (primarily those using outside evaluators):

Home   Who We Are   Grantseeking   **Programming**   Knowledgebase

☒ W.K

EVALUATION TOOLKIT

Sign up f
Newslett

New Publications   ◄ ►
Show
All

**Systems Concepts in Evaluation: An Expert
Anthology** - This volume was supported by a
grant from the W.K. Kellogg Foundation, which
is increasingly using systems thinking
approaches to our work. It is...

Overview
▶ Publications and
Resources

Toolkit Overview
▶ Where to Start
▶ Evaluation Approaches
▶ Evaluation Questions
▶ The Evaluation Plan
▶ Budgeting for an Evaluation
▶ Hiring and Managing an
Evaluator
Additional Resources

Toolkits

Toolkit Overview

This toolkit is designed to provide our grantees with guidance as they undertake evaluating ar
learning from their work. It is targeted primarily at those grantees who will be working with an
external evaluator or conducting their own rigorous internal evaluations, but we believe anyon
is seeking to design a useful evaluation can benefit from it.

The tools and approaches in this toolkit are based on our mission and evaluation philosophy a
built upon our Evaluation Handbook. The toolkit has seven sections (the links to these section
located in the left hand column and are available on every page of the toolkit):

1. **Where to start**: Describes some of the first issues to address in beginning an evaluati

2. **Evaluation approaches**: Gives some detail on different approaches to evaluation anc
how they are related to hiring an evaluator and designing the evaluation.

3. **Evaluation questions**: Gives suggestions on developing the questions that will guide
evaluation work.

4. **Evaluation plan**: Provides details on the major components of an evaluation plan, inc
data collection and analysis, reporting, and assuring use of findings.

5. **Budgeting**: Shows how to create an initial evaluation budget.

6. **Hiring and managing evaluators**: Suggests things to consider in selecting and mana
the best evaluator for your project.

7. **Additional resources**: Links to useful on-line resources on evaluation.

Please provide your feedback on our toolkit.

Site Map • Contact • Privacy Policy

Beyond the very practical concerns of increasing one's chances at being funded, the well conceived grant project quite simply requires some evaluative aspect to enable both grantee and funder to ultimately determine if it succeeds or not. The form the actual evaluation plan takes will be different in each case, but is obviously closely tied to the initial objectives for the grant project and is designed with measurable outcomes in mind, so that the grantee will be able to report back about its accomplishments to the funder at the end of the grant period. The evaluation component of your proposal might be one or two paragraphs or one or more pages, depending on the nature of the project.

Typically the evaluation component of your proposal will be part of the project description. And it makes sense to match the scope and complexity of the evaluation component to that of the project. For example, if you are asking for funds to buy an additional computer for your agency, it is probably not necessary to develop an elaborate plan to assess its impact on your operations. On the other hand, if you are requesting a significant amount of funds to conduct a scientific experiment involving multiple researchers utilizing sophisticated equipment, you should provide details on specific mechanisms to determine whether the methodology described in your proposal will have achieved your goals and objectives and will have had the desired results.

Keep in mind that not all funders require a formal evaluation: some want monitoring reports only. In this case, it is up to you to first find out what is needed and then to decide whether a formal evaluation plan is an essential aspect of the project or not. Many of the grantmakers interviewed for this book, however, told us that a sound evaluation component based on measurable outcomes, is the hallmark of a proposal they are likely to fund. You will want to remain flexible about precisely how you will evaluate your project, because in discussions about the proposal, some funding representatives may want to further help you shape the evaluation. In the words of Bruce Esterline of the Meadows Foundation: "We ask the applicant to tell us how they will measure their own effectiveness. Sometimes we have to prod them to be more deliberate and precise about what they are going to evaluate."

Types of Evaluation

It is essential to describe your plans to evaluate your project in such a way as to clearly indicate that you are serious about honestly assessing its potential for success. Some evaluation plans measure the product; that is the end result. Others assess the process; that is the ongoing activities. You may find that either or both will be appropriate for evaluating your particular project, depending on the nature of your operations and the project's objectives. No matter which type of evaluation you choose, you will want to describe how you will collect the information you need, how data will be analyzed, and by whom.

Whether you are measuring the process, the product, or both, there are two types of data to gather: qualitative and quantitative. Most sound evaluation plans include both types.

Qualitative evaluation methods include interviews, focus groups, questionnaires, notes compiled by objective observers, and/or surveys. A picture of the whole that reflects multiple perspectives should emerge from these methods. For example, an evaluation of a swimming program for toddlers might include a formal observation and written notes regarding the instructional activities that comprise the swimming lessons and a parent questionnaire in order to understand how the techniques used affected the child's learning experience.

Quantitative evaluation methods are more formal in their execution and numerical in their output. Quantitative means are used to generate statistics that demonstrate the program's effectiveness, via such metrics as test scores or numbers of participants. For example, an evaluation of the same swimming program for toddlers might include the age and number of children participating and how many reached certain milestones and passed the swimming test.

Crafting the Evaluation Component

Putting together a solid evaluation module for your grant proposal is a skill that most grantseekers will want to develop. Today's grants decision-makers may well assume that a well-crafted evaluation plan is an indication of a well-run organization, one they can have confidence in and one that is worthy of their investment of funds. It instills confidence in the funder. In the words of Danah Craft of Sun Trust Bank, Atlanta foundation, "Having a good evaluation component in place helps position the grantseeker for the next grant."

We already mentioned that it is critical to match the evaluation to the project. A key point to keep in mind also when writing the evaluation section of your proposal is that it should proceed in a linear fashion, from the objectives and activities of your project description to the anticipated outcomes and then to the ultimate impact on the audience you serve.

One fundraiser we know suggests that it might be helpful to think of this linear progression in reverse chronological order. Start by envisioning the anticipated impact of your grant project, then list the outcomes, then the activities you will engage in to achieve these outcomes, and finally describe your initial objectives. This approach will help make your evaluation section compelling in a more futuristic way. Your evaluation should be the primary vehicle for assessing the degree to which the activities successfully meet the stated outcomes. It should entail very specific indicators of success. This means you will need to have a vision for success (ideally a vision that the funder shares, sometimes referred to as "theory of change") when you set out to construct your evaluation component. And you will want to review and refer back to your objectives and activities to ensure that you can point to a causal relationship between the procedures you're adopting, the strategies behind them, and the outcomes of the project.

To help construct a solid evaluation component, ask yourself the following questions:

- What do you consider success to be?

- What do you suppose the funder considers success to be?

- Are you using qualitative or quantitative measures, or both?

- What specific evaluative mechanisms do you plan to utilize, e.g. observation, surveys, interviews, tests, etc.?

- What format will you use in the body of your proposal to depict the various stages of the evaluation, e.g. descriptive text, tables, charts, diagrams, etc.?

- Will the evaluation be performed by in-house staff or by an outside consultant?

What follows are several examples of evaluation components from grant proposals that funders shared with us. They are notable for their variety in content and format and tend to focus for the most part on assessment of the processes entailed in each grant project. The final excerpt is from a proposal that the Foundation Center submitted to the Clark Foundation and is an example of an evaluation component that is outcomes-based.

The first example is from a proposal for its newcomers program that Southeast Community College submitted to the Cooper Foundation. This is an excerpt from a longer evaluation plan. You will note that the proposal writer chose to use a table format, a common vehicle for depicting an evaluation and its projected results, and to separate the evaluation processes into "objective" (quantitative) and "subjective" (qualitative) measures. Also indicated is the frequency and timing of the various stages of the evaluation efforts and who will be involved in each stage of activity.

Southeast Community College—Evaluation Component (excerpt)

Criteria	Evaluation Process	Timeline	Staff
By the end of year one, at least 80 English-language learners will receive academic and career advising through the Newcomers Educational Center.	**Objective Evaluation:** Project records will track number of students served and the type of services provided. *Evaluation instrument:* Students will complete a survey indicating strengths and weaknesses of the program.	Quarterly	Project
	Subjective Evaluation: Advisory Committee meetings will be held to discuss program management and improvements.	Quarterly	PC and PD, Advisory Committee
	Reporting: An annual report will be made to the administration, funders, and other stakeholders outlining the lessons learned and project accomplishments.	Annually	PC and PD

The next quite different example is from a proposal that the Arts & Business Council of Miami submitted to the Dade Community Foundation. The Council quickly sketches the evaluation plan for its project to increase awareness of the arts among its targeted audience base.

The Arts & Business Council will measure the success of the Amplifying Arts Audiences Initiative through a variety of methods, including:

- The success of mapping 25 arts facilities will be measured by successfully creating seat diagrams of each space and leveraging this information to increase performance opportunities in underserved and neighborhood facilities.
- Teaching facilities managers and arts groups that perform in the facilities how to use the tools to maximize ticket sales will be measured by evaluations and anecdotal evidence.
- The success of developing the collective marketing initiative and the blueprint for the Virtual Box Office will be measured by feedback from arts groups and facilities managers on the effectiveness of the tools.
- The success of educating arts executives and arts marketing professionals on using technology and web sites to effectively reach new audiences will be measured with evaluation forms filled out by participants.
- The Amplifying Arts Audiences task force will also conduct focus groups with arts executives and potential arts consumers.

And here is the evaluation section of the WomensLaw.org proposal to enhance its web site submitted to the Blue Ridge Foundation of New York. Note the highly specific benchmarks the organization has established.

WomensLaw.org has a strong commitment to quality and easy-to-use services. To ensure that the website is effective and the information accessible, we will use several methods of evaluation.

Website use. Each month we will collect data on website use, tracking how many users are hitting which pages and noting which states are getting an increase in visits. We also keep track of emails, noting the state for which information is requested and the needs expressed or types of information requested. We will also track the communications on our listserv or bulletin boards.

User and Agency Evaluations. In order to ensure that we are providing the information that is most needed in an accessible format, we will send out a questionnaire to users of the site who agree to participate and to domestic violence agencies throughout the country. We will also post an optional questionnaire on the website for users who would like to give their feedback.

Benchmarks. We have set benchmarks for WomensLaw.org, which will also help illustrate the success of this project. By the end of year 2003, we anticipate achieving the following:

1. 60,000 visitor sessions per month (use for Oct. 2002 was 15,035 visitor sessions)

2. 30,000 unique visitors per month (use for Oct. 2002 was 6,642 unique visitors)

3. 500 domestic violence agencies reporting that they are using the site with their clients

4. 400 email info requests per month (current avg. use is 130 requests per month)

5. 150 bulletin board or listserv users per month

Finally, here is an example of the evaluation section from a proposal submitted by the Foundation Center to the Clark Foundation for the Center's First Steps & Next Steps project, a fundraising capacity-building program for New York-area nonprofits.

EVALUATION

Outcome thinking will inform our strategies for evaluation of First Steps & Next Steps II. At the beginning of the program, participants and fundraising advisors will discuss desired outcomes for participation, and we will assess progress toward these outcomes on an ongoing basis. We will use the following methods to gather information on the outcomes of FS&NS II, both in building participants' knowledge and skills and in yielding tangible benefits to their organizations:

Evaluation of classroom components: Participants will complete evaluation forms following each module, giving feedback on its content and delivery, self-evaluating the knowledge they gained, and listing action steps they will take from the session to improve their fundraising efforts.

Evaluation by fundraising advisors and guest presenters: In debriefing meetings, fundraising advisors and guest presenters will assess participants' learning, based on observation during the workshops, discussion with participants, and the group's e-mail communication between and after the workshops.

Feedback summary: At the conclusion of the program, participants will complete a feedback summary to indicate the level of overall satisfaction with the program and to identify aspects of the program that were most useful and least useful to them.

Tangible benefits to nonprofits: During the program and three months, six months, and one year after its conclusion, we will gather information on nonprofits' gains as reflected by the Indicators of Success listed above on pp. 2–3.

Movement along the matrix of under-resourced organizations: In assessing the status of participating organizations, the Foundation Center established a scales-and-ladders matrix to capture the spectrum of conditions of under-resourced nonprofits, ranging from "In Crisis" to "Safe." FS&NS II fundraising advisors, along with participants, will determine where each organization falls on this matrix at the beginning of the program and upon completion of the program.

Who Will Conduct the Evaluation?

Determining who will conduct the evaluation is often a challenge for the nonprofit grantseeker, but an essential aspect of the evaluation component of your proposal. Many grantseekers find evaluation quite intimidating, not only because of the potential costs of such an effort, but because they have little experience with it. The fact is that funders usually leave it up to the nonprofit to determine who will conduct the evaluation. And the vast majority of evaluations of most foundation grant projects are conducted by in-house program staff. When the nonprofit's own staff or volunteers engage in evaluative activities, therefore, it is important that they go beyond simply tracking program outputs to determining the actual outcomes of the grant project and the ultimate impact on the project's beneficiaries.

Outside evaluators, on the other hand, fulfill the need for the application of rigorous design grounded in the social sciences to the evaluation plan and its implementation. These experts bring credibility, objectivity, research and analytical skills, and expertise that most nonprofits simply lack. They can also provide confidentiality in data gathering where needed. The types of evaluation that outside consultants typically conduct include formal needs assessments, environmental scans, financial analyses, focus groups, and interviews. Funders that require outside evaluators tend to be among the larger ones, and typically this requirement applies to complex, relatively expensive grant projects only.

The good news for grantseekers is that often when an outside evaluator is required, the funder will either permit the nonprofit to include the cost of such an evaluation as a separate line item in the project budget or will provide its own evaluator. To quote Robert Crane of JEHT Foundation: "When we want an outside consultant's validation of a particular project, we will fund the cost separately." And from Robert Jaquay of the George Gund Foundation, "We will initiate evaluation from the outside, if is called for, and we will pay for it."

Determine Funder Preferences

As with all other aspects of proposal writing, if the funders' requirements vis a vis evaluation are unclear, you should ask about them. This is still an area where there is great disparity among funder preferences. To quote Marilyn Hennessy of the Retirement Research Foundation when asked her opinion of how evaluation was being handled today: "This is a mixed bag. More funders are trying to find out the impact of the money they spend. But this is being done with varying degrees of sophistication and through in-house staff and consultants. The focus on evaluation is causing angst among nonprofits. There is a need for greater balance, to both get the needed information and to respect the time and dollars needed to produce the information for funders."

We would be remiss if we failed to point out that for some funders evaluation remains a relatively controversial issue. In a time when grant dollars are increasingly competitive to secure, one can question the value of those spent on administrative efforts as opposed to direct service provision. Nancy Wiltsek of the Pottruck Family Foundation expressed the following opinion. "There is a backlash about getting measurable outcomes from grantseekers. What are they really able to do? They should be able to define success for themselves, be clear about how they measure that success, not promise what they can't deliver, and ultimately feel good about what they are doing. It is more than just outcomes."

Conclusion

Evaluation of a grant project is not something that the grantseeker should treat lightly. This outcomes-based means of measuring success is becoming as important in grantmaking as it is in business or government. When approaching what is still a daunting task for many proposal writers, the very first thing you should do is to find out exactly what the prospective funder's requirements are regarding evaluation of its grants. This information will help shape the construction of a useful evaluation plan and an effective evaluation component as part of the project description of your grant proposal. But evaluation is more than just what the funder wants. It is a guiding principle and an important mechanism for the nonprofit to ensure that it accomplishes what it sets out to do. It is evident that evaluation is fast becoming an important aspect of the grant proposal, and while not as significant as the statement of need or the budget, careful consideration and skill are required in putting it together.

7

Developing the Proposal: The Budget

The project description provides the picture of your proposal in words. The budget further refines that picture with numbers. A well-crafted budget adds greatly to the proposal reviewer's understanding of your project. Or as Bob Wittig of the Jovid Foundation says: "The numbers paint a picture. Budgets provide depth. Be strategic about it."

The budget for your proposal may be as simple as a one-page statement of projected expenses. Or your proposal may require a more complex presentation, perhaps a spreadsheet including projected support and revenue and notes explaining various items of expense or revenue. The most important point is also the most obvious. As Leslie Silverman of the Bill & Melinda Gates Foundation reminds us: "The budget should be aligned with your objectives."

Expense Budget

As you prepare to assemble the budget, go back through the proposal narrative and make a list of all personnel and nonpersonnel items related to the operation of the project. Be sure that you list not only new costs that will be incurred if the project is funded but also any ongoing expenses for items that will be allocated to the project. Then get the relevant numbers from the person in your agency who is responsible for keeping the books. You may need to estimate the proportions of your agency's ongoing expenses that should be charged to the project and any new costs, such as salaries for project personnel not yet hired. Put the costs you have identified next to each item on your list.

It is accepted practice to include as line items in your project budget any operating costs of the agency that will be specifically devoted to running the project. Most commonly, these are the costs of supervision and of occupancy. If the project is large relative to the organization as a whole, these line items might also include telephone, utilities, office supplies, and computer-related expenses. For instance, if one of three office phone lines will be devoted to the project, one-third of the monthly cost of maintaining phone service could legitimately be listed as a project cost.

There are other costs incurred by your organization that benefit your project indirectly. These can be called overhead costs, administrative costs, supporting services, or shared costs. They are the costs of running your organization: rent, utilities, maintenance, general liability insurance, and staff to perform administrative duties, such as payroll or accounting functions. These items support all programs within your organization, and you would incur these costs whether or not you operated the particular project you are budgeting for. They are often referred to as the "indirect costs" of your project.

Examples of typical costs that might be considered indirect include:

- Administrative staff
- Audit fees
- Equipment rental
- Fundraising costs
- Insurance
- Legal fees
- Meetings of the board of directors
- Occupancy (rent and maintenance)
- Utilities

Since some foundations will not award grants for general operating support, it is in your organization's best interest to try to recover a portion of these costs with each project grant you prepare. After all, your project could not exist if these overhead items were not available to support its activities. To accurately depict the full costs of your project, you need to allocate some of these costs to your project.

There are two methods commonly used to add indirect costs to a project budget. The first, which is by far the most common, entails adding a percentage for indirect costs. Some funders have an allowable percentage of your project's direct costs that you can add for indirect costs. A second method is a line item by line item allocation. In this method you identify specific overhead expenses that you will add to your project budget based on certain formulas. Both methods require consultation with your organization's financial officer, bookkeeper, or other accounting professional.

It is important to include indirect costs in your project budgets because programs do not exist in isolation. You need funding from some source to cover these costs—to pay for your organization's support services (such as the bookkeeper, fundraiser, or your human resources department) and to pay for other overhead items, such as rent and telephone expenses.

Funders may have policies regarding the percentage of overhead that they will allow in a project budget. Some do not allow any overhead at all to be included. If possible, you should find out about the overhead policy before submitting your proposal to a particular foundation, because you may need to explain to that funder how you will cover overhead costs from other sources.

Your list of budget items and the calculations you have done to arrive at a dollar figure for each item should be summarized on worksheets. You should keep these to remind yourself how the numbers were developed. These worksheets can be useful as you continue to develop the proposal and discuss it with funders. They are also a valuable tool for monitoring the project once it is under way and for reporting after completion of the grant.

A portion of a worksheet for a year-long project might look like this:

Item	Description	Cost
Executive director	Supervision	10% of salary = $10,000 Benefits at 25% = $2,500
Project director	Hired in month one	11 months full time at $35,000 = $32,083
Tutors	12 working 10 hours per week for 13 weeks	12 x 10 x 13 x $4.50 = $7,020
Office space	Requires 25% of current space	25% x $20,000 = $5,000
Overhead	20% of project cost	20% x $64,628 = $12,926

With your worksheets in hand, you are ready to prepare the expense budget to accompany your grant proposal. For most projects, costs should be grouped into subcategories, selected to reflect the critical areas of expense. All significant costs should be broken out within the subcategories, but small ones can be combined on one line. It is common practivce to divide your expense budget into personnel and nonpersonnel costs. Personnel subcategories might include salaries, benefits, and consultants. Subcategories under nonpersonnel costs might include travel, equipment, and printing—just to name a few items—with a dollar figure attached to each line.

Two expense budgets follow. The first example is from the East Side House proposal for an evaluation project submitted to the Altman Foundation.

EAST SIDE HOUSE
Evaluation Consultant Budget

Expenses	Total
Consultant (fee and expenses)	$ 50,000
Staff	
Executive Director	15,000
Assistant Executive Director	20,000
Deputy Director of Community Centers	15,000
Deputy Director of School Programs	8,000
Director of Information Technology	10,000
Subtotal	$ 68,000
Other Than Personnel	
Database Development	17,000
Staff Training	15,000
Survey/Tools Development	12,000
Subtotal	$ 44,000
Total Expenses	**$162,000**

The second example is from the Arts & Business Council of Miami, Inc. proposal to the Dade Community Foundation. It includes a separate column for funds requested from the Community Foundation as distinguished from other sources.

Expenses Line Item	Total Cash Expenses	Dade Community Foundation Funds	Other Funds for Proposed Project	In-Kind Contributions
Project Staff: (Position): Coordinator	$5,000	$2,500	$2,500	$0
Project Staff: (Position): Training Coord	1,000	0	1,000	0
Project Staff: (Position):	0	0	0	1,000
Services sub-contracted to key partners	7,500	3,000	4,500	0
Consulting Services	3,500	0	3,500	0
Other contracted services	7,000	3,000	4,000	5,000
Materials/Supplies				
Marketing/Publicity/Advertising	2,000	1,000	1,000	2,000
Printing & Copying	1,500	500	1,000	1,000
Postage & Delivery	100	0	100	0
Travel—Local				
Travel—Out of Country				
Equipment Rental	500	0	500	0
Equipment Purchase				
Space Rental for project activities	2,000	0	2,000	1,000
Total Expenses	**$30,100**	**$10,000**	**$20,100**	**$10,000**

Support and Revenue Statement

For the typical project, no support and revenue statement is necessary. The expense budget represents the amount of grant support required. But if grant support has already been awarded to the project, or if you expect project activities to generate income, a support and revenue statement is the place to provide this information.

In itemizing grant support, make note of any earmarked grants; this will suggest how new grants may be allocated. The total grant support already committed should then be deducted from the "Total Expenses" line on the expense budget to give you the "Amount to Be Raised" or the "Balance Requested."

Any earned income anticipated should be estimated on the support and revenue statement. For instance, if you expect 50 people to attend your performance on each of the four nights it is given at $10 a ticket, and if you expect that 20 of them will buy the $5 souvenir book each night, you would show two lines of income, "Ticket Sales" at $2,000 and "Souvenir Book Sales" at $400. As with the expense budget, you should keep backup worksheets for the support and revenue statement to remind yourself of the assumptions you have made.

Because an earned income statement deals with anticipated revenues, rather than grant commitments in hand, the difference between expenses and revenues is usually labeled "Balance Requested," rather than "Amount to Be Raised." The funder will appreciate your recognition that the project will earn even a small amount of money—and might well raise questions about this if you do not include it in your budget.

Now that your budget is complete, take the time to analyze it objectively. Be certain that the expense estimates are neither too lean nor on the high side. If you estimate too closely, you may not be able to operate within the budget. You will have to go back to funders already supporting the project for additional assistance, seek new donors, or underwrite part of the cost out of general operating funds. None of these alternatives is attractive.

Consistently overestimating costs can lead to other problems. The donor awards a grant expecting that all of the funds will support the project, and most will instruct you to return any funds remaining at the end. If you have a lot of money left over, it will reflect badly on your budgeting ability. This will affect the funder's receptiveness toward any future budgets you might present.

Finally, be realistic about the size of your project and its budget. You will probably be including a copy of the organization's financial statements in the appendix to your proposal. A red flag will be raised for the proposal reviewer if the budget for a new project rivals the size of the rest of your operation.

If you are inexperienced in developing proposal budgets, you should ask your treasurer or someone who has successfully managed grant funds to review it for you. This can help you spot obvious problems that need to be fixed, and it can prepare you to answer questions that proposal reviewers might raise, even if you decide not to change the budget.

Budget Narrative

A budget narrative portion is used to explain any unusual line items in the budget and is not always needed. If costs are straightforward and the numbers tell the story clearly, explanations are redundant.

If you decide a budget narrative is needed, you can structure it in one of two ways. You can create "Notes to the Budget," with footnote-style numbers on the line items in the budget keyed to numbered explanations. Or, if an extensive or more general explanation is required, you can structure the budget narrative as straight text. Remember, though, that the basic narrative about the project and your organization belong elsewhere in the proposal, not in the budget narrative.

The following is an example of a budget with an accompanying footnoted narrative from a proposal of Canal Community Alliance.

Canal Community Alliance
Radio Canal Remote Studio Project Budget
As of April 4, 2003

Project Expenses	CCA	Milagro Foundation	Marin Arts Council	The Bothin Foundation	Project Budget	Notes
			Amount Requested			
Construction of office and studio space	$8,250				$ 8,250	a
Mixing Board				$ 4,000	4,000	b
MAC I Book				1,800	1,800	c
Pro-Tools Music Editing Software				1,500	1,500	d
Microphones		$ 250			250	e
Microphone stands		100	$150		250	f
Headphones			270		270	g
Speakers			80	20	100	h
1 Dual CD player		500			500	i
2 CART machines		1,200		1,750	2,950	j
Dedicated telephone line				550	550	k
Internet services for a year				200	200	l
Furniture				1,400	1,400	m
Carpet				1,500	1,500	n
Cables and wire adapters				400	400	o

Project Expenses	CCA	Milagro Foundation	Marin Arts Council	The Bothin Foundation	Project Budget	Notes
2 Wood doors with small window		700		650	650	p
Sound proofing material and installation				800	1,500	q
Curtains/drapes for windows				400	400	r
Radio Engineer @ $50/hr x 50 hours				2,500	2,500	s
Total Expenses	**$8,250**	**$2,750**	**$500**	**$17,470**	**$28,970**	

a. Remodeling and construction of office and studio space at CCA Teen Center.

b. Mixing board will be used to produce interviews and radio segments.

c. Laptop computer will be used in the production room which is a former closet and has no room for a desktop computer.

d. Music editing software for 3 computers @ $500 each

e. 5 mikes x $50 each

f. 5 mike stands x $50 each

g. 6 headphones @ $45 each

h. 4 speakers @ $25 each

i. CD player will be used to play music on the air.

j. Radio cart machines will be used to record and play PSAs, radio segments, and interviews. This includes one DLPS Cart-play @ $1,150 and one DLRS Cart-record @ $1,800.

k. Installation of a phone line for transmitting radio signal to and from San Rafael High School's transmitter.

l. Cost for DSL internet service for one year.

m. Furniture for meetings and production use. This includes a round table with chairs, 3 desk chairs, & a table for the mixing board.

n. The teen center does not have any carpet. Carpet is needed for Radio Canal's office and studio space.

o. Cables and wiring for installing equipment.

p. 2 solid wood doors with a small window for production rooms; includes installation.

q. Sound proofing material and installation.

r. Curtains will be used as part of soundproofing on a wall with windows.

s. Technical consultant to select, wire and install all radio equipment.

The budget, whether one page or several, is now ready to include in the proposal document. Keep a copy of it with your backup worksheets in a special folder. The materials in this folder will assist you in tracking actual expenses as the project unfolds. They will enable you to anticipate lines that are in danger of going over budget or areas where you might have extra funds to spend, so that you can manage effectively the grant funds that you receive. These materials will also be extremely helpful when it comes time to write the grant report. An example of a program budget will be found in the sample proposal in Appendix A.

8

Developing the Proposal: Organization Information and Conclusion

Organization Information

Normally the résumé of your nonprofit organization should come at the end of your proposal. Your natural inclination may be to put this information up front in the document, but it is usually better first to sell the need for your project and then your agency's ability to carry it out.

It is not necessary to overwhelm the reader with facts about your organization. This information can be conveyed easily by attaching a brochure or other prepared statement or by providing brief information and then referring the funder to your organization's web site, if you have one. In two pages or less, tell the reader when your nonprofit came into existence; state its mission, being certain to demonstrate how the subject of the proposal fits within or extends that mission; and describe the organization's structure, programs, and special staff expertise. Here is an example from the Next Generation proposal to the Agape Foundation.

Organization Information

Since our founding three years ago, Next Generation has reached close to 5,000 young people in Marin County and beyond. We have educated thousands of youth, helped engage hundreds of young leaders, planned dozens of successful events and direct actions, generated extensive media coverage and succeeded in changing policies and practices countywide and in local schools.

Our Peace Campaign educates students about the war in Iraq and its tremendous cost, as well as U.S. foreign policy in general, and helps young people to take grassroots action for peace. Last year, Next Generation youth partnered with local government officials and our county's Youth Commission to persuade our county government to unanimously pass a resolution opposing the war in Iraq and calling for a withdrawal of U.S. troops. We held educational events and brought young anti-war veterans into local schools and communities, to share their stories and their opposition to the war. Our "Fund Our Town, Not the War," march drew significant media coverage and more than 100 people—including U.S. Congresswoman Lynn Woolsey—for a rally and march through San Rafael, CA, highlighting the cost of war to local agencies like police and fire departments, libraries, and schools, and concluding with a forum at City Hall featuring every top city official, including the police and fire chiefs, and town council members. Our actions at the local military recruitment center and our vigil mourning the 2000th U.S. soldier killed in Iraq and calling for an end to war drew more than 100 youth and adults, as well as front-page media coverage.

Next Generation's programs integrate peace/anti-war work with sustainability outcomes. We recognize that war is not sustainable in terms of social justice issues and environmental concerns, and that social and environmental sustainability promotes peace. In order to address some of the root causes of conflict, our Sustainable Schools Initiative is helping to achieve peace and justice by changing the way we live and creating more responsible institutions. We were proud to be one of the main organizations behind the Marin Earth Day 2005 festival, and our workshops, guides and resources have helped students to expand school recycling programs, to start school gardens, and to convince their clubs to switch to fair trade, organic clothing. Some are even working with their schools to shift to solar power. These efforts support workers and the environment—and they build peace and goodwill.

Discuss the size of the board, how board members are recruited, and their level of participation. Give the reader a feel for the makeup of the board. (You should include the full board list in the appendix.) If your agency is composed of volunteers or has an active volunteer group, describe the functions that the volunteers fill. Provide details on the staff, including numbers of full- and part-time staff and their levels of expertise.

Describe the kinds of activities in which your staff engage. Explain briefly the assistance you provide. Describe the audiences you serve, any special or unusual needs they face, and why they rely on your agency. Cite the number of people who are reached through your programs.

Tying all of the information about your nonprofit together, cite your agency's expertise, especially as it relates to the subject of your proposal.

This information, coupled with the attachments you will supply in the appendix, is all the funder will require at this stage. Keep in mind that funders may wish to check with other sources to learn more about your organization and its performance.

These sources might include experts in the field, contacts established at organizations similar to your own, other funders, or even an agency such as the Better Business Bureau Wise Giving Alliance, which issues reports on some of the larger, national nonprofits.

In the next example, Dress for Success Atlanta briefly describes its history to The Community Foundation for Greater Atlanta, Inc.

> Our mission is "to support low-income women in their quest for self-sufficiency by providing interview and career clothing, ongoing professional and personal development, and role models who have overcome and triumphed in similar circumstances."
>
> Dress for Success Atlanta (DFSA), formerly Working Wardrobe, was founded in 1997 by Deborah Wolf. Ms. Wolf created the organization after seeing numerous highly-skilled applicants through her medical staffing agency who could not be placed in professional positions because they did not have appropriate interview attire. She urged her friends and colleagues to help her with donations of gently-used suits and accessories and to volunteer as Personal Shoppers to assist clients in finding just the right outfit for an interview. Ms. Wolf secured donated space from the Apparel Mart. Until 1999, DFSA was an all-volunteer organization. As the client base grew and additional program components were added, it became clear that a full-time, salaried program director was needed to manage volunteers and inventory, work with community partner organizations who refer clients, and oversee administrative and fundraising activities.

Conclusion

Every proposal should have a concluding paragraph or two. This is a good place to call attention to the future, after the grant is completed. If appropriate, you should outline some of the follow-up activities that might be undertaken, to begin to prepare your funders for your next funding request.

This section is also the place to make a final appeal for your project. Briefly reiterate what your nonprofit wants to do and why it is important. Underscore why your agency needs funding to accomplish it. Don't be afraid at this stage to use a bit of emotion to solidify your case.

The following two examples come from proposals submitted to The Frances L. & Edwin L. Cummings Memorial Fund. The first is a brief but powerful concluding statement from the Groundwork proposal.

Conclusion

In a relatively short amount of time Groundwork has developed, funded, and launched a respected institution serving over 600 youth and 1,000 families in one of New York City's most at-risk and underserved communities. A full-time Support Services Coordinator is essential to meaningfully accommodate the growing demand for support services as we become a recognized and established presence in the community. It is our sincere hope that The Frances L. & Edwin L. Cummings Memorial Fund will partner with us once again over the upcoming year as we work to build "Powerful Youth for Powerful Communities."

The second example is excerpted from the Common Ground proposal for its S2Hi program.

Conclusion

S2Hi has created an unprecedented level of communication and cooperation among service providers and clients, and has proven that chronic homeless individuals are indeed "housing ready." The project's collaborative approach and high success rate have also led to significant changes in the policies and practices of both service providers and government agencies. As we approach our goal of reducing the homeless population of West Midtown by two-thirds by the end of 2006, we seek to maximize the program's impact by helping other organizations to replicate our program model in other New York City neighborhoods and by ensuring our clients' housing stability.

Private funding was absolutely essential to Common Ground's initial launch and implementation of S2Hi. A $50,000 grant from The Frances L. & Edwin L. Cummings Memorial Fund will enable us to reach our goals for reducing street homelessness in West Midtown, follow-up with clients to ensure their longer-term success, and continue sharing our work with organizations throughout the City. We urgently request your support.

9

Variations on the Project Proposal Format

In the preceding chapters we presented the recommended format for components of the standard proposal. In reality, however, not every proposal will slavishly adhere to these guidelines. This should not be surprising. Sometimes the scale of the project might suggest a small-scale letter format proposal, or the type of request might not require all of the proposal components or the components in the sequence recommended here. The guidelines and policies of individual funders will be your ultimate guide. Many funders today state that they prefer a brief letter proposal; others require that you complete an application form. In any case, you will want to refer to the basic proposal components (see Chapter 2) to be sure that you have not omitted an element that will support your case.

What follows is a description of a letter proposal and of other format variations.

A Letter Proposal

The scale of the project will often determine whether it requires a letter or the longer proposal format. For example, a request to purchase a $300 fax machine for your agency simply does not lend itself to a lengthy narrative. A small contribution to your agency's annual operating budget, particularly if it is a renewal of past support, might also warrant a letter rather than a full-scale proposal.

What are the elements of a letter request? For the most part, they should follow the format of a full proposal, except with regard to length. The letter should be no more than three pages. You will need to call upon your writing skills because it can be very hard to get all of the necessary details into a concise, well-articulated letter.

As to the flow of information, follow these steps while keeping in mind that you are writing a letter to an individual funding representative. It should not be as formal in style as a longer proposal would be. It may be necessary to change the sequence of the text to achieve the correct tone and the right flow of information.

Here are the components of a good letter proposal, with excerpts of relevant sections of a letter proposal from St. Ann's School to the Independence Community Foundation.

Ask for the gift: The letter should state why you are writing and how much funding is required from the particular foundation.

Dear Ms. Gelber,

St. Ann's is a Pre-K to eighth-grade fully accredited Catholic grammar school serving a very diverse ethnic population. Some students are not Catholic. Our enrollment has increased in the last two years through outreach and marketing efforts, and we believe it will continue to grow in the coming years. One of our fifty-year-old boilers needs replacement, and we are requesting funds to do this. We have been quoted a price of $59,000, and our hope is that one half may come from your foundation. We have secured the remainder from three sources: the parish, alumni and a matching grant from the diocese. Any additional funds will be met by fund-raising events. The time frame is rather acute, as the installation of a new boiler needs to be completed before the onset of cold weather.

Describe the need: In a compelling manner, tell the funder why there is a need for this project, piece of equipment, etc.

As a Catholic school, our financial resources are very limited. Our tuition is as affordable as we can possibly make it, and we offer discounts for families with more than one child enrolled. Although a number of Catholic schools have closed, we have been able to maintain enrollment and financial stability through careful financial management and cost control. We have a very active parents committee and their effort to raise funds and volunteer for various activities is yet another reason for our success. Our diverse student population has benefited from this stability, and the result is outstanding academic achievement. We are very hopeful that we can continue to provide a learning environment with a dedicated staff and faculty and a community for our parents and students for many years to come.

The need for a new boiler is an exceptional case that we believe warrants this action. Our normal operations are met in our budget with some allowance for extraordinary expenses. This is a major capital expense. If we can secure partial funding from your foundation, we can also secure a matching grant from the diocese which will cover most of the remaining cost. We also anticipate some additional cooperation from our vendor to help control the expense of this installation. Although we do have the option of repairing the current unit, such a repair would be almost half the cost of a new unit and we might expect only five years of service before major repairs or replacement would be required. From these standpoints, an investment in a new boiler is the wisest choice. Since we now have the means to apply for grant funds through the efforts of a parent volunteer, it seems prudent to seek such funds.

Explain what you will do: Just as you would in a fuller proposal, provide enough detail to pique the funder's interest. Describe precisely what will take place as a result of the grant.

The installation of a new boiler has several benefits. Obviously, a reliable source of heat in the cold months is necessary. We are the daily custodian of 250 students ranging in ages from four to thirteen, and we would be less than responsible if the building was unsuitable for learning in the winter. With a new unit, we will have a service warranty, hence maintenance savings over a number of years. We also expect fuel savings of a considerable magnitude. The investment in a new boiler now will see savings this coming school year. We have contracted with a respected and reliable vendor for this project. They have already equipped the building with a new oil tank and have demonstrated their commitment to working with us in cost control.

Provide agency data: Help the funder know a bit more about your organization by including your history, brief description of programs offered, number of people served, and staff, volunteer, and board data, if appropriate.

St. Ann's was founded in 1954 and has provided quality education and spiritual guidance for our students. We are fully accredited by Middle States Association. We hold our students to the highest academic standards. St. Ann's is a safe learning environment. Our facility features a gymnasium, library, science lab and computer lab. Our services include a full-time registered nurse, a guidance counselor, peer tutoring, a full-time reading specialist, music classes, Spanish classes for grades seven and eight, early drop-off and a supervised after-school program for our working parents. Our activities include track and basketball teams, school band and choir, the Girl Scouts and special events for our community of parents and students. All of this is possible through the dedication of our faculty, staff, involved parents and parishioners at St. Ann's.

Include appropriate budget data: Even a letter request may have a budget that is a half-page long. Decide if this information should be incorporated into the letter or in a separate attachment. Whichever course you choose, be sure to indicate the total cost of the project. Discuss future funding only if the absence of this information will raise questions.

Close: As with the longer proposal, a letter proposal needs a strong concluding statement. But it can be short and concise.

Thank you for your time in evaluating this inquiry. We await your reply.

Regards,

Attach any additional information required: The funder may need much of the same information to back up a small request as a large one: a board list, a copy of your IRS determination letter, financial documentation, and brief résumés of key staff. Rather than preparing a separate appendix, you should list the attachments at the end of a letter proposal, following the signature.

It may take as much thought and data gathering to write a good letter request as it does to prepare a full proposal (and sometimes even more). Don't assume that because it is only a letter, it isn't a time-consuming and challenging task. Every document you put in front of a funder says something about your agency. Each step you take with a funder should build a relationship for the future.

Other Variations in Format

Just as the scale of the project will dictate whether a letter or a full proposal is indicated, so the type of request will be the determining factor as to whether all of the components of a full proposal are required.

The following section will explore the information that should appear in the proposal application for five different types of requests: special project, general purpose, capital, endowment, and purchase of equipment.

SPECIAL PROJECT

The basic proposal format presented in earlier chapters uses the special project proposal as the prototype, because this is the type of proposal that you will most often be required to design. As stated previously, foundations tend to prefer to make grants for specific projects because such projects are finite and tangible, and their results are measurable.

GENERAL PURPOSE

A general purpose proposal requests operating support for your agency. Therefore, it focuses more broadly on your organization, rather than on a specific project. All of the information in the standard proposal should be present, but there will not be a separate component describing your organization. That information will be the main thrust of the entire proposal. Also, your proposal budget will be the budget for the entire organization, so it need not be duplicated in the appendix.

Two components of the general purpose proposal deserve special attention. They are the need statement and program information, which replaces the "project description" component. The need section is especially important. You must make the case for your nonprofit organization itself, and you must do it succinctly. What are the circumstances that led to the creation of your agency? Are those circumstances still urgent today? Use language that involves the reader, but be logical in the presentation of supporting data. For example, a local organization should cite local statistics, not national ones.

The following is an example of a need statement from a general purpose proposal submitted by South Asian Youth Action (SAYA!) to Independence Community Foundation.

As you know, SAYA! is the only organization of its kind in New York City providing youth development programs for underserved and needy low-income South Asian youth. In our work with these youths, it is evident that the community still faces the following challenges:

1. Despite the long history and presence of South Asians in New York City, the community has been largely underserved in terms of their needs being identified and addressed through social and community services.

2. SAYA! youth attend the most under-resourced and overcrowded schools in Queens. For instance, Newtown High School, which is just a few blocks from our center, is the most crowded school and is operating at 206% capacity. John Adams High School, a school that is 75% South Asian, is at 162% capacity. Richmond Hill High School and W.C. Bryant High School are operating at 185% and 155% capacity respectively. An article from the *Queens Gazette* shows a correlation between these most crowded schools and the results of students' Regents exams.

3. SAYA!'s youth are attending schools such as John Adams High School, a Title I school with a 43.49% graduation rate, or WC Bryant High School, where there is a 52.3% graduation rate. Indeed, if you account for discharges, these rates drop even lower. Our youth typically have little or no access to additional academic assistance in their schools.

In such a situation, it is crucial that SAYA! continue to provide its desperately needed academic services to low-income South Asian youth to work toward achieving its mission of creating social change and opportunities for South Asian youth to realize their fullest potential. For the past eight years, we have been successfully addressing key needs of youth in the community. However, we have only made tiny inroads, given the scale and escalation of the problem and need to continually do more. As such, funding from foundations such as the Independence Community Foundation becomes critical.

1. Wilson, Linda J. "Queens Scores Better Than NYC Average But Overcrowded", *Queens Gazette*, 2001.
2. City of New York Department of Education, Class of 2004 Four-Year Outcomes.

Consider including details on recent accomplishments and future directions as seen in this additional excerpt from the South Asian Youth Action proposal.

Academic and College Preparation Program

SAYA!'s Academic and Career Preparation Program gives South Asians youths the tools to navigate the educational system and succeed academically. SAYA! is able to bridge the gaps in the New York City public school system that disproportionately affect South Asian immigrant youth who are English language learners or have acculturation needs.

The academic services SAYA! offers include SAT, SHSAT, and Regents preparation, one-on-one tutoring, and college guidance. The SAT prep courses occur twice a year for ten weeks and serve at least 55 students overall. The SHSAT classes meet for six weeks twice a year for a total of 15 students. Regents preparation is a one-on-one service and is based on need. Youth may meet with their instructor throughout the year or for a few weeks. Usually they meet weekly for two hours. College advising is also a one-on-one service open to all students, but generally it is most utilized by those in the SAT classes. This service is also based on need and is facilitated by the Academic Program Coordinator.

Program Component	Projected Number of Youth Served
SAT Preparation Classes and College Advising (guidance on college selection and scholarships; college visits)	55
SHSAT Preparation Class	15
One-on-One Tutoring (including Regents preparation)	20
TOTAL	90

SIGNIFICANT PROGRAM ENHANCEMENTS

In the upcoming 2005–2006 program year, SAYA! has designed our programs to be integrated with the Academic and College Preparation Program. In the past, SAYA! has encouraged all of our youth to take advantage of our academic supports. Yet, as an increased commitment to our holistic model, SAYA! will now actively include academic assistance and college guidance as a component of the leadership development programs. Each youth in the Young Men's Leadership Program, Desi Girls on 'da Rise, and ARISE will be assessed by their Program Coordinator based on academic need. The Program Coordinator will work with the youth and the Academic Program Coordinator to ensure that the young person is receiving appropriate provision in the areas of academics and college preparation.

CAPITAL

A capital proposal requests funds for facility purchase, construction, or renovation, or possibly land purchase or long-term physical plant improvements. Today many institutions include other items in a capital campaign, such as endowment funds, program expansion, and salaries for professors. But, for our purposes, we will discuss the more traditional definition of capital, that is, "bricks and mortar."

All of the components of a proposal will be included in a capital request. Differences in content will be found mainly in the need statement, the project description, the budget, and the appendix.

The need section in a capital proposal should focus on why the construction or renovation is required. The challenge is to make the programs that will use the facility come alive to the reader. For example, your agency may need to expand its day care program because of the tremendous need in your community among working parents for such support, the long waiting list you have, and the potential educational value to the children. Your proposal will be less compelling if the focus of the need statement is purely related to space considerations or to meeting building code requirements.

Following is an excerpt from a capital proposal for The Children's Institute.

Four interrelated problems have hampered the Children'sInstitute's ability to provide the programs and all of the services originally anticipated. Those problems are: (1) an increase in the numbers seeking help from TCI; (2) a lack of space preventing the creation of new programs; (3) a lack of space has resulted in overcrowding and negatively impacted the instructional and therapeutic programs for current students and (4) a lack of space has negatively impacted personnel needs, professional development activities and establishment of a research and community outreach program.

1. *Increase in those seeking help:* Numerous reports and studies underscore the growing incidence of learning and behavioral problems among the types of children served by TCI. Statistics compiled by the New Jersey State Board of Education on December 1, 2003, indicate that of the 1,381,523 school-aged children in the public system ranging in age from 3-21 years, 225,780 (16.3%) are classified with disabilities impacting their learning. Nearly 6% of these special education school-aged children, totaling 12,978 due to severity of their disabilities, are referred to approved private schools for the disabled. Of the students referred to programs for the behavioral disabled (this category includes students with Aspergers Syndrome) 23% are referred to private schools, and of children referred to autistic programs, 28% are referred to private schools.

Since moving into our current facility, we have experienced an increase in referrals beyond our original projections. Within one year, student enrollment was at full capacity. This resulted in having to establish an extensive waiting list of students in need and appropriate for the program. The waiting list has been averaging approximately 90 students per year.

2. *Lack of space prevented creation of new programs:* An Early Intervention Program for children below the age of three, which was originally planned to be initiated when we moved into our facility, has not been implemented due to a lack of space. The implementation of this program is important, considering that research indicates that the prognosis for students is greater when they receive educational and therapeutic interventions at a younger age. Each year TCI receives a number of requests for this program.

Further, a great need has arisen to expand the career education program to accommodate the needs of students 14 years of age and older.

Finally, we need separate and different age appropriate environments. TCI serves students ranging in age levels from 3-21 years of age. School programs include: Preschool, Elementary, Middle, Secondary School and Career Education. Considering the different cognitive and social-emotional and physical levels of the students in each program, additional space is needed to create separate, distinct learning environments.

3. *Lack of space has resulted in overcrowding and negatively impacted the instructional and therapeutic program for current students:*

The following student programs are being provided in less than ideal settings:

- occupational and physical therapy
- reading remediation
- career education
- world language instruction
- parent-teacher conferences
- student performances
- student testing
- eating and socialization
- science
- health and fitness

4. *Lack of space to address personnel needs and professional activities including:* work space; professional development; research; community outreach; day care and meetings. In summary, ironically TCI's success jeopardizes the school's ability to do even more for the students who need so much special assistance to succeed.

The project description component of a capital proposal includes two elements. The first is the description of how your programs will be enhanced or altered as a result of the physical work. Then should come a description of the physical work itself. The funder is being asked to pay for the latter and should have a complete narrative on the work to be undertaken. You might supplement that description with drawings, if available. These could be external views of the facility, as well as interior sketches showing people using the facility. Floor plans might help as well. These need not be formal renderings by an artist or an architect; a well-drawn diagram will often make the case. Photos showing "before" and drawings indicating what the "after" will be like are also dramatic adjuncts to the capital proposal.

The budget for a capital proposal will be a very detailed delineation of all costs related to the construction, renovation, etc. It should include the following:

- Actual brick-and-mortar expenses: These should be presented in some logical sequence related to the work being undertaken. For example, a renovation project might follow an area-by-area description, or a construction project might be presented chronologically. Don't forget to include expenses for such items as construction permits in this section.

- Other costs: Salaries, fees, and related expenses required to undertake the capital improvements. Be certain to include in your budget the projected costs of architects, lawyers, and public relations and fundraising professionals. Many capital proposal writers fail to adequately anticipate such "soft" costs.

- Contingency: Estimates for actual construction costs often change during the fundraising and preconstruction periods. It is therefore a good idea to build a contingency into the budget in case costs exceed the budgeted amounts. A contingency of 10 to 20 percent is the norm; more than that tends to raise a proposal reviewer's eyebrows.

Here is the budget for the two-phase Children's Institute construction project.

Proposed Project

TWO-PHASE CONSTRUCTION PROJECT WITH MULTI-PURPOSE ROOM.

Phase I: High School & Career Education Center Addition

2 floors @ 10,000sf each = 20,000sf @ $230/sf = Construction Cost	$4,600,000
Associated Renovations/Alterations to Existing Space Construction Cost	$40,000
Total Construction Cost Phase I	**$4,640,000**

Projected Additional Associated Costs:

• Architecture & Standard Engineering Fees (Structure/MEP)	$400,000
• Specialty Consultants (Traffic/Technology, etc.)	25,000
• Site Work	725,000
• Legal/Experts/Planner	250,000
• Fundraising	300,000
• Contingency	350,000
• Furnishing	200,000
Total	**$2,250,000**

OVERALL PROJECTED COSTS FOR PHASE I	**$6,890,000**

Phase II: Multi-Purpose Therapy Center/Daycare/(5) Classrooms

a. 1 Floor: Area includes multi-purpose room (2,669sf), Therapy, Daycare, and 2 Classrooms = 7,958sf

2 Floor: Area Includes 3 Classrooms & Support Spaces = 3,136sf

Total: 11,094sf @ $240/sf = $2,662,560

b. Renovations/Alterations to Existing Space (Pre-School, Life Skills Apt., Offices) 3,700sf @ $150/sf = $550,000

Total Construction Cost Phase II	**$3,212,560**

Projected Additional Associated Costs

• Architecture & Standard Engineering Fees (Structure/MEP)	$50,000
• Specialty Consultants (Traffic/Technology etc.)	—————
• Site Work	25,000
• Legal/Experts/Planner	—————
• Fundraising	150,000
• Contingency	200,000
• Furnishing	<u>125,000</u>
Total	**$550,000**
OVERALL PROJECTED COSTS FOR PHASE II	**$3,762,560**
COSTS PHASE I + PHASE II	**$10,652,560**

The appendix to a capital proposal may be expanded to include floor plans and renderings if they do not appear within the proposal text. If a brochure has been developed in conjunction with the capital campaign, this could be sent along as part of the appendix package.

ENDOWMENT

An endowment is used by a nonprofit to provide financial stability and to supplement grant and earned income. Often campaigns, designed like capital drives, are mounted to attract endowment dollars. A proposal specifically requesting funding for endowment may resemble either a special project or a general operating application, depending on whether the endowment is for a special purpose, such as scholarships or faculty salaries, or for the organization's general operations. Your focus will be on the following components: the need statement, the program description, and the budget.

The need statement for an endowment proposal will highlight why the organization must establish or add to its endowment. Points to raise might include:

- the importance of having available the interest from the endowment's corpus as an adjunct to the operating budget;

- the desire to stabilize annual income, which is currently subject to the vagaries of government or other grants;

- the value of endowing a particular activity of your organization that lacks the capacity to earn income or attract gift support.

The project description will cover the impact of endowment dollars on the programs of your nonprofit. Provide as many details as possible in explaining the direct consequences of these dollars. Indicate if there are naming or memorial opportunities as part of the endowment fund.

The budget will round out all of this data by indicating how much you are trying to raise and in what categories. For example, there might be a need to endow 75 scholarships at $10,000 each for a total of $750,000.

EQUIPMENT

Frequently, organizations have a need to develop a free-standing proposal for purchase of a piece of equipment, be it MRI equipment for a hospital or a personal computer for program staff. Purchasing a piece of equipment might require only a brief letter proposal, but the scale or significance of the purchase may dictate a full proposal. Again, the need statement, the project description, and the budget will be primary.

In the need statement, explain why the organization must have this equipment. For example, this hospital has no MRI equipment, and people in the community have to travel great distances when an MRI test is required.

Then in the project description, explain how the equipment will alter the way services are delivered. For example: "The new MRI equipment will serve some 500 people annually. It will assist in diagnoses ranging from structural problems in the foot to tracking the development of a lung tumor. The cost per procedure will be $1,000, but it will save millions in unnecessary surgical procedures."

This budget may be the easiest you will ever have to prepare. Indicate the purchase cost for the equipment, plus transportation and installation charges. Consider whether staff training to utilize the equipment properly and the added expenses of maintenance contracts should be included in your budget with the cost of its purchase.

10

Packaging the Proposal

Writing a well-articulated proposal represents the bulk of the effort in preparing a solid proposal package. The remaining work is to package the document for the particular funder to whom it is being sent, based on your research and your contact with that funder to date (as described in Chapters 11 and 12).

Be sure to check the foundation's instructions for how and when to apply. Some foundations will accept proposals at any time. Others have specific deadlines. Foundations will also differ in the materials they want a grant applicant to submit. Some will list the specific information they want and the format you should adopt. Others will have an application form. In the course of the interviews for this book, it became apparent that an increasing number of foundations are developing an application form or a specific proposal format. Many are posting these as guidelines for grantseekers on their web sites. Whatever the foundation's guidelines, pay careful attention to them and follow them.

Grantmakers are extremely frustrated with applicants who do not take the time to find out what is in their application guidelines. It is in the grantseeker's best interest to follow the grantmaker's advice. Otherwise there are delays in reviewing the application while the grantmaker waits for the missing items. Foundation and corporate giving representatives express dismay at having review of worthy proposals delayed sometimes for up to a year because of requested items that are not included.

Of equal concern to grantmakers is the submission of attachments that are not required by the guidelines. Nonprofit applicants would be well advised to refrain from adding any unnecessary attachments—ever! Rather, interesting items not included in the proposal package might be sent to the prospect as part of good cultivation later on.

In the following pages we will discuss the packaging of the document, including:

- cover letter or letter of transmittal;

- cover and title pages;

- table of contents; and

- appendix.

The Cover Letter

Often the cover letter is the basis for either consideration or rejection. As Hildy Simmons, formerly of J. P. Morgan Private Bank, told us in the past, "The cover letter is key. It should be clear and concise and make me want to turn the page. Here are a few dos and don'ts:

- Do make a specific request. It's inconvenient if we have to dig for it.

- Do include a couple of paragraphs about why you are applying to us. But don't quote back to us our own contribution report.

- Do note references but don't name drop."

Elizabeth Smith of the Hyams Foundation tells us: "The cover letter is the first thing that I read." Christine Park of Lucent Technologies Foundation provides this recommendation: "Make your case quickly in the cover letter; provide the detail in the proposal." Maria Mottola of the New York Foundation notes: "This section makes a difference. We learn who wants this project to happen. It tells the story of the why and the how."

What a waste of your agency's resources to invest time, energy, and money developing a proposal around a terrific project and then not have it read! To avoid this happening, be clear, be succinct, and state immediately why the project fits within the funder's guidelines. For example, you might state, "Our funding research indicates that the XYZ Foundation has a special interest in the needs of children in foster care, which is the focus of this proposal." If the proposal does not fit the foundation's guidelines, this should be acknowledged immediately in the cover letter. You will then need to provide an explanation for why you are approaching this foundation.

If you had a conversation with someone in the funder's office prior to submitting the proposal, the cover letter should refer to it. For example, you might say, "I appreciate the time Jane Doe of your staff took to speak with me on December 1 about the Foundation." But do not imply that a proposal was requested if in fact it was not.

Sometimes in a discussion with a funder you will be told, "I can't encourage you to submit because. . . . However, if you want, you can go ahead and submit anyway." In this case, you should still refer to the conversation, but your letter should demonstrate that you heard what the funder said.

The cover letter should also indicate what the reader will find in the proposal package. For example: "You will find enclosed two documents for your review. The first is a concise description of our project. The second is an appendix with the documents required by the Foundation for further review of our request."

Cite the name of the project, a précis of what it will accomplish, and the dollar amount of the request. For example: "Our After School Recreational Program will meet the educational and recreational needs of 50 disadvantaged Harlem children. We are seeking a grant of $25,000 from the Foundation to launch this project."

In the concluding paragraph of the cover letter, you should request a meeting with the funder. This can take place at the funder's office or on site at your agency. Also indicate your willingness to answer any questions that might arise or to provide additional information as required by the funder.

In summary, the cover letter should:

- indicate the size of the request;
- state why you are approaching this funder;
- mention any prior discussion of the proposal;
- describe the contents of the proposal package;
- briefly explain the project; and
- offer to set up a meeting and to provide additional information.

Who should sign the letter? Either the chairman of the board or the chief executive officer of your agency should be the spokesperson for all proposal submissions. Some funders insist on signature by the chairman of the board, indicating that the proposal has the support and endorsement of the board. However, signature by the executive director may allow for a sense of continuity that a rotating board chair cannot provide. If your group has no full-time staff, then the issue is resolved for you, and the board chairman should sign all requests. This would hold true also if your agency is in the process of searching for a new chief executive.

The proposal cover letter should never be signed by a member of the development staff. These individuals do the research, develop the proposals, and communicate with the funder, but generally they stay in the background when it comes to the submission of the proposal and any meetings with the funder. The individual who signs the cover letter should be the same person who signs subsequent correspondence, so that the organization has one spokesperson.

Variations may occur under special circumstances. For example, if a board member other than the chairperson is directly soliciting a peer, the cover letter should come from him or her. Alternatives would be for the letter to be signed by the chairman of the board and then for the board member to write a personal note on the original letter, or to send along a separate letter endorsing the proposal.

Here is an example of a cover letter from East Side House to the Altman Foundation. It includes:

- a specific request;

- a description of broader impact;

- an offer to meet.

June 3, 2005

Karen L. Rosa
Executive Director
Altman Foundation
521 Fifth Ave., 35th Fl.
New York, NY 10175

Dear Ms. Rosa,

I write to ask the Altman Foundation's support for East Side House through a $75,000 grant, which will underwrite an experienced Evaluation Consultant.

To better serve our constituents, East Side House plans to address our evaluation systems across the agency, finding more effective ways to measure success and identify remedial resources when needed. This project is critical to our future work in Mott Haven, and our Board of Managers considers it a top priority.

To this end, East Side House will work with an Evaluation Consultant who can provide proven expertise and evaluation training for staff to create a successful and sustainable assessment system for each of our programs, which touch over 8,000 lives annually. This initiative will increase our organizational capacity, our ability to report on our participants' successes, and ultimately our ability to leverage funding from additional sources.

I would be delighted to meet with you to discuss our request, and to show you our current educational programming for the residents of Mott Haven. Please do not hesitate to contact me with any questions.

Sincerely,

John A. Sanchez
Executive Director

cc: Stephen R. Seiter, Board of Managers

Here is another example of a cover letter. This is from Next Generation to the Agape Foundation. It conveys:

- excitement;

- a specific request;

- an offer to answer questions or provide more information;

- handwritten note at the bottom.

Next Generation
Empowering young activists
www.gonextgeneration.org

January 27, 2006

Dear Karen and the Agape Foundation Board,

It is with great enthusiasm that I submit the enclosed grant proposal on behalf of Next Generation, a grassroots organization that empowers young people to work for peace, sustainability, and our democracy.

Next Generation seeks funding for our Youth Peace Campaign, which helps young people to learn about U.S. foreign policy and military spending, gain activists skills, organize at the grassroots, and work for peace. Our youth are currently organizing to create a youth movement that can help end the war in Iraq and prevent future wars.

Our organization has developed a diverse fundraising plan that includes foundation grants, but we have found it difficult to secure funding for our youth-led peace work. Agape's contribution of $2,000 will allow us to spend more time and resources educating and mobilizing young people to learn the truth about U.S. foreign policy and work for peace at this crucial time.

Thank you in advance for considering our request. Please do not hesitate to contact me with any questions or requests for additional information.

Sincerely,

Roni Krouzman
Founding Director

Thanks so much for all your help, Karen!

Cover Page and Title

The cover page has three functions:

1. to convey specific information to the reader;

2. to protect the proposal; and

3. to reflect the professionalism of the preparer.

You should personalize the information on the cover page by including the name of the funder. You might present the information as follows:

A PROPOSAL TO THE XYZ FOUNDATION

---

or

A REQUEST DEVELOPED FOR THE XYZ FOUNDATION

Then note the title of the project:

A CAMPAIGN FOR STABILITY

Provide key information that the funder might need to contact your agency:

Submitted by:
The Nonprofit Organization
40 Canal Street
New York, NY 10013

Mary Smith   Susan Jones
Executive Director   Director of Development
212-935-5300 x23   212-935-5300 x21
212-935-9660 (fax)   212-935-9660 (fax)
                              e-mail: SJones@aol.com

It is possible that your cover letter will be separated from the rest of the proposal once it arrives at its destination. Without key information on the cover page, the funder could fail to follow up with your agency. You are being kind to your prospective funder when you remember to add the following:

- phone extension or direct telephone line for both the person who signed the letter and a primary staff contact;

- fax number for your organization; and

- e-mail addresses for both the signer and staff contact, if available, since it is becoming increasingly common for funding representatives to contact the grantseeker via e-mail with questions and requests for additional documentation.

The cover page from the Groundwork proposal serves as an example.

Groundwork

For Powerful Youth and Powerful Communities

A Proposal for Funding the Family Resource Center

Contact: Richard Buery, Jr.
Co-Founder & Executive Director
595 Sutter Avenue
Brooklyn, NY 11207
tel: 718-346-2200 ext. 112
fax: 718-346-2020
rbuery@groundworkinc.org
www.groundworkinc.org

The title you assign to your proposal can have a surprisingly significant impact on the reader. It should reflect what your project is all about. "A CAMPAIGN FOR STABILITY" tells the reader that there is a formal effort taking place and that the result will be to bring stability to nonprofit organization. It is short and to the point, while being descriptive.

There are a few suggestions for developing the title for a proposal:

- Don't try to be cute. Fundraising is a serious matter. A cute title implies that the proposal is not a serious attempt to solve a real problem.

- Do not duplicate the title of another project in your agency or one of another nonprofit that might be well-known to the funder. It can cause confusion.

- Be sure the title means something. If it is just words, try again, or don't use any title at all.

Coming up with the title can be a tricky part of proposal writing. If you are stuck, try these suggestions:

- Seek the advice of the executive director, the project director, or a creative person in the organization or outside.

- Hold an informal competition among staff and/or volunteers to see who can come up with the best title.

- Go to the board with a few ideas and ask board members to select the one that makes the most sense.

- Jot down a list of key words from the proposal. Add a verb or two and experiment with the word order.

Let's take a look at a few actual titles and evaluate their effectiveness.

Title	Effectiveness
Forward Face	Arouses interest but does not tell you anything about the project.
	This is a proposal that seeks funds for facial reconstruction for disfigured children. With the help of the nonprofit group involved, the children will have a new image with which to face the future. The title is a pun, which is cute but not very effective.

Title	Effectiveness
Vocational, Educational Employment Project	This title tells us that three types of services will be offered. The project serves disadvantaged youth, which is not mentioned. The effectiveness of this title could be improved if the population served were somehow alluded to.
Building a Healthier Tomorrow	This title implies that construction will occur, and indeed it is the title for a capital campaign. It also suggests that the construction is for some kind of health facility. This proposal is for a YMCA to improve its health-wellness facilities. Thus, the title is very effective in conveying the purpose of the proposal.

You should evaluate any titles you come up with by anticipating the reaction of the uninitiated funding representative who will be reading this proposal.

Table of Contents

Obviously, for letter proposals or those of five pages or less, a table of contents is not required. For proposals of ten pages or more, a table of contents is essential.

Simply put, the table of contents tells the reader what information will be found in the proposal. The various sections should be listed in the order in which they appear, with page numbers indicating where in the document they can be located. The table should be laid out in such a way that it takes up one full page.

Following the proposal format we have recommended, a table of contents would look like this:

TABLE OF CONTENTS	PAGE
Executive Summary	1
Statement of Need	2
Project Description	4
Budget	7
Organization Information	9
Conclusion	10

By stating where to find specific pieces of information, you are being considerate of the proposal reader, who might want an overview of what information is included and also might want to be selective in the initial review.

A sample follows. It is from a proposal for WomensLaw.org.

Table of Contents

The Appendix

The appendix is a reference tool for the funder. Include in it any information not included elsewhere that the foundation or corporate grantmaker indicates is required for review of your request. Not every proposal requires an appendix.

The appendix should be stapled together or bound separately from the proposal narrative. Because it usually contains information that the funder has specifically requested, keeping it separate makes it easy for the funder to find those items. The appendix may have its own table of contents indicating to the reader what follows and where to find it.

A sample table of contents to a proposal appendix, taken from the Ali Forney Center proposal, follows:

Ali Forney Center

Attachments

1. Board of Directors List
2. Operating Budget
3. Current Funding Sources
4. Copy of IRS 501(c)3 Letter
5. Audited Financial Statements

You may wish to include any or all of the following items in the appendix:

1. *A board list.* This should contain the name of each board member and that person's business or other affiliation. Adding further contact information such as address and telephone number is optional. The reader will use this to identify people he or she knows or whose names are familiar.

An excerpt from the board list of King Manor Museum serves as an example:

BOARD OF DIRECTORS KING MANOR ASSOCIATION OF L.I., INC.

PRESIDENT
Robert V. Edgar
Manager, Donor Services, The New
York Community Trust

VICE PRESIDENT
Richard C. Yeretzian, Esq.
Yeretz & Yeretzian

TREASURER
Christopher J. Merritt
Assistant Vice President, Cord Meyer
Development LLC

SECRETARY
Anne Jacobosky
Assistant Regional Commissioner,
Social Security Administration

EXECUTIVE DIRECTOR
Mary Anne Mrozinski

Walter F. Brewster, Jr.
AJR Services Group

Rev. Percival G. Brown
Rector, Grace Episcopal Church

Gerald J. Caliendo
Gerald J. Caliendo, Architect, P.C.

Charlotte Pickman Gertz
Associate Professor, Modern
Languages, Molloy College

Ben Harris
Founder & Operator, Early Bird Car &
Limousine Service

Mary A. Kidd
Executive Director, Chaka Chinyelu
Foundation
York College Commemorative
Community Quilt Committee

Charles G. Meyer, Jr.
President, Cord Meyer Development
LLC

Carl Mileo
Branch Manager, Astoria Federal
Savings Bank

Clayton A. Prugh, Esq.
Humes & Wagner

3/02

2. ***Your nonprofit's IRS Letter of Determination.*** This document, issued by the IRS, indicates that your agency has been granted 501(c)(3) status and is "not a private foundation." Gifts made to your organization are deductible for tax purposes. This letter is usually requested by funders. Foundations can give most easily to publicly supported organizations, and corporations want their gifts to be tax deductible. If your organization is religiously affiliated or a government entity, you might not have such a letter, and you should explain that fact to the funder.

3. *Financial information.* The operating budget for the current fiscal year and the latest audited financial statement or balance sheet are often appropriate to include. Some funders request your latest 990 in order to assess the financial stability of your organization. If your agency is religiously affiliated, or if for some other reason you do not file a 990, you will need to explain this fact to a funder that requests it. You may want to include a list of donors for the past fiscal year by name and size of gift. Grantmakers also want to know which foundations and corporations currently are being approached to help with the project under review, as well as who has already funded the project. An excerpt from Operation Exodus Inner City's support list follows.

Operation Exodus Inner City List of Supporters

Funding Sources	2003–2004*	2004–2005	2005–2006
Anonymous Corporate Donor	$1,500	$1,000	
Anonymous Foundation Donor			$20,000
American Chai Trust			4,000
Assurant Foundation			2,500
Lily Auchincloss Foundation			10,000
Barker Welfare Foundation		6,000	6,000
Edith C. Blum Foundation	500		500
Robert Bowne Foundation		20,000	29,000
Brick Presbyterian Church	4,000		
The Louis Calder Foundation**		15,000	30,000
Colgate Palmolive	3,000	3,000	3,000
Columbia Neighborhood Fund	500	500	250
Con Edison	500	1,000	2,000
Daniels Foundation	1,000	5,000	10,000
Fifth Avenue Presbyterian Church	5,000	5,000	
The Glickenhaus Foundation	2,500	2,500	2,500
William T. Grant Foundation		5,000	5,000
Hope for New York	13,000	2,500	17,000
Madison Avenue Presbyterian Church		5,950	5,000
Marsiano Foundation	850	4,000	1,000
Metzger-Price Fund, Inc.	1,500	850	
Morgan Stanley Foundation	4,000	1,000	
Newman's Own	10,000		10,000
New York Christian Resource Center	2,000		

Funding Sources	2003–2004	2004–2005	2005–2006
New York Mercantile Exchange Foundation		2,500	5,000
Latino Pastoral Action Committee			4,700
PASE			2,000
Pinkerton Foundation		30,000	33,000
Rite Aid Foundation		5,000	
Starr Foundation		25,000	
St. James Church			6,000
TJX Foundation		5,000	
Varnum De Rose Trust		5,500	5,500
Laura B. Vogler Foundation		25,000	
Washington Square Fund	10,000		10,000
TOTAL	**$59,850**	**$153,800**	**$223,950**

*Note: OEIC's fiscal year begins September 1st and ends August 31st
** The Louis Calder Foundation has committed to a $60,000 grant for the ASP and SAP programs over two years; the first $15,000 was allocated to 04-05, $30,000 will be allocated to 05-06, and the last $15,000 will be allocated to 06-07.

4. ***Résumés of key staff.*** If the background information on key staff members is not included as part of the project statement of the proposal, it should be included in the appendix.

5. ***Organizational chart.*** Include this if you feel it would be helpful.

Do not include in the appendix anything that is not required by the funder or deemed essential to making your case. The key is to give the funder what is needed for review of your proposal without making the package look overwhelming. For example, many nonprofits like to add press clippings to the appendix. If they make the package appear unnecessarily bulky and are tangential to the grant review, they should be sent to the funder at another time when they will receive more attention. However, should these clippings be essential to the review of the request, then by all means include them.

At this stage of assembling the proposal, you have a cover letter and two additional separately packaged components: the proposal narrative and the appendix. If each is clearly identifiable, you will save the funder time and energy in the initial review of your proposal.

Packaging

Packaging refers to both the physical preparation of the documents and their assembly.

PHYSICAL PREPARATION

Every proposal package should be individually prepared for each funder. This permits you to customize the submission in order to reflect the interests of a specific funder and to show them that you've done your homework. This is the point at which you need to double-check the guidelines for a funder's specific requirements for the proposal package. Karen Topakian of the Agape Foundation had this to say: "Answer the questions that we ask of you. This is not busy work; they are things we need to know. Don't ignore them. We can't evaluate your proposal without the answers. You run the risk of the board rejecting your proposal if you omit an answer. If a question doesn't apply to your organization, indicate that; don't just omit it." And Lita Urgarte of The Community Foundation for Greater Altanta reminds us: "Do the research. It is frustrating when we receive applications from people who clearly did not read the instructions. Look at our web site. Read our guidelines. Follow the instructions."

With today's word-processing software, it will be relatively easy to customize the cover letter, title page, and other components of the package that have variables in them. For those components that are photocopied, be sure that the originals you are working from are crisp and legible. For example, if your IRS Letter of Determination is in poor condition, write to the Internal Revenue Service at I.R.S., Exempt Organizations Determinations, P.O. Box 2508, Cincinnati, OH 45201 (or call toll-free 1-877-829-5500), and ask for a fresh copy of the letter. The request must be on your organization's official letterhead. The letter should contain your organization's name, address, taxpayer ID number, and a daytime telephone number, and it must be signed by an officer with that person's title. For the other documents, copy from originals whenever possible.

ASSEMBLY

When a proposal arrives in a funder's office, any binding is usually removed before the proposal is reviewed. Therefore, do not waste money on binding for the proposal and the appendix. Simply staple each document, or use a plastic strip to hold together each document. Christine Park of Lucent Technologies Foundation says: "Bells and whistles are distracting and not necessary. Please don't send CDs, 3-ring binders and pages with plastic sleeves. I undress the thing when I get it. Save yourself the time and energy, packing material and postage."

You have three documents: the cover letter, the proposal, and the appendix. The latter two are separately stapled. In all likelihood, these documents will require a manila envelope. Be certain that the addressee and return address information are printed clearly on the envelope. You might want to put a piece of cardboard in the envelope to protect the documents. Then insert the three documents with the cover letter on top, followed by the proposal and the appendix.

With regard to the funder's address, if you are following the procedure recommended in Chapter 11 for submitting this request, you will have had a conversation with the funder's office prior to submitting the proposal. Use that opportunity to verify the address and the name of the person to whom the package is to be sent.

Of course, the prior advice assumes you will be mailing in a proposal to a funder. Many of the grantmakers interviewed for this book indicate that they now accept proposals as documents attached to e-mail cover letters. Others say they expect to do so in the very near future. David Odahowski of the Edyth Bush Charitable Foundation opines: "We are trying to figure out what we have to do and how to do it right before we move to electronic submission." Still others are considering online application forms that grantseekers fill out and submit electronically. The John S. & James L. Knight Foundation has adopted a staged approach to the question of electronic submission. Julie Brooks tells us about it: "In January 2006, we started accepting LOIs submitted only on our online system. Proposals will follow early in 2007. We are developing the capability for proposals right now and will test in the fourth quarter of 2006. We plan on accepting reports online in 2008. Our goal is to be 100% online in all our interactions by 2008. This is a great opportunity to capitalize on technology. Operating electronically will speed up the processing of requests and reports. We will be able to streamline the process for both the internal and external audiences." In many instances, however, the attachments such as the IRS designation letter, audited financials, and the organization's Form 990 still need to be mailed separately. David Palenchar of the El Pomar Founation puzzles over this issue: "We rely a lot on the financial information. We ask for so many documents that can only be sent in hard copy. Since we are going to ask for those to be mailed, what's the benefit?"

The grantmakers we interviewed suggest a few tips for those transmitting proposals electronically. First, don't wait until the last minute to submit the proposal just because you no longer need to rely on the U.S. mail. Second, be sure the document gets to the correct person. You can verify receipt by sending a follow-up e-mail query after the document was sent or by calling to be sure it was received. Third, don't send "broadcast" proposals by e-mail since they will receive no more serious consideration than mass mailings did in the past.

11

Researching Potential Funders

Early on in the proposal process it is essential that you identify the foundations and corporations you will be asking to support your organization. With this list of potential supporters in hand, you will be able to tailor your proposal to the unique funding interests of each grantmaker.

In this chapter we review the principles of effective research and the factors to consider in shaping your list of prospective funding sources. Then we describe the types and uses of resources available to create your prospect list, and the steps to take in assessing the best prospects for your organization.

The Importance of Doing Your Homework

The key to success is doing your homework. Identifying potential funders requires serious, time-consuming research, but most grantseekers determine that it is well worth the effort. The foundation and corporate executives we interviewed for this *Guide* consistently advise grantseekers to pay special attention to the research effort. Here's some expert advice from Robert Crane of the JEHT Foundation: "Foundations are idiosyncratic. Since no two are alike, formulas for approaching them generally do not work. Do your research. Know who you are going to and how to approach them."

The objective of your funding research is to find funders who have the same interests and values as your organization. Foundation trustees and staff generally care deeply about the problems of society and struggle to determine the most effective strategies they can use to produce the greatest impact with their funding dollars. When they describe their programs on their web site or in their printed literature, or when they announce new areas of interest, these are the result of careful planning and strategy. As a grantseeker it is your responsibility to thoroughly review all the available information about a funder to determine if your organization's programs are a potential match with the funder's stated interests. To quote Lita Ugarte of the Community Foundation for Greater Atlanta, Inc., "The majority of grantseekers who come to us have done their homework. We strongly encourage those who haven't to go to our web site and look at our materials and then give us a call back. We find that they come back to the conversation more prepared with questions and ideas."

As you conduct your research, be realistic in your expectations. Foundations and corporations cannot meet all, or even most, of your needs. The vast majority of the money given to nonprofits is actually donated by individuals. As already noted, foundations and corporations currently provide 16.8 percent of all philanthropic dollars, but their grants can make up an important part of your support.

Before You Begin

Successful fundraising depends on making the right match between your organization and appropriate funders. And, as in most relationships, both parties must have common interests and motivations for that relationship to work. Determining your options for funding from foundations and corporations requires a thorough examination of where these common interests converge. Before you begin the research process it is a good idea to review your organization's attributes and clearly define its program and financial needs so that you can match those requirements to funders' potential interest and capacity to give. Your objective here is to think of your organization's work in ways funders will connect to it. Ask yourself the following questions:

- ***Do you have a clear picture of the purpose of the program or project for which you are seeking support?*** It is generally a good idea to have at least a detailed outline of your project or a preliminary proposal in hand before you begin your foundation and corporate funding research. What you have written about your organization's unique characteristics, and the specific details of your project, will equip you with the facts and terminology you need to find funders with similar interests.

- ***What is your organization's mission?*** Know your organization's guiding principals and fundamental goals. For example, let's assume you represent an organization whose mission is "to strengthen the lives of diverse communities by assisting individuals in attaining their goals for self-sufficiency." Think about the important concepts here— "strengthen the lives of diverse communities" and "attaining their goals for self-sufficiency"—and how these key phrases might connect to funders with similar missions or stated programmatic interests.

- ***Can you describe the audiences served by your organization's programs?*** Does your organization serve the general population, or does it address the needs of one or more specific racial, ethnic, age, gender, or other group, such as Asians, Latinos, immigrants, people with disabilities, women, or youth?

- ***Where does your organization operate its programs?*** You should be able to describe the geographic scope of your activities, such as in what town, city, county or state you perform your services. Does your program have a national or international focus, or are there specific countries in which your organization operates?

- ***What are the distinctive features of your project/organization?*** Are you collaborating with, or do you have an affiliation with another organization? Do your services generate income? Are you creating a model program that other organizations can replicate? Does your organization provide direct services, or are you an advocacy or research group? Your organization or project may have other features that distinguish its activities. In each example here, there are some funders that may look more favorably on an organization that meets one or more of these criteria.

- ***Do you know the total dollar amount needed from foundations for your organization or project?*** When you create an outline for your proposal, you will be deciding whether you are seeking general support for your organization or support for a specific project. If you are seeking project support, you must create a budget to determine the amount of money you will need for a specific time frame (see Chapter 7). Then, through your funding you will determine how much of the funding you need is likely to come from one or more foundations and corporations versus other sources.

- ***What is the grant amount you are seeking?*** Before you start your research it can be helpful to consider the general size of the grants you are seeking. This, in turn, will help you gauge the number of funders you will need to fully fund your project. For example, if your project budget is $80,000, are you seeking four grants of $20,000 each, or two grants of $40,000 each? Your organization's annual budget and the size of the project budget, as well as the giving capacity of various funders and their typical grant range will help determine the answer to this question.

The Research Process

Once you have taken a careful look at your organization's program, its specific assets, and the ways it can connect to funder interests, you are ready to create your prospect list. Researching potential sources of grants is a two-step process. First you compile a list of prospects that is as comprehensive as possible. Second, you refine your list by researching all the available information on each funder. And that step will help you to evaluate each prospect to ensure that there is a good "fit." At the same time, you will prioritize the top prospects among your potential supporters.

Step 1: Creating Your Preliminary Prospect List

In this first step of the research process, you are looking for funders who meet, at least, these two important criteria:

- Program interests that match your organization's needs or have a demonstrated pattern of giving in your area of interest;

- Giving in the geographic area in which your organization operates, or that have no stated restrictions as to where they give.

Like the individuals and corporations who established them, foundations and corporate giving programs differ dramatically from each other in their giving interests. A number of key resources will help you focus on those funders whose priorities most closely match your organization's interests. Try to be inclusive at this first stage for your research. If preliminary investigation makes you think that a specific foundation or corporate donor should be on the list, go ahead and include it. Let further research you conduct on that funder tell you otherwise.

These resources will help you compile your prospect list:
- Foundation and corporate databases and directories
- News sources
- Grantmaker web sites and publications
- IRS Form 990-PF

Availability of Resources

In accordance with its mission of strengthening the nonprofit sector by advancing knowledge about U.S. philanthropy, the Foundation Center provides free public access to funding resources at five library/learning centers (in New York, Atlanta, Cleveland, San Francisco, and Washington, DC) and more than 300 Cooperating Collections throughout the U.S. Visitors to the five Center-operated sites have access to the Center's databases (the *Foundation Directory Online* and *FC Search),* its content-rich web site, and a vast collection of fund raising and philanthropic materials. The Cooperating Collections also provide free access to the *Foundation Directory Online* or *FC Search*, the Center's web site and a core group of other Center publications. The balance of the fundraising materials available are unique to each site and often reflect the regional focus of the collection. The Center provides free and fee-based training in the grantseeking and proposal writing process at its library/learning centers, Cooperating Collections, and throughout the country, as well as in the "virtual" classroom at its web site.

Foundation and Corporate Databases

Because of its broad coverage of the grantmaking universe and its ability to search for multiple funder characteristics, many grantseekers start their research with the Foundation Center's highly regarded *Foundation Directory Online* or alternatively the CD-ROM version of this database, *FC Search,* (see foundationcenter.org/marketplace/fdcdchrt.pdf for a comparison chart showing the features of both databases).

The *Foundation Directory Online* is available at several subscription levels, each providing access to additional information. These examples assume you are using the highest subscription level, the *Foundation Directory Online Professional,* which contains more than 88,000 foundations and corporate givers. It is easily searched for potential funders using four separate databases devoted to Grantmakers, Companies, Grants, and 990s.

FOUNDATION

Grantmakers database. A good initial strategy is to begin your search for funders in the *Foundation Directory Online's* Grantmakers database where you will be searching funder profiles. For example, let's assume you represent a nonprofit in Chicago that is seeking funding for a theater program. Using the *Foundation Directory Online's* predetermined index terms you can create a few simple searches that combine subject interests with geographic criteria:

- *Search 1:*
  Geographic Preference: Illinois
  Field of Interest: Arts

- *Search 2:*
  Foundation City: Chicago
  Field of Interest: Performing arts, theater

Both Searches 1 and 2 use appropriate beginning strategies. Search 1 uses broad terms to retrieve a potentially larger list of prospective funders, while Search 2 is more targeted to the organization's exact funding interests and geographic location. Whether you start with a broad or a narrower search strategy is partially determined by the number of funders you think you might retrieve and your personal preferences.

A successful search result will include a list of foundations and/or corporations that have a demonstrated interest in your subject area *and* your geographic location. You can then research each funder on the list by first reviewing its profile.

Here is a partial view of a foundation's profile in the *Foundation Directory Online.*

Foundation Directory Online - Microsoft Internet Explorer

FOUNDATION DIRECTORY ONLINE
PROFESSIONAL

The Chicago Community Trust
Copyright © 2007 The Foundation Center

«Previous Record | Next Record»
Print Page
Close Window

| Profile | Grants | News/Jobs/RFPS | Publications | People | 990s |

Profile

The Chicago Community Trust
111 E. Wacker Dr., Ste. 1400
Chicago, IL 60601
Telephone: (312) 616-8000
Contact: For grants: Ms. Sandy Phelps, Grants Mgr.
FAX: (312) 616-7955
E-mail: info@cct.org
TDD: (312) 856-1703
Grant inquiries E-mail: grants@cct.org
URL: http://www.cct.org

Donor(s): Albert W. Harris; and members of the Harris family.
Type of grantmaker: Community foundation.
Background: Established in 1915 in IL by bank resolution and declaration of trust.
Purpose and activities: Established for such charitable purposes as will best make for the mental, moral, intellectual and physical improvement, assistance and relief of the inhabitants of the County of Cook, State of Illinois. Grants for both general operating support and specific programs and projects in the areas of health, basic human needs, education, arts and humanities, and community development; awards fellowships to individuals in leadership positions in legal community service organizations.

Internet

It is always a good strategy to assume that you will conduct several different searches. While initially you may have the inclination to locate just those funders that match your exact interests, this is not always the best approach. This strategy may yield good results, but you may be excluding other funders that have not supported the precise program you are seeking to fund, but that may be interested in your organization anyhow.

Other funding criteria can also be added to your search strategies, such as the audience that benefits from your program. In our example the intended population group is African Americans.

- *Search 3:*
  Geographic Focus: Illinois
  Field of Interest: Arts and African Americans/Blacks

- *Search 4:*
  Grantmaker City: Chicago
  Field of Interest: Performing arts, theater, and African Americans/Blacks

The *Foundation Directory Online*'s Grantmakers database allows you to select from 11 different criteria to create other variations in your search strategies, such as adding the type of support you are seeking (seed money, capital support, etc.) or searching for something very specific using the keyword search feature to find terms that might appear in a foundation's profile.

CORPORATE GRANTMAKERS

The fundraising strategies of many nonprofit organizations include seeking support from corporations. Corporations may provide support to nonprofits in a variety of ways. Some corporations give only through a private foundation, while others give only through direct corporate giving programs. Still others use both vehicles to support nonprofits in their communities. If a corporation has a foundation, then a 990-PF will be available for that funder, just as with other private foundations. If the corporation has a direct giving program, it is not required to file a publicly available report on gifts awarded under that program. This can make it difficult to unearth information on a corporation's nonfoundation giving. However, some corporations have special sections of their web sites devoted to their philanthropy, and others issue guidelines on their giving.

In seeking grants from corporations it is important to consider their motivations for funding nonprofit organizations. Unlike foundations, corporations do not exist to give money away. Their allegiance, instead, is to their customers, shareholders, employees, and—most of all—to the bottom line. It is fair to assume that although many corporations award grants out of a combination of altruism and self-interest, most corporations will seek some benefit from their charitable activities. As a grantseeker, it is up to you to determine which attributes of your organization will be attractive to each corporation on your prospect list. For example, a local orchestra or a community center may receive funding because it serves the interests of corporate employees and the larger community, while a clinic providing health services to Latinos may be funded in part because the corporation wants to enhance its image among members of that population.

A good place to start your search for potential corporate donors is the *Foundation Directory Online*.

Companies database. *The Foundation Directory Online* contains information on more than 4,000 company-sponsored foundations and other corporate giving programs. These corporate givers are also available in the Grantmakers database, but selecting this one allows you to search corporate-specific data. For example, since corporations generally contribute in the geographic areas in which the company operates, you can search to find corporations that have headquarters, subsidiaries, or plants in your local area or that have international operations in countries in which your organization operates programs.

- *Search 5:*
  Subsidiary City: San Diego

- *Search 6:*
  Subsidiary State/Country: Brazil

The Companies database can also be searched by a corporation's business type to find corporations that might have an affinity with your organization. For example, in addition to cash grants, you may uncover a potential funder in your state whose product donations would benefit your work, as in the sample search below.

- *Search 7:*
  Business Type: Computer and office equipment
  Company State: Connecticut

Here is the company profile of the Xerox Corporation that resulted from the above search.

In addition to searching for corporate attributes that match your organization's goals, you should also search grantmaker records in the *Foundation Directory Online*'s Grantmakers database for stated philanthropic programs and the Grants database described below for demonstrated funding patterns.

Corporate databases such as the Charities Aid Foundation's *CCInet* or the Foundation Center's *Corporate Giving Online* can also be helpful in identifying potential corporate support. Other research tools include print sources such as *Corporate Philanthropy Report*, a periodical published by Aspen Publishers; the *National Directory of Corporate Giving*, published by the Foundation Center; and resources on foundation and corporate giving published by various regional associations of grantmakers.

Grants database. Another research strategy is to search the actual grants awarded by funders that share your organization's interests. To quote Andrew Lark of the Frances L. and Edwin E. Cummings Memorial Fund: "Look at our past grants.

This will often help to indicate the likelihood of your grant application's future success." The *Foundation Directory Online*'s Grants database contains more than 700,000 grants awarded by the nation's largest foundations. Examining a foundation's grants history helps illustrate how it has translated its mission and program interests into the actual funding of specific organizations and projects. It also can help reveal recent funding patterns.

A beginning approach is to search for grants to organizations in your city or state for purposes similar to your project. Using the same theater program example as we did for our grantmakers search, we can perform the following searches:

- *Search 8:*
  Recipient State: Illinois
  Subject: Arts

- *Search 9:*
  Recipient City: Chicago
  Subject: Performing arts, theater

Here again you will notice that we can search broadly—looking for organizations within a state and a broad subject category—and also by using more specific criteria.

Another research strategy using the Grants database is to find out which foundations are funding other agencies with similar interests operating in your community. These foundations may be likely sources of support for your own organization as well. For example, we can look for donors to an organization we know runs a program similar to our own in the Chicago area by searching on that organization's name.

- *Search 10:*
  Recipient Name: Black Ensemble Theater Corporation

A successful search result will include a list of recently awarded grants to this organization; a sample grant record is shown below.

```
┌────────────────────────────────────────────────────────────────┐
│ 🔲 Foundation Directory Online - Microsoft Internet Explorer  _ □ ✕ │
├────────────────────────────────────────────────────────────────┤
│                                                                  │
│        FOUNDATION DIRECTORY ONLINE                               │
│                                  PROFESSIONAL                     │
│                                                                  │
│  © 2007 The Foundation Center      «Previous Record | Next Record»│
│                                              Print Page           │
│                                              Close Window         │
│                                                                  │
│  GO TO FOUNDATION»                                               │
│                                                                  │
│  Recipient:            Black Ensemble Theater Corporation        │
│  Location:             Chicago, IL                               │
│  Recipient url:        http://www.blackensembletheater.org/      │
│  Type of recipient:    Performing arts, theater                  │
│  Grantmaker:           The Chicago Community Trust, IL           │
│  Grantmaker geographic IL                                        │
│  focus:                                                          │
│  Grant amount:         $25,000                                   │
│  Year authorized:      2005                                      │
│  Description:          For arts education program on West side,  │
│                        Cultural Arts School Enhancement Program  │
│  Type(s) of support:   Program development                       │
│  Subject(s):           African Americans/Blacks; Arts education; │
│                        Performing arts, theater                  │
│  Recipient EIN:        362852762                                 │
│                        Most Recent IRS filings: 990              │
│                                                                  │
│                            «Previous Record | Next Record»       │
│                                              Close Window         │
│                                                                  │
│ 🔲                                          🌐 Internet           │
└────────────────────────────────────────────────────────────────┘
```

Similar to the Grantmakers database, the Grants database can also help you find funders that have awarded grants for specific types of support, or by key word to find something very specific, such as funding for a "mime troupe."

990 database. Also in the *Foundation Directory Online*, the 990 database can be helpful in uncovering smaller grants and/or grants awarded by smaller foundations that are not covered in the Grants database. All foundations regardless of size are required to file a 990-PF tax return with the IRS each year, and all public foundations with revenues of $25,000 file Form 990. Among other data, a foundation's 990-PF contains a list of grants for each year. The 990 database works by searching every word in its database of more than 325,000 990-PFs and 990s. This database can be searched using key words that might be in the description of a grant, such as "arts" or "theater," or by searching by an organization's name to find grants to organizations similar to yours.

The 990 database, of course, can also be used to find a specific 990-PF for a foundation that you want to learn more about. You can also locate 990-PFs using Foundation Finder, a free search tool accessed through the Foundation Center's web site, and they are also available on other sites like Guidestar.org and the web sites of certain state attorneys general. While the 990-PF will not give you as much information about a foundation as its web site, annual report, or printed guidelines, it is the only source of information for the majority of small and medium-sized foundations that do not issue these other information sources. Among other useful data on a 990-PF, reviewing two or three years' worth of a foundation's grants can uncover patterns in giving to certain organizations and projects similar to your own.

In addition to the databases in the *Foundation Directory Online* and the 990-PFs filed by private foundations, sometimes lists of a nonprofit's donors, which may also be prospects for your organization, will be found on its web site or in its annual report. Other nonprofits may occasionally thank funders in a local newspaper, and arts organizations often list their donors in event programs.

News Sources

News sources that cover philanthropy can also be helpful in creating and refining your prospect list. One such source is *The Chronicle of Philanthropy*, a biweekly news source covering philanthropy and the nonprofit world, including articles on foundations and other grantmakers, coverage of recently issued annual reports, and announcements of recently awarded grants. In addition to using it as a source to keep current on the foundation field, subscribers to the print version can acquire a password to search back issues by key words. This can be helpful, for example, in uncovering a recent article on a specific foundation, or a list of recent grants in a specific subject area.

The Foundation Center's *Philanthropy News Digest* (PND) is another resource you can use to help you create your prospect list. PND is a daily online news service providing abstracts of philanthropy related articles covering the major media, funder press releases, and other news sources. It also provides interviews, commentary, and profiles of foundation and nonprofit leaders and the organizations they represent. Because PND's archives can be searched using any words in its text, it can be useful in uncovering recent articles in your subject area or information about a specific grantmaker. Another source that can be searched by subject area is the Center's *RFP Bulletin*, a compilation of recently released requests for proposals issued by foundations. By scanning these news sources regularly, plus the local newspapers and journals in your community, and any newsletters produced by local grantmakers or grantmaker associations, you can add potential funders to your prospect list. You can sign up for free e-mail versions of these resources through the homepage of the Foundation Center's web site.

Grantmaker Web Sites

While the majority of grantmakers do not have web sites (only about 7,000 do), those foundation web sites that do exist provide information that can help you determine if your nonprofit's programs are a good fit with a funder's priorities. Typical web site contents can include a brief history of the foundation, program descriptions, recent grants lists, and application guidelines. Some also contain electronic versions of the foundation's annual reports. The breadth of information on grantmaker web sites can vary significantly from one foundation to another. Although the quantity of information available often correlates with a funder's size, sometimes you will come across a small foundation with a very comprehensive web site, and the reverse may be true as well.

Since the information on a foundation's web site is likely to be the most *current* data available, it is important that you review all the information that is relevant to your organization's potential solicitation of that funder. Remember, this is one of the few primary sources of data available for a foundation, other than its 990-PF or annual report. And it is often the best place to read about a foundation's interests in its own words. To quote Ilene Mack of Hearst Foundation, Inc.: "Our web site provides specific information on what we do and what we don't do. As a result of grantseekers visiting our site, turndowns have decreased and proposals include most of the backup information we require. It is really a timesaving device."

The Foundation Center helps grantseekers to identify which foundations and corporate giving programs have web sites. At the Center's own web site you can search via Foundation Finder, which has links to the home pages of funders that have web sites. Also, the *Foundation Directory Online* and *FC Search* allow you to visit a grantmaker's web site by clicking a link in its profile.

Grantmaker Guidelines

A foundation or a corporate giver's application guidelines provide critical information for the grantseeker. Guidelines generally provide a description of the types of programs and organizations grantmakers will and will not fund, as well as other restrictions on their giving. Some contain detailed program descriptions, while others only briefly mention the funder's main areas of interest. In addition, they usually indicate any specific application procedures and deadlines for submitting proposals.

If a grantmaker does not have this type of information on its web site, check the funder databases or directories you are using to see if the funder indicates that it has published guidelines. Even if you have a copy of a funder's guidelines, it is always a good idea to check to make sure you have the most recent version. Although foundations tend to "stay the course" for several years, it is not unheard of for a grantmaker to make a major change to its program focus or revise its applications procedures.

Foundation Annual Reports

If a foundation publishes an annual report, it can be a valuable asset in researching that funder. It is important not only for determining current giving patterns but also for anticipating future trends. The annual report reflects the personality, style, and interests of a foundation. More than 2,600 foundations currently publish annual reports. These documents can often be found at a foundation's web site and in PubHub at the Foundation Center's web site. Many can still be requested in print format directly from the foundation, although some funders are now issuing them only online.

In reading an annual report, you should look most closely at two sections. First, read the statement by the chairman, president, or chief executive. Look for clues that reveal the foundation's underlying philosophy. What are the problems in society that the foundation wants to address? What kind of impact does its leadership hope to make with the foundation's funds? This section will also reveal any new or changed program areas. Such shifts in direction can present you with a significant window of opportunity, if your project happens to fit within new areas the foundation intends to explore.

Another section to examine carefully is the list of grantees for the past year or years. Check the grants list against what the foundation says it wants to fund. You are looking for clues that will illustrate specific areas of interest and how the foundation implements its stated priorities in the grants it awards.

Step 2: Evaluating Your Prospect List

In this next stage of your research you will be evaluating the funders on your prospect list by gathering important information on those funders whose guidelines or funding patterns most closely match your organization's funding needs. As you research the funders on your initial list of prospects, you will be looking for answers to the following questions:

- ***Does the funder accept applications?*** You may find it surprising that some do not. You'll want to find this out early in the research process so you don't waste your time. However, even when the funder says it does not accept applications and/or gives only to preselected organizations, you should not completely disregard it as a prospect, if your research shows that it has the potential to be a very good fit. Check to see if anyone on your board of directors, staff, or volunteers knows someone connected to the foundation and/or begin to cultivate the prospective funder by sending a letter introducing your organization.

- ***Has the funder demonstrated a real commitment to funding in your subject field?*** Check to see that the funder's stated mission, program descriptions, and/or recently awarded grants indicate that there is a match with your organization's funding needs. Sometimes you may come across one or more grants by a particular foundation in your subject area, but they may be the exception to the rule. They may be grants awarded for reasons other than a specific commitment to that field such as a special relationship between a board member and the recipient. Other foundations have historic and continuing relationships with particular organizations, perhaps due to a specified interest of the donor, which may cause them to fund activities outside of their current giving guidelines.

- ***Does it seem likely that the funder will make grants to organizations in your geographic location?*** Most foundations and corporations have stated geographic limitations. Although it isn't necessary for a funder to have awarded grants in your state or city, prior giving in your geographic area is a good indication that a funder may be interested in your project. Check the funder's guidelines for specific geographic limitations, and be on the lookout for local or regional giving patterns, or concentrated giving in rural or urban areas that might exclude your project.

- ***What are the financial conditions that may affect the foundation's ability to give?*** In general, a foundation's prior level of giving is a good indication of its capacity to give in the future, since foundations must pay out five percent of their assets each year. However, this amount can increase if the funder has recently received a large contribution, possibly from the donor. Also, foundations are affected by economic conditions. In a strong economic environment a foundation's assets will often increase, and in a slow economy assets will often decline, reducing the amount of funding that is available to nonprofit grantseekers.

- ***Does the funder give to the same nonprofit groups every year, or have they committed their resources many years into the future?*** Some foundations fund the same organizations each year and have few grant dollars left to support new grantee's projects. Check a funder's list of grants for the past two to three years to discern patterns like this that would limit your chances of funding. Other funders make multiyear grant commitments that can limit the amount of funds they have available for new projects. Grants lists should indicate such long-term funding commitments as well.

- ***Does the amount of money you are requesting fit within the funder's typical grant range?*** You are looking for patterns in the foundation's past giving. If your research shows that a grantmaker's largest grant over the past few years is $25,000, you should not ask for $40,000. At the same time you should be looking for more subtle distinctions, such as the giving range in the particular subject area for which you seek funding. Also remember that some funders may give first-time grantees smaller grants until they have an established relationship with your organization.

- ***Does the funder have a policy prohibiting grants for the type(s) of support you are requesting?*** Some foundations will not make grants for the general support of your organization. Others will not provide funds for endowments, building projects, or equipment. Determine whether the funder is willing to consider the type of support you need.

- ***Does the funder usually make grants to cover the full cost of a project or does it favor projects where other funders will participate?*** Unless you are seeking funding for a very small project, it is unlikely that a first-time donor will fund an entire project. Most funders assume that grantseekers will be approaching multiple funders for their project, asking each to contribute a portion of the needed funds.

- ***Does the funder put limits on the length of time it is willing to support a project?*** Some foundations favor one-time grants, while others will continue their support over a number of years. However, it is rare to find a grantmaker that will commit funding to an organization for an indefinite period of time.

- *What types of organizations does the funder tend to support?* As part of your research, check to see if the funder favors large, well-established groups such as universities and museums, or supports smaller, community-based groups. Some funders will support a wide range of organizational types, while others will not. Lists of past recipients can provide good insight into this matter, whereas it may not be stated in a funder's printed guidelines.

- *Does the funder have application deadlines?* Note carefully any information you uncover regarding deadlines and board meeting dates so that you can submit your proposal at the appropriate time. Some funders have application deadlines, while others review proposals on a continuing basis.

- *Do you or does anyone on your board or staff know someone connected with the funder?* You will want to gather background information on the funder's current trustees and staff. In doing so you may find some connections between your organization and a potential funder that will make it easier to approach the funder. While knowing someone who is affiliated with a prospective funder usually is not enough to secure a grant, it does tend to facilitate the process (see Chapter 12 for more on donor cultivation).

Refining Your Prospect List

The importance of answering all of the above questions to the best of your ability and doing a thorough job in your research cannot be overstated. To quote Andrew Lark once again: "Each foundation has its own unique traits and characteristics. Do good research. Learn about them. For greater success, approach multiple grantmakers at one time with *targeted* (not 'one-size-fits-all') grant requests."

As you winnow and prioritize your list you may be tempted to focus all your efforts on one or two "ideal" funders. You should resist this temptation. As long as the funder's guidelines and the other information you uncover do not rule out your organization as a potential grantee, you should keep it on your list. A funder may not have stated the exact specifications of your program as a particular area of interest, but your program may still fit within its broader funding goals.

For those funders that remain on your list, those that match your organization's interests most closely and have the ability to provide the greatest financial support will rise to the top of your list. But don't forget about the others that have made it through your preliminary screening. For example, smaller funders can play a significant role in your overall funding strategies. Remember, this year's small grants may turn into future years' larger grants, and both large and small funders have the ability to become long-term supporters. Also, funders that may turn you down this year because your project is not an exact fit with their interests, may be impressed by your organization's work and may look favorably at your next request.

12

Contacting and Cultivating Potential Funders

Making the Initial Contact

Once you have determined that a foundation is a likely funder, then you must initiate contact. Some foundations prefer that you call first to see if your project fits their specific guidelines. Be aware, however, that this is not a popular step with all funders.

If you decide to call first, be sure you don't appear to be going on a fishing expedition. Funders find this particularly annoying. Your conversation needs to make it clear that you have read the guidelines and want further clarification on whether your particular project would fit. You are not making a solicitation by telephone.

Funders caution that, if you do call, listen carefully to what is being said. Julie Brooks of the John S. & James L. Knight Foundation comments: "We encourage phone calls. We want open communications with the public about our grantmaking process, objectives and strategies. We find that a discussion up front often clears up questions and prevents the grantseeker from going down the wrong path." Jonathan Goldberg of the Surdna Foundation adds: "People call frequently. We talk to them about pre-proposal information. This helps them in clarifying information and helps us by reducing the number of applications that don't fit."

On the other hand, the grantmaker we interviewed cautioned that you should also listen for the "no".

There are three objectives to the initial call:

- It promotes name recognition of your group.

- It tests the possible compatibility between the potential funder
  and your agency.

- It permits you to gather additional information about the funder and about
  possible reaction to your project before you actually submit your proposal.

How should you proceed? First, rehearse what you will say about your
organization. You may be given just a few minutes by the foundation or corporate
representative. Also, have on hand the background information you have compiled
about the potential funder and how much and what you would like them to fund.
If there is a prior relationship with your nonprofit group, be fully aware of the
details. In the words of Elizabeth Smith of the Hyams Foundation: "It is best if
grantees do their research and then call. Then, staff is available by phone to answer
unique questions."

Second, make the call. It would be great if you could speak directly with the
president of the foundation or senior vice president in charge of corporate
contributions. But this will not often happen. Be satisfied with anyone who
can respond to your questions. In the process, don't underestimate the importance
of support staff. They can be very helpful. They can provide you with key
information and ensure that your proposal is processed promptly. Be sure to obtain
the name of the person you do speak with so that reference to this conversation
can be made when you submit your formal request. This may be your contact
person for future calls and letters.

What should you say? Be prepared to:

- Introduce your agency: give the name, location, purpose, and goals.

- State up front why you are calling: You have done your homework. You
  believe there is a fit between the grantmaker and your organization.

- Inquire if you can submit a proposal: be specific about which one and the
  hoped-for level of support.

- Request an appointment: few funders are willing to grant the request for a
  meeting without at least an initial proposal on the table, but it's always
  worth inquiring about this. As a matter of fact, each time you speak with a
  funder, you should ask if a face-to-face conversation would be appropriate.

Variations will emerge in each call, so you must be sharp, alert, and ready to respond. At the same time, try to seem relaxed and confident as the discussion proceeds. Remember that you are a potential partner for the prospective funder.

Many foundations have no staff or limited office support. Some corporations assign their philanthropic activities to executives with very heavy workloads. The point is, repeated calls may go unanswered. Above all, be persistent. Persistence will set your agency apart from many nonprofits whose leaders initiate fundraising with determination but quickly lose heart. If you cannot get through to a potential funder on the telephone, send a letter of inquiry designed to gain the same information as the call. If your letter goes unanswered, then be prepared to submit a request anyway.

The message here is that, like people, every foundation is different. Foundations, in fact, are made up of people. It is important to listen to and to respect what the funding representative is telling you about preferred styles of approach.

The Letter of Inquiry

Many grantmakers today are requesting that applicants provide a brief letter of inquiry (or intent) about their project before submitting a complete proposal. Just like the introductory phone call, this letter, often referred to by the acronym LOI, is used by funders as a simple screening device, enabling the grantmaker to preclude submission of an inappropriate application and to encourage the submission of proposals with funding potential. It also enables those grants decision-makers who prefer to be involved in the shaping of a proposal at the very earliest stages to do so. The letter of inquiry can be useful to the grantseeker, since it saves time compiling lengthy documents and attachments for proposals that are unlikely to be favorably received.

The requirement to submit a preliminary letter of intent is not always a plus for the grantseeker. In the first place, it is an extra step, requiring that additional time be factored into the application cycle. Second, some view this procedure as a way for the funder to cut off an application before the grantseeker has had the opportunity to fully portray the benefits of the project. And finally, you need to have the full proposal, at least in draft form, before you can submit a letter of intent, which in a sense is a highly compacted proposal with most of the components covered, albeit briefly. David Ford of Richard and Susan Smith Family Foundation tells us: "The letter of intent should be up to three pages, plus a budget. It should describe who the group is, what they want to accomplish, their growth plan, and how our grant will help enable them to meet their goals."

Christine Park of Lucent Technologies Foundation says: "The letter of intent saves everyone time. We will respond and if there's a possibility for a partnership, we will share next steps."

A talent for précis writing is definitely required to get the letter of inquiry just right. It should not be longer than two to three pages.

What follows is a letter of inquiry from Neighbors Together to Independence Community Foundation:

September 21, 2005

Ms. Marilyn Gelber
Executive Director
Independence Community Foundation
182 Atlantic Avenue
Brooklyn, NY 11201

Dear Ms. Gelber:

It has been a privilege to work with the Independence Community Foundation over the past year to strengthen Neighbors Together's capacity to improve our low-income community. As you know form my work with Stuart Post, Neighbors Together is in the process of implementing a strategic plan to expand our key programs, enabling us to put more emphasis on the long-term empowerment of our lowest-income neighbors. I would like to request $20,000 of organizational support from the Independence Community Foundation for the coming year to help us put this place into action.

Neighbors Together is committed to ending hunger and poverty in Ocean Hill-Brownsville, the lowest-income community in Brooklyn. Our mission is deeply grounded in our belief in the dignity and potential of each person. Since 1982 we have been fighting hunger on three levels:

- Our soup kitchen alleviates the immediate crisis by providing hot, nutritious meals to 300 people a day, six days a week;

- Our Homelessness Prevention and Empowerment Program addresses the struggles which go hand-in-hand with hunger: unemployment, lack of education, homelessness, addiction, inadequate health care;

- Our neighborhood-directed advocacy and community development efforts strive to transform social structures that result in poverty and hunger.

STATEMENT OF NEED

While in many ways our community has improved in the past five years with a surge in housing development, we continue to see 250-300 people every day in our soup kitchen; we continue to see a large number of people struggling with addiction and mental illness, unemployed people with very inconsistent work histories, people who are working full-time but not making ends meet because of rising rental costs; we continue to see a community overwhelmed by violence and despair.

Neighbors Together conducted a community needs assessment this spring with coordination by students in the Milano Graduate School of New School University. From this process, including interviews with current clients, we found that our clients are the most marginalized and challenging to engage, and there are not adequate services in our area to address their needs. While our clients all struggle due to our society's lack of respect for and lack of opportunities for low-income people, most of them have additional personal struggles (mental illness, addiction, depression, physical disabilities) that make it extremely difficult to achieve stable, engaging lives.

The majority of our unemployed clients really want to work, but they do not have the education, training or life skills to hold employment consistently. Seventy-eight percent of our clients have been out of work for more than a year. Some other significant client statistics:

- 94.5% of our clients have incomes of less than $12,000 a year ($1,000 a month).
- 66% of our clients have government benefits as their primary income; 13% receive no income at all other than family donations; 13% are employed; 5% receive unemployment benefits; 2% receive retirement or pension benefits.
- 95% of our clients use soup kitchens at least once a week; 88% use them at least a few times a week; 66% use food pantries at least once a week.
- 78% of our clients are between 30 and 60 years old; 12% are over 60; 10% are 18-30 years old.
- 78% of our clients have children, but of those only 12% have children living with them.

GENERAL OVERVIEW OF ACTIVITIES

At the end of an extensive planning process, the board of directors and staff met to discuss how to make the most significant impact on our community. Based on all of our research, the board and staff decided that Neighbors

Together should build on the strength and demand of our three major programs by moderately expanding each of them in order to deepen our impact on the lives of our current clients.

Specifically, we plan to:

1. Expand our Emergency Hunger Relief program by offering an evening meal four days a week in addition to lunch six days a week;

2. Expand our Homelessness Prevention and Empowerment Program by adding a full-time Social Worker who can provide consistency, develop therapeutic relationships with clients, expand our case management focus, and coordinate extended opportunities for client growth through workshops and support groups;

3. Expand our Advocacy and Community Development program by adding a full-time Community Organizer who can provide more consistent empowerment opportunities for our clients to get actively involved in improving their community and the situation of low-income people throughout the city, state, and county;

4. Adding an evening meal requires and creates an opportunity to expand the kitchen assistant training program by adding a third Kitchen Assistant to the staff;

5. Our strength lies in the supportive community we create with our clients, so we will expand this by opening our dining room as a community space for congregating before, during, and after the meals we serve;

6. To accomplish these goals we will need a new location, which should increase the dignity of our clients by doubling the seating space in the dining room to 36, providing a bathroom off the dining room for client use, and creating office space that ensures greater client privacy when meeting with staff;

7. In order to adequately supervise these program expansions, we will need to expand our board from 10 to 15 members and hire part-time fundraising/administrative support for the Executive Director.

Our immediate need is to locate a new facility that will allow us to move in by the end of 2005. Due to the severe deterioration of our current space, we will need to move out as soon as possible. We are lucky to have recently acquired substantial funding for this move, due to the sale of property owned by the organization; so this expedited timeline for moving seems reasonable.

Once we have moved, we will solidify goals and objectives for our programs and secure the funding for program expansion. We hope to phase in new staff and begin our evening meal in early- to mid-2006.

PLANNED OUTCOMES

We naturally have high hopes for the impact our expanded activities will have. We have particular outcomes that we are anticipating from this beginning stage, and we also expect that planned outcomes may change once staff are hired to guide the work. As of now, we hope to provide 100 additional meals each day in our evening meal program, work closely with 50 clients to make detailed case management plans including increased referrals to mental health and addiction treatment, and increase the number of people involved in community development campaigns on a sustained basis from 15 to 30 people by the end of the fiscal year. We also plan to spend a significant amount of time solidifying a model of case management that will fit the realities of our clients and staffing our pattern.

ORGANIZATIONAL CREDENTIALS

Neighbors Together has close working relationships with all of the leading anti-hunger organizations in New York City: the Food Bank for New York City, City Harvest, the United Way of New York City, the New York City Coalition Against Hunger, the Hunger Action Network of New York State, and many others. Neighbors Together is prominently featured in these organizations' publicity materials, and members of our staff are regularly invited to speak at their conferences for the anti-hunger network. Most significantly, in September 2004, Neighbors Together was named Agency of the Year by the Food Bank for New York City, which has over 1,200 member programs throughout the five boroughs.

ESTIMATED BUDGET

Neighbors Together's fiscal year is November 1 to October 31, so we are currently in the process of finalizing our operating budget for FY 2006. In order to implement our strategic plan, we anticipate increased facility expenses as well as increased staffing costs. As we phase in new staff over the next six to eight months, we anticipate our total expenses for the fiscal year to be $517,570. We expect continued support from past funders during this exciting phase of our development, and we are forming relationships with new partners, including the Robin Hood Foundation, which has indicated that they are very interested in funding Neighbors Together at a significant level.

CONCLUSION

The Independence Community Foundation has been a key partner in the development of our strategic plan over the past year. In a brief amount of time, we have been able to work together to make concrete plans for the empowerment of one of the lowest-income communities in New York City. I would be grateful for the opportunity to submit a proposal for continued funding from the Independence Community Foundation, and I welcome any questions you may have. Thank you for your support and your commitment to our mission of ending hunger and poverty in our community.

Sincerely,

Ed Fowler
Executive Director

Some grantmakers have online application forms that function as letters of inquiry. What follows are instructions for submission of an online letter of inquiry from the W. K. Kellogg Foundation's web site.

English • Spanish • Portuguese

W.K. Kellogg Foundation - Online Grant Application
Instructions

Instructions

* Red text indicates a required field.

*Target Geographic Area	Geographic area intended to be served by this project. Select all that apply.
*Organization Type	
*	
*Organization Name	Legal name of the organization according to IRS (for U.S.) or IRS-equivalent (non-domestic) [255 chars max]
Other Organization Name	Any other names or common references [255 chars max]
*Address	
	[100 chars max per line]
*City	[35 chars max]
*State/Province	[100 chars max]
*Zip/Postal Code	[50 chars max]
*Country	
*Phone Number	[50 chars max]
Fax Number	[50 chars max]
Website	[255 chars max]
*Salutation	
*First Name	[20 chars max]
Middle Initial	
*Last Name	[20 chars max]
*Title	[256 chars max]
Use Organization Address?	
*Address	
	[100 chars max per line]
*City	[35 chars max]
*State/Province	[100 chars max]
*Zip/Postal Code	[50 chars max]
*Country	
*Phone Number	[50 chars max]
Fax Number	[50 chars max]
*Email Address	[100 chars max]
*Language	Please indicate the language of this request.
*Proposed Name of Idea	Provide the proposed name of your

If you are not able to complete the application at this time, enter your e-mail to **save your data ONCE just before exiting**. You will be sent an e-mail with a URL to return to your information at a later time. You will be able to return to the data for up to 30 days.
Email Address:

Save

Instructions

	idea [100 chars max]
*Purpose Statement	*Provide a brief description of what will be accomplished as a result of the project.* *[1000 chars max]*
*Summary of Request	*Provide a brief summary of your idea. This should include an overview, the goals and outcomes, and target beneficiary. [1000 chars max]*
Grantee Project ID	*If you have your own ID or reference for the project, enter it here.* *[50 chars max]*
*Previous contact with WKKF staff	*Have you discussed this request with a Kellogg Foundation staff member?*
If yes, please indicate the name (s) of W.K. Kellogg Foundation staff and when and where you contacted them so that we can share this information with them.	

Previous   Next   Cancel

While the letter of inquiry has its pluses and minuses from the grantseeker's perspective, this is still required by many funders as a preliminary step in the process. And writing such a letter is a skill that proposal writers need to develop.

Submitting the Proposal

Actually submitting the proposal may seem anticlimactic considering the amount of preparation that has gone into identifying and researching the prospective funders and putting together the various components. But eventually there comes the time to submit the full proposal to the funders on your list.

Checklists may prove useful at this point. You may wish to check and double-check one last time to ensure that all requirements of the funder have been met and that all of the pieces of the proposal package are there in the proper sequence. Above all, you will want to be sure that you submit the proposal in accordance with the funder's deadline. If possible, whether you use regular mail, e-mail, or are applying online, send in your proposal at least two weeks in advance of the deadline. This enables the funder to request additional information, if needed.

Grantseekers often wonder whether they should mail in their proposals, send by overnight mail or messenger, or hand-deliver them. By far the best choice is the least expensive one. Use regular mail unless there is a very good reason to do otherwise.

The Role of Technology in the Application Process

New grantseekers may be under the impression that all of their contact with grantmakers will take place electronically. While grantmakers have come a long way in harnessing technology to facilitate the submission process, as is reflected in their comments in successive editions of this *Guide,* they still have a long way to go. Nonetheless, technology is making inroads into the grantmaking world. As we've seen some foundations have developed online pre-proposal forms for prospective grant applicants to submit as a required preliminary step in the process. A few grantmakers, especially those in the corporate world, now *require* granseekers to submit their proposals via online applications at their web sites. The vast majority, however, still prefer proposals to be submitted the old fashioned way, by mail.

THE INTERNET

As noted in the previous chapter, only about 10 percent of foundations have web sites, but for those that do, they are extremely helpful as a means for grantmakers to deliver important information about guidelines and application procedures efficiently and inexpensively, and for grantseekers to find up-to-the minute information about the foundations they are applying to. The web has enabled grantmakers to make the entire process of accepting and evaluating proposals and determining whom to fund much more transparent. Many grantmakers report a reduction in requests for printed guidelines and annual reports (hence reduced printing and postage costs) as a result of having a web site. The grantmakers we spoke to are actively monitoring visits to their web sites and say that they are pleased at the amount of traffic.

ONLINE APPLICATIONS

Despite the growing use of the web by grantmakers for a variety of purposes related to the grant application process, very few funders actually accept proposals electronically, either as online applications or as e-mail attachments. Letters of inquiry or draft proposals may be submitted electronically (and a small number of foundations require this first step), but in general, at some point along the way, most grantmakers will require a hard copy of the final proposal you submit. Those we interviewed cited a number of reasons for this requirement: Some point out that proposals are difficult to read on the computer screen, particularly if you are scanning a good number of them. Others note that their decision-making procedures entail sending along proposals that pass initial screening to all of their board members, and even if foundation staff members are proficient with computers, their board members may not be. Quite a few mentioned a preference for hard copy proposals (with substantial margins) so that they can make notes in those margins. And many of the grantmakers we queried reminded us that since the attachments, e.g. the IRS designation letter, the organization's 990, and audited financial statements, still need to be submitted by mail, they might as well accompany the full proposal.

E-MAIL AS A COMMUNICATIONS VEHICLE

The majority of our grantmakers indicated that they are using e-mail to communicate with grant applicants. According to them, e-mail makes the routine back and forth of sharing and verification of information related to the grant request go much more easily. Accepted protocol for most grantseekers is to wait until the grantmaker initiates e-mail communication or until you are invited to respond to a query or submit additional documentation via e-mail, rather than beginning this process yourself. As you can imagine, program officers at the larger foundations worry about receiving more e-mail messages from grant applicants that they can possibly read and respond to. And several of our interviewees expressed a familiar concern about this method of communication—that it is easy to misconstrue the meaning of what is being said. As already noted, it is a rare grantmaker who will accept an unsolicited proposal as an e-mail attachment.

Due Diligence As Practiced by Grantmakers

You may wonder what actually happens to your proposal once it arrives at the offices of your prospective funder. In the course of our conversations with grantmakers for this edition of the *Guide* we heard a great deal about what they referred to as "due diligence," a term that has migrated to the nonprofit world from the legal and financial professions. In this context it relates to the careful scrutiny and consideration of your request for funding. Here in brief we describe what is likely to happen at a staffed foundation. But keep in mind, there is no "typical" situation when it comes to grants decision-making, and foundations may differ considerably from one another in the procedures they adopt.

THE LOG-IN

Not surprisingly, many grantmakers have computer systems that enable them to track the receipt and review of your funding request. A staff person enters into the system all of the pertinent information about your proposal, including organization name and contact information, the title of the project, the amount of the request, a summary of the project (ideally comprised from your executive summary), and your recent relationship with this particular funder, if any.

Often at this stage the cover letter and appendix materials are separated out and placed in a folder while the proposal narrative and project budget are forwarded to a program officer, staff member, or trustee for initial review.

INITIAL REVIEW

To save time, the program officer or another assigned staff member will quickly review the executive summary, budget and other key sections of the proposal document to make certain that the project serves a geographic area and/or audience that is of interest to the grantmaker. Requests that are clearly outside of the grantmaker's guidelines are likely to be sidelined at this stage.

At this juncture, there may also be a quick review of the attachments to your proposal and any additional information the grantmaker needs may be requested. If this data is not complete, you may receive a letter or a phone call asking for the missing elements. Most grantmakers insist that *all* of the required information be in place before the decision-making process proceeds. Not having everything they need to make a decision may result in consideration of your proposal being delayed to a future board meeting, something most grantseekers wish to avoid. So it goes without saying that a prompt reply to a request for additional information is essential on the grantseeker's part.

ALIGNMENT

The proposals that are now being looked at very carefully have all of their attachments and have been determined to fit the grantmaker's guidelines. The program officer now wants to be certain that the project aligns with the grantmaker's mission and current specific interests. Does this project complement and/or enhance other projects the grantmaker may be supporting? This is particularly important if the grantmaker is in the midst of a well-publicized initiative of one kind or another.

Special attention is then paid to the ability of the organization to implement the project. Grants decision-makers will analyze the organization's track record, its staff and board leadership, and the reputation of the nonprofit in the community. Equally important, of course, is the perceived value of the grant project. Does it make sense as described? Is it likely to have the intended impact? As you can see, all of the components of your grant proposal as outlined in this *Guide* will come into play in responding to the various screens the grantmaker applies to your request.

REFERENCES

In considering your proposal the grants decision-maker is likely to speak with internal and external sources familiar with your organization. Having a staff or board member at the foundation who is already knowledgeable about you and your project and can serve as its champion, while rare, is extremely helpful at this point. Grantmakers may also speak to representatives of other nonprofits whom they know and trust to see if they are familiar with your organization and its work. There may also be conversations with other grantmakers, especially your current and past foundation and corporate donors, to learn how your agency handles the grantee relationship and its responsibilities. A few of the grantmakers we interviewed admitted to conducting internet searches to learn more about grant applicants, along with referring to local media sources. All of these efforts are aimed at determining the credibility and reliability of the potential grantee, to ensure that the organization will be able to deliver on the promise implied in its grant request.

FINANCIAL SCRUTINY

Grants decision-makers most often look for organizational stability and project sustainability. Based on your project and/or operating budget, your audited financial statement or balance sheet, and the most recent 990 you filed with the IRS, they may conduct an analysis of the overall fiscal soundness of your agency. They'll look for patterns of growth. They'll want to know if administrative expenses seem to be in line with your operating budget and with what they know other similar organizations are spending on such items.

Finally comes the issue of sustainability. They'll ask themselves if it appears that your project or organization will be able to attract the full support it needs to operate this program. How will it sustain itself over time? Is there a possibility that it will generate enough earned income ultimately to be self-supporting, or is there a finite period for this grant project after which no additional funds will be needed? Grants decision-makers may even speak with other potential donors to assess the possibilities for joint funding or collaboration in support of your grant project.

THE BOARD'S ROLE IN THE PROCESS

Depending on funder size and type, board members may play a more or less active role in the decision-making process. Board involvement seems to fall into three general categories.

For many foundations with professional staff, the members of the board receive only a summary of each project being recommended for funding with a suggested grant level. They may or may not also receive a list of nonprofits whose applications are *not* being recommended for support. In most instances a board member may ask to see the full proposal and request additional staff review of the project, although this rarely occurs. This type of board validation of experienced program officer recommendations is fairly common at the larger foundations and may invoke some discussion at the board meeting. But this is usually done under the guise of requests for clarification only.

At some foundations board members receive staff-prepared summaries and then are asked to cast a ballot that helps generate the actual agenda for the board meeting. There will be some projects which everyone agrees should be funded or denied and thus require no further examination. The remaining projects form the basis for the "docket" at the board meeting. These funders tend to have one lone staff member or a small number of staff and to attract board members who are willing to be a fairly involved with the foundation and hands-on in their approach.

At some foundations, especially family foundations and those without staff that are run by volunteers or family or company attorneys or accountants, the board members are actively engaged in all aspects of the decision-making process. They may receive and review every single proposal. They may conduct site visits to grantee organizations. They may invite some or all of the grant applicants to give presentations at the board meeting. In these instances it is the board itself that makes final decisions on each grant proposal.

As is evident, the due diligence process described here is not a "one size fits all" procedure. Each grantmaker has its own variation on the theme. But all of these efforts are aimed at developing objective ways of learning as much as possible about prospective grantees to ensure that precious grant monies are expended on the best possible applicants and on projects with a high potential for achieving success.

Cultivating the Potential Funder

Don't forget to continue to communicate once you have submitted your proposal. Cultivation of the funding prospect can make the critical difference between getting a grant and getting lost in the shuffle.

Knowledge of the funder's situation, and of that particular grantmaker's procedures for processing proposals, can be extremely helpful in developing your cultivation strategy.

Funders are flooded with proposals. Even if they turn down all that are clearly outside their guidelines, they still get many more than their budgets will allow them to fund. To cite just one example, Bruce Esterline of The Meadows Foundation shared the following statistics that he had at his fingertips: "Over 1,000 proposals go through a formal review process. Forty percent of those requests are selected for an in-depth review. Out of that group, about fifty percent—200–220—are funded annually. All applicants receive written notification of the foundation's decision.

We receive 50 to 100 calls from agencies that received rejections; and we try to respond and explain our rationale to all of them."

The ways in which foundations operate differ widely. At some small family foundations, the donor himself or herself will review all requests. At the larger foundations, a first cut is usually made to eliminate those that are out of program, then program officers review proposals in specific areas and must take each proposal through a staff review process before a recommendation goes to their board of trustees. Foundations vary greatly in the precise manner in which they review proposals and how these are shared with members of the board. Here is how Marilyn Hennessy describes the process at the Retirement Research Foundation: "The board makes all grant decisions. Six weeks before the board meeting, board trustees receive proposal summaries (usually ten or twelve at a time and each eight to 20 pages in length) accompanied by a ballot describing the proposal and the staff's recommendations. The trustee has four options: 1) approve; 2) decline; 3) ask for a consultant review; 4) discuss. Ballots are mailed back to the office in advance of the meeting so that we have a summary of the proposal votes by the time of the meeting. Probably one-third are unanimous decisions and two-thirds are subject to discussion (no unanimous vote). This ballot process is a way to structure our grant agenda. The trustees get a list of those proposals that are outside of our guidelines; these are called 'staff declines,' and these actions are ratified by the board."

Foundations frequently work closely with the grantseeker in developing the request. Victoria Kovar of the Cooper Foundation tells us: "We provide as much support as the grantseeker requests from us. I review draft applications and provide suggestions, and editing in some cases." Bob Wittig of the Jovid Foundation says: "I always encourage organizations new to our foundation to call me first and discuss their funding idea before they submit." And Lita Ugarte of The Community Foundation for Greater Atlanta adds: "Build the relationship. Call before you apply. Call after you are declined. Develop the relationship. While it is hard for applicants to understand what this means, many foundation staff members want to get to know applicants." Finally, Michele Pritchard of the Peyton Anderson Foundation sums it up for many of the grantmakers we interviewed: "Communicate with the foundation. If you keep us informed, we will have a successful relationship no matter the outcome. Don't surprise the grantmaker."

Several forms of cultivation may be particularly valuable after the proposal is submitted:

- Communication by phone or e-mail;

- Face-to-face meetings;
- Using board contacts; and
- Written updates and progress reports.

Follow-up by Phone or E-mail

Normally you should plan to call or send an e-mail about two weeks after the proposal package is mailed. The primary purpose of this communication is to make sure that the proposal has been received. You have requested a meeting in the cover letter and offered to supply any additional information required to help the funder consider your request. You should therefore ask if it is appropriate to schedule a meeting at the foundation or corporate office or a site visit at your agency. Be sure to ask about the process and timing for the review of your proposal. This will guide you as to when you might call back or send updated information.

Call periodically thereafter to check on the status of your proposal. If you have had no response in the expected time frame, call to find out if there has been a change in the schedule. Ask the same types of questions as you did previously: Is additional information required? When will the proposal be reviewed? Would the foundation or corporate representative like to meet? Be brief. There is a fine line between being helpful and being too pushy.

Each time you call, be prepared to answer the program officer's detailed questions about any aspect of the proposal or of your agency's work. You should also expect to receive calls or e-mails from your program officer during the course of the proposal review.

Marilyn Hennessy of Retirement Research Foundation describes this kind of communication as follows: "More often, we are communicating with grantseekers on questions about their proposal or to seek clarity on what they have said, and as part of that process they provide us with additional information." And Bruce Esterline of The Meadows Foundation states: "We welcome this, especially via e-mail. But, if we are doing our job well, the program officer would be keeping applicants updated on their status."

It helps to stay in touch by phone or e-mail. This gives you a chance to find out what is happening with your proposal and to share information with the foundation or corporate funder.

When appropriate, follow up the phone conversation with a note or e-mail message about the next step you plan to take or confirming any new information you provided over the phone. While phone communication is often the most convenient way to keep in touch, you need to be sure that any agreement or information that is critical to a successful outcome of the review process is put in writing.

Face-to-Face Meetings

Appointments can be very hard to obtain and typically occur at the initiative of the grantmaker. Many funders will not agree to a meeting until the proposal is under active consideration. This might entail assigning it to a program officer, who would then be the person to meet with you. Even when the foundation or corporate representative is intensely interested in your project, he or she may believe that a meeting would not be helpful in arriving at a recommendation on your request. However, some foundations insist on a site visit for most or all of the groups to which they make grants. While some program officers will not meet with applicants until a proposal has been submitted, others say that they would prefer that the proposal be submitted only after a meeting. To quote Julie Farkas of Consumer Health Foundation: "This has always been tremendously important to us. For prospective grantees, we always visit them at their site in the community because the leadership, staff and location are all critical to our decision-making process and, ultimately, the program's success or failure."

When you are offered an appointment, you should view this as a very special opportunity. It is one that you must prepare for carefully. To quote Peter Bird of the Frist Foundation: "The visit helps clarify ideas about the project, the operation, and the nonprofit's board."

First, be sure that the right team is selected to attend the meeting. If your nonprofit agency has staff, the chief executive officer or executive director should go. The CEO should be able to answer specific questions relating to the project. The other member of the team should be a volunteer, preferably from the board. The presence of the volunteer underscores the fact that the board is aware of and supports the work of the organization. Under the right circumstances, a member of the program staff can be a helpful adjunct, or you might bring along someone who benefits from the good work of your organization. But don't overwhelm the funder by bringing too many additional people to the meeting. Clear with the funding representative precisely how many people are welcome. If time permits, call a day in advance to confirm the date and remind the funder who is coming.

Invite the prospective funder to visit your organization. A site visit obviously allows you to introduce the funding representative to a wider range of people involved in your agency or project.

Next, prepare for the meeting. Compile background information about the foundation or corporation. You should be careful to note any prior interaction with the funder, especially if it was less than positive. Develop a profile of the person(s) with whom you are meeting, if this information is available in standard biographical sources, on the Web, or via the grapevine. Your peers in the nonprofit world who are grant recipients might shed some light on the personality and idiosyncracies of the funder.

Create a role for each of the participants. It is critical that no one sits idle. There should be a dialogue and rapport among the meeting participants.

Last, know precisely what you want to accomplish in the meeting. You won't leave with a check in hand, but you do need to decide in advance what information you want to share and to obtain. David Grant of the Geraldine R. Dodge Foundation addresses preparedness this way: "Good advice is to ask the grantmaker what to prepare for the meeting, and don't do it at the last minute. The best-prepared people simply show us that they go about everything they do with high standards for themselves. We want to see not only the work being considered for funding, but also evidence that the agency is a high functioning organization."

You should expect to accomplish a great deal through the simple process of meeting face-to-face with the funder. The meeting will establish a personal relationship between the representatives of your organization and of the funding agency. Despite our high-tech world, giving is still a highly personal activity. Hence, the better your rapport with the donor, the more likely it is that financial support will be forthcoming.

Along with getting to know the people at your agency, this will be an opportunity for the funding representative to gain a much better understanding of your group's work. Hearing from knowledgeable people about your mission, programs, and dreams will allow the funder to ask questions, to refine information, and to correct misperceptions.

Bruce Esterline of The Meadows Foundation describes what the grantmaker should seek to achieve at a meeting this way: "Become familiar with the foundation: our guidelines; what we fund; look at the most similar grant recipients. Talk to other grantees that have worked with the foundation. Treat the meeting like a job interview. Show how your proposal fits within the foundation's interests. Try to promote a good exchange of views and ideas. Be able to answer all kinds of questions about your agency and the proposed project. Finish by identifying the next steps in the application process."

The staff and trustees of the Frances L. & Edwin L. Cummings Memorial Fund shared the following evaluation form, detailing the questions they ask themselves as part of a site visit.

THE FRANCES L. & EDWIN L. CUMMINGS MEMORIAL FUND

TRUSTEE'S SITE VISIT EVALUATION

I. GENERAL INFORMATION

Name of Organization:

Location:

Date of site visit: Board Member:

Other Attendees:

II. PROGRAM INFORMATION

1. Rate Executive Director with respect to the following:
   (Scale: 1=Excellent, 2=Very Good, 3=Good, 4=Fair, 5=Poor)

   Understanding of his/her job

   Leadership

   Relationship to staff

   Understanding of needs of community being served

   Effective communicator of ideas

   Dedication to job

   Ability to respond under pressure—deal with critical problems

   Additional comments:

2. Is the organization overloaded with professionals, property lien, or understaffed for program efficiency?

   _____

   _____

   _____

3. Does this organization have a proven track record in general? Specifically or as to this program(s)?

   _____

   _____

   _____

4. Does this organization have the potential to expand to meet increasing needs of the community? (If this organization is already expanding/expanded, has it done so in a manageable fashion?)

_____

_____

_____

5. Is this organization offering innovative programs or are they replicating/duplicating others' efforts?

_____

_____

_____

III. BOARD OF DIRECTORS

1. Is the Board of Directors an "active" or a "paper" Board? Explain.

_____

_____

_____

2. Using the same scale as above, rank the Board of Directors with respect to:

   Leadership

   Relationship to staff

   Dedication to achieving stated objectives of the organization

   Personal knowledge of organization's daily activities

   Amount of time personally committed to organization

   Personal financial commitment

   Distribution of responsibility among Board Members

   Additional comments:

IV. FACILITIES

1. Is the space effectively utilized?   Yes   No   Describe.

_____

_____

2. Is the atmosphere conducive to the programs being operated? Yes   No
   If no, please explain.

   _____

   _____

   _____

V. PROPOSAL INFORMATION

1. Is there a need for this kind of service in the community? Are other agencies
   already providing the same kind of service(s)? If so, is the proposal(s)
   unique in any respect?

   _____

   _____

   _____

2. Are the goals of the proposal(s) aggressive enough? Too aggressive?

   _____

   _____

   _____

3. Is the budget for the proposal(s) realistic?

   _____

   _____

   _____

4. Is the proposal(s) cost-effective in its anticipated results?

   _____

   _____

   _____

5. Has the program(s) been well-planned?

   _____

   _____

   _____

6. Is the Board/Staff committed to undertaking the project(s) regardless of Cummings Fund support? (If so, how?)

_____

_____

_____

VI. FINANCIAL INFORMATION

1. What is the overall present financial situation of this organization?

_____

_____

_____

2. Additional comments/Summary:

_____

_____

_____

_____

_____

_____

_____

_____

During a face-to-face meeting, the funder will gain a much better sense of the project for which you are seeking support. Critical information about the proposal, such as the need, methods for addressing it, and the capability of your group to run the program, might be covered during discussion. For this reason, be sure to review the proposal carefully before the meeting.

You must assume responsibility for the agenda of the meeting. Be prepared to:

- *Use an icebreaker.* The first few times you attend a meeting with a funder, it can be nerve-racking. Break the tension by telling an amusing anecdote, by relaying a true incident of interest to the group, or by commenting about the view or an object in the room where the meeting takes place.

- *Introduce all of the meeting participants by name, title, and/or role.* This way the funder will know the players and be clear to whom specific questions should be addressed.

- *Get down to business.* Once introduced, the participants should promptly move on to the real purpose of the meeting: Your group hopes the funder will become a partner with you in getting your project off the ground.

- *Remind the funder about the mission and history of your agency.* Be thorough but brief in this review.

- *Describe the programs you offer.* Again, be succinct, but be certain that the funder has a good overview of your services. This is important in case the project submitted for funding proves not to be of interest. The funder may request a proposal relating to a different aspect of your agency's work, having achieved a good grasp of the whole program.

- *Describe the project for which you are seeking support.* It is critical that you demonstrate the conviction that success is likely. Provide the necessary detail for the funder to understand the problem being addressed and your agency's proposed response to it.

- *Keep a dialogue going.* It is easy to speak at length about your organization. But it is also easy to bore the funders and, even worse, for you to come away from the meeting not having gained any relevant new information about this grantmaker. Whenever possible, try to elicit the funder's reactions. Inquire about current programs they have funded that address similar problems. Treat the grantmaker as a potential partner. Remember, their dollars have significance only when combined with programs. Listen carefully to their responses, comments, and questions. This dialogue will clue you into the real interests and concerns of this potential funder. Don't assume anything.

- ***Obtain a clear understanding of the next steps.*** You should determine the following: if anything more is needed for review of the request; when the proposal will come up for review; and how the agency will be notified about the outcome. If, as a result of this conversation, it is clear that the proposal is unlikely to be funded, you should ask what you might do to resubmit this or another proposal.

A great deal can be accomplished in a well-crafted meeting, whether at their place or yours. You don't want this process spoiled by extending it for too long. Once it is clear that the objectives have been achieved, you need to summarize the next steps to be taken by both sides and move on to a cordial goodbye. End the meeting while the "good vibes" are still being felt by both sides.

Here is an example of a thank-you letter submitted to a funder by the executive director of East Side House, subsequent to a face-to-face meeting.

October 26, 2005

Ms. Donna Highlander
Vice President
The Teagle Foundation
10 Rockefeller Plaza, Rm. 920
New York, NY 10020-1903

Dear Donna:

I write to thank you and Cheryl Chang for your visit yesterday. Joy Ferguson, Ana Maldonado, John Ventura and I very much enjoyed meeting you both and showing you the College Preparatory and Leadership (CPL) Program.

We are proud of the success our students have attained through the CPL Program and of our capable staff, who invest so much in our youth. The generous support of The Teagle Foundation has played an important role in making this success possible.

I would be delighted to answer any further questions you might have about our program; please do not hesitate to call me at 718.665.5250. In the meantime, I thank you for your consideration of our work.

Sincerely,

John A. Sanchez
Executive Director

cc: Ms. Cheryl Chang, Program Assistant

Using Board Contacts

A contact from one of your board members with a peer affiliated with the foundation or corporate funder you are approaching will usually reinforce the relationship you are building.

How do you discover if your board members have contacts that can help with raising funds? First, circulate to all of the members of your board the names of the officers and directors of the foundations and corporations you plan to approach. Ask your board members to respond to you by a certain date about those whom they know. Then work one-on-one with individual board members, developing a strategy for them to utilize their contacts. Another approach is to meet with the board members to talk about individuals with whom they can be helpful. You may find contacts with funders that you had not intended to approach, where having an entree will make a difference.

Knowing that you have board-to-board contact is not enough. You must assist your board member in capitalizing on this relationship on behalf of your nonprofit group. First, develop a scenario with the board member focusing on how to approach the contact. The more personal the approach, the better it is. Second, assist your board member with understanding why this funder would want to help your organization, finding the right language to discuss your agency and your funding needs, and drafting correspondence as needed. Then make sure that the board member makes the promised contact after the proposal has been submitted. Periodically remind this individual of the next step to be taken. The groundwork you have done is wasted if the board member never follows through.

Be forewarned that staff of foundations and corporate grantmakers may be concerned about your board members contacting their board members. This is particularly true of professionally staffed foundations where program officers may consider it inappropriate or may view it as interference. Some funders feel strongly that an agency should not use a board contact, even if they have one.

Still others report that their trustees are encouraged to indicate their interest in a project. At a minimum, staff want to know in advance that a board contact will be used. In the opinion of Danah Craft of Sun Trust Bank Atlanta Foundation: "Having a board contact makes a difference for family foundations—it is like a major gift solicitation. For a corporate foundation it makes less of a difference." And Julie Farkas of the Consumer Health Foundation had this suggestion: "The Board member might share information, if requested, but then recuse him or herself from the vote."

Where you already are in contact with the foundation staff, it is critical to discuss a board contact with them before it is set in motion. Finally, keep in mind that relying on board contacts can backfire. At some foundations, if a board member has had contact with an agency, he or she is expected to disqualify himself from discussion about the specific proposal.

Written Updates and Progress Reports

Written communication helps a foundation or corporate donor learn more about your group and reminds them that you need their support. You should plan to send materials selectively while your proposal is under review. Here are some ideas for what you might send:

- summary reports on what is going on in your organization;
- financial information, such as a new audit;
- newsletters, bulletins, brochures, or other frequently issued information;
- updates/reports on specific projects; and
- newspaper or magazine articles on the project for which you have requested support, the work of your nonprofit, or closely related issues.

It is usually not necessary to customize the materials, but a brief accompanying note always helps to reinforce your relationship with the funder.

The Frances L. & Edwin L. Cummings Memorial Fund provides an example of a cultivation letter from Groundwork. The use of acronyms usually is not advisable, but in this case the funder is well aware of what they stand for.

May 16, 2006

Ms. Elizabeth Costas
Administrative Director
The Frances L. & Edwin L. Cummings Memorial Fund
501 5th Avenue, Suite 708
New York, NY 10017-6103

Dear Ms. Costas:

Thank you so much for hosting Jamali and me at your offices last week to discuss the importance of her position in the Family Resource Center. It was a good conversation and I hope the information you were able to gather was helpful.

As you requested, I have included the following information concerning our method of evaluation, for your review:

- Screen shot from the PMA
- Highlights of Annual Goals and Outcomes
- Most recent Philiber Report
- Copy of our most recent GW report card

If you should need anything else, please do not hesitate to reach out at (718) 346-2200 ext. 112 or rbuery@groundworkinc.org. I would be happy to further discuss our method of evaluation, once you've had a chance to review the enclosed materials.

I look forward to being in touch with you soon.

Regards,

Richard Buery
Executive Director

Listservs and E-newsletters

Don't overlook the possibility of selective e-mail contact with prospective funders, if they have communicated with you that way in the past or have indicated a preference for this vehicle for providing updates. A concise e-mail message with, perhaps, a link to an appropriate area of your web site or other coverage of your activities, can have a significant impact. Repeated or unnecessary e-mail messages directed at funding program officers can prove annoying, however.

Some agencies have developed listservs or broadcast e-mail services to keep various constituents apprised of recent developments. It would be wise not to add a funder's e-mail address to your listserv without prior permission to do so. On the other hand, this is a very convenient way to keep donors and prospective funders aware of your agency's accomplishments if they agree to it. In general, such cultivation is welcomed by today's grantmaker.

Even after your project has concluded, don't forget to continue to cultivate your donors. Fundraising is all about relationship building. Kathleen Ceverny of the Cleveland Foundation puts it very succinctly: "Communication is important and a challenge."

13

Life After the Grant—or Rejection

The Initial Follow-up to a Grant

You've just received a grant from a foundation or corporation. Congratulations! What should you do? First of all, you should celebrate. Include everyone in your agency who contributed to this wonderful outcome. Thank them for their help and remind them about what this means for your organization.

Next, send a thank you letter to your funder. This seems so obvious that one would think it hardly worth stating. Yet a number of the grantmakers interviewed for this book responded to the question, "What is the best thing an organization can do after receiving a grant?" with the simple response: send a thank-you letter.

Here are three sample thank-you letters. The first is from Sponsors for Educational Opportunity and goes into some detail about what the grant will help SEO achieve.

August 2, 2005

J. Andrew Lark, Esq.
Co-Trustee
The Frances L. & Edwin L. Cummings Memorial Fund
501 Fifth Avenue, Suite 708
New York, NY 10017

Dear Mr. Lark:

On behalf of SEO and the young people we serve, please accept my heartfelt thanks for The Frances L. & Edwin L. Cummings Memorial Fund's $30,000 contribution in support of the "Starting Off Strong" ninth-grade component of our Scholars Program.

This grant will enable us to recruit more ninth-grade students, expand our college preparation services for them and help them fulfill their potential. By intervening early with these students and teaching core skills, our services extend far beyond simply getting students into college – we help them thrive there and establish successful careers. These students will be well-educated leaders of color for the next generation.

The support provided by the Cummings Memorial Fund is critical in enabling us to open doors for young people from underserved communities, and to push our students to even higher levels of academic and personal achievement.

Thank you for your support of SEO's students. Together, we are making a tremendous difference in the lives of deserving young people.

Best regards,

William A. Goodloe
President & CEO

cc: Grace Allen

The next example from Highbridge is quite brief and to the point.

Highbridge Community Life Center
Brother Edward Phelan
Executive Director

August 4, 2005

J. Andrew Lark, Esq.
The Frances L. & Edwin L. Cummings Memorial Fund
501 Fifth Avenue, Suite 708
New York, NY 10017-6103

Dear Mr. Lark:

We received your generous donation of $50,000. This award will support the Program Manager for our Recreation Center.

Once again, we are very grateful for your contribution.

Sincerely yours,

Brother Edward Phelan
Executive Director

The final example of a thank-you letter from Careers Through Culinary Arts Program refers to the first installment of a multiyear grant and underscores the partnership with the funder.

July 24, 2006

Norman L. Peck
Chair
The Peter Jay Sharp Foundation
545 Madison Avenue
New York, NY 10022

Dear Norman:

We just received the first installment of $200,000 on the $350,000, three-year grant from The Peter Jay Sharp Foundation. On behalf of our board, staff, and especially the students we serve, I want to thank you and the other Directors for the Foundation's extraordinary generosity. This gift will help us enormously with our goals for training and preparing teachers as well as students for entry-level certification. The results of our efforts over the next three years should dramatically improve the NYC public school culinary programs.

All of us at Careers Through Culinary Arts Program are inspired by your continued interest in the work we do. Thanks in no small part to The Peter Jay Sharp Foundation, C-CAP has made incredible strides in the past few years. As one of our most valued partners, I hope you share our feelings of pride and accomplishment and look forward to our future endeavors.

Thank you for helping us bring the culinary arts to underserved high school students both here in NYC and around the country.

Kindest regards,
Richard Grausman
Founder and President

cc: Edmund Duffy; Barry Tobias

The foundation representatives we interviewed expressed a concern that needs to be taken to heart. Appreciate the investment that has just been made in your agency. Recognize that it is not just an institution that is supporting you but the actual people within that institution. Remember that the grants decision-makers feel good about the commitment to invest in your organization. They may even have had to fight for you in the face of opposition by other staff and board members. Show your thanks and appreciation for this vote of confidence.

Grantmakers want to ensure effective communication after a grant is awarded. They remind us that a grant is a contract to undertake a specific set of activities, and they want and need to know what has transpired.

Remember the watchword of all fundraising: communication. A telephone call to say "thank you," an update on recent activities, or an announcement of additional funding committed or received are all ways to keep in touch after the grant is made.

Grant Reporting

If a foundation has specific reporting requirements, you will be told what they are. Usually reporting requirements are included in the grant letter; sometimes you are asked to sign and return a copy of the grant letter or of a separate grant contract. These "conditions," which a representative of the nonprofit signs, sometimes require timely reports that are tied to payments.

Here is the Cooper Foundation Grant Agreement form.

SAMPLE AGREEMENT

[GRANTEE ORGANIZATION] (Recipient) hereby accepts this grant from the Cooper Foundation (Foundation) in the amount of [GRANT AMOUNT] and agrees to comply with the following terms and conditions.

1. The grant funds will be used solely for [PROJECT TITLE OR PURPOSE]. If unable to proceed with the activities described in the proposal dated [PROPOSAL DATE], Recipient agrees to contact the Foundation in writing. Substantive changes in the program, budget or use of the grant funds must be submitted in advance, in writing, and approved by the Foundation in writing.

2. In the case of a contingent grant, Recipient agrees to provide information that the contingency has been met prior to the Foundation making payment. This grant is contingent upon [CONTINGENCY DESCRIPTION].* The deadline for this information is [DATE]. Failure to provide this information may result in the grant monies being rescinded. Any request to extend the deadline or change the nature of the contingency must be submitted an advance to the Foundation in writing.
   * *Examples: raising the full project budget; receipt of necessary information or permissions; confirmation that a particular position has been filled, etc.*

3. The grant term shall start at the date of approval and end [PROJECT END DATE].

4. If any grant funds remain unused at the end of the grant term, Recipient agrees to contact the Foundation to determine whether to return the funds or expend them for another purpose.

5. Recipient agrees to provide written reports, including program and financial information, by [REPORT DATES]. *This section used when interim reports are required for multi-year grants.*

6. Recipient agrees to provide a final report by [DATE]. The final report must include the organization's most recent audited financial statements and current financial reports.

7. Recipient may not seek additional funding from the Foundation during the grant term or for 12 months after the last payment date, whichever is later.

Recipient certifies that its 501(c)(3) status with the Internal Revenue Service remains in full force and effect, and that we are not a private foundation within the meaning of section 509(a) of the Internal Revenue Code.

For [GRANTEE ORGANIZATION]:

Board Chair or President

_____   _____   _____
Signature   Print Name   Date

Chief Executive Officer

_____   _____   _____
Signature   Print Name   Date

For the Foundation:

Art Thompson, President   _____   _____
                                              Signature   Date

What follows are the Grant Letter and Grant Agreement used by the
Agape Foundation.

Agape Foundation
Fund for Nonviolent Social Change

Roni Krouzman
Next Generation Youth Peace Campaign
51 Essex Street #2
San Anselmo, CA 94960

Dear Roni,

Congratulations! On April 30, 2006, the Agape Foundation's Board of Trustees
awarded a grant of $2,000 from the David R. Stern Fund (check #3135) to the
Next Generation Youth Peace Campaign for its educational and charitable
work. This grant is for support to fund the Youth Peace Campaign, which helps
young people to learn about US foreign policy and military spending, gain
activist skills, organize and work for peace. Information about the Stern Fund is
enclosed.

The length of the grant is six months, at which time your organization will
submit a final written report to the Agape Foundation explaining how the
monies were spent and provide copies of receipts that reflect those expenses.
Please include a statement describing how Agape helped you achieve your
goals, moved the organization forward, won a campaign, etc. Please use the
enclosed form to submit that report. **This report is due November 1, 2006.**

No funds engendered through this grant shall be used for political lobbying or
for illegal purposes.

The Agape Foundation requests, as a condition of this grant, that a
representative of your organization sign all copies of this Grant Letter and the
enclosed Grant Agreement, keeping a copy of each for your files and returning
the originals to the Agape Foundation. Also, let us know if this is one of the
project or organization's first grants. (We love to be first!)

For the duration of the grant period, please place Agape on your mailing list and keep us updated on media coverage of your project. Please publicly acknowledge the Agape Foundation, e.g., in your newsletters, brochures, film credits, etc. We would also like to link our websites to keep our donors and other interested parties informed of our work. Our URL is http://www.agapefdn.org.

Sincerely,

Karen Topakian
Executive Director

Signed/Title/Date: Roni Krouzman/Director/5-2-06
                    Next Generation Youth Peace Campaign

AGAPE FOUNDATION BOARD OF TRUSTEES GRANT AGREEMENT

On Sunday, April 30, 2006, the Agape Foundation (Grantor) awarded a grant of $2,000 from the David R. Stern Fund to Next Generation Youth Peace Campaign (Grantee) for purposes stated in the Grant Letter accompanying this Grant Agreement. The Grantee agrees and consents to the following conditions of this grant:

1. Grantee shall use the grant solely for the purposes stated in the accompanying Grant Letter and the Grantee shall repay the Grantor any portion of the amount granted which is not used for the purposes of the grant.

2. Grantee shall submit a final report and financial accounting to Grantor. Such a report shall describe the progress the Grantee has made toward achieving the purposes for which this grant was made and it shall detail by copies of receipts all expenditures made form the granted funds.

---

3. Grantee shall not use any portion of these grant funds for the following:

    a) to carry on propaganda or otherwise attempt to influence specific legislation, either by direct or grassroots lobbying;

    b) to influence the outcome of any specific public election;

    c) to make grants to individuals on a non-objective basis;

    d) to support any non-charitable or non-educational activities;

    e) to support any illegal activities.

4. If this grant is made for the purpose of capital equipment or for endowment, Grantee shall submit reports to the Grantor for this taxable year and for Grantee's two succeeding taxable years describing the use of the principal and income (if any) described from the granted funds.

IN WITNESS WHEREOF, this Grant Agreement is signed this date

1 May, 2006

Roni Krouzman
(Officer, Next Generation Youth Peace Campaign)

Karen L. Topakian, E.D.
(Director or Trustee, the Agape Foundation)

When a foundation provides formal reporting guidelines, in most cases there will be dates when the reports are due. If a funder has given you specific dates for reporting, develop a tickler system to keep track of them. If you can tell now that you'll have a problem meeting these deadlines (such as your auditors are scheduled for March, and the audited financial report is due in February), discuss this with the funder immediately. If the foundation staff has not heard from the grantee within a reasonable time period after the reports are due, they will call or send the grant recipient a note to follow up.

Some funders want reports at quarterly or six-month intervals, but most request an annual report and/or a final report, two to three months after the conclusion of the project. Even for grants of fairly short duration, foundations often express the desire to receive an interim report. Unless otherwise stated, an interim report can be informal.

The Cleveland Foundation issues very specific reporting instructions. Its Grant Report Preparation Guidelines provide a useful framework to guide agency staff in drafting a report to any funder. While these guidelines are designed for the

Cleveland Foundation's grantees, they provide a reliable model for reports to other foundations that may not be as specific in their requirements.

The following guidelines are reprinted in their totality with permission from the Cleveland Foundation:

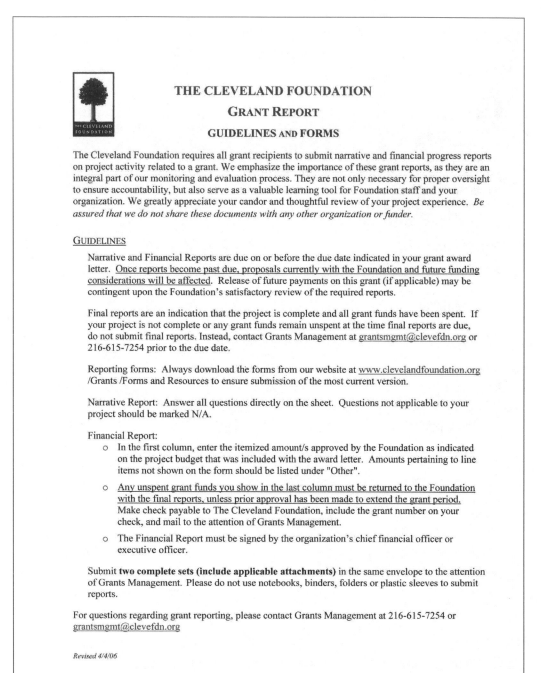

THE CLEVELAND FOUNDATION
GRANT REPORT
GUIDELINES AND FORMS

The Cleveland Foundation requires all grant recipients to submit narrative and financial progress reports on project activity related to a grant. We emphasize the importance of these grant reports, as they are an integral part of our monitoring and evaluation process. They are not only necessary for proper oversight to ensure accountability, but also serve as a valuable learning tool for Foundation staff and your organization. We greatly appreciate your candor and thoughtful review of your project experience. *Be assured that we do not share these documents with any other organization or funder.*

GUIDELINES

Narrative and Financial Reports are due on or before the due date indicated in your grant award letter. Once reports become past due, proposals currently with the Foundation and future funding considerations will be affected. Release of future payments on this grant (if applicable) may be contingent upon the Foundation's satisfactory review of the required reports.

Final reports are an indication that the project is complete and all grant funds have been spent. If your project is not complete or any grant funds remain unspent at the time final reports are due, do not submit final reports. Instead, contact Grants Management at grantsmgmt@clevefdn.org or 216-615-7254 prior to the due date.

Reporting forms: Always download the forms from our website at www.clevelandfoundation.org /Grants /Forms and Resources to ensure submission of the most current version.

Narrative Report: Answer all questions directly on the sheet. Questions not applicable to your project should be marked N/A.

Financial Report:
- o   In the first column, enter the itemized amount/s approved by the Foundation as indicated on the project budget that was included with the award letter. Amounts pertaining to line items not shown on the form should be listed under "Other".

- o   Any unspent grant funds you show in the last column must be returned to the Foundation with the final reports, unless prior approval has been made to extend the grant period. Make check payable to The Cleveland Foundation, include the grant number on your check, and mail to the attention of Grants Management.

- o   The Financial Report must be signed by the organization's chief financial officer or executive officer.

Submit **two complete sets (include applicable attachments)** in the same envelope to the attention of Grants Management. Please do not use notebooks, binders, folders or plastic sleeves to submit reports.

For questions regarding grant reporting, please contact Grants Management at 216-615-7254 or grantsmgmt@clevefdn.org

Revised 4/4/06

THE CLEVELAND FOUNDATION

FINANCIAL
GRANT REPORT

Check one:

_____ **Interim Report**

_____ **Final Report** *(Final report should include financial activities covering the entire grant period showing all funds expended)*

Organization Name: _____

Grant Number: _____

Date of this Report: _____

Project Title: _____

	Cleveland Foundation Total Grant Amount	Amount Expended to Date	Balance of Grant Funds
Personnel Expenses			
Salaries and Wages			
Fringe Benefits			
Non-Personnel Expenses			
Contract Services/Professional Fees			
Office Space			
Equipment/Supplies			
Staff/Board Development			
Travel/Related Expenses			
Indirect Costs			
Other			
TOTAL	$	$	$

Signature: _____ **Date:** _____

chief financial office or executive officer

Name: (please print) _____

chief financial office or executive officer

Telephone: _____ **Email:** _____

Revised 4/4/06

THE CLEVELAND FOUNDATION

NARRATIVE
GRANT REPORT

Please check one: ___ **Interim Report** ___ **Final Report** *

Organization Name: _____

Grant Number: _____

Project Title: _____

Reporting Dates: From: _____ To: _____

Signature: _____

Name *(please print)*: _____ **Date:** _____

Email: _____ **Telephone:** _____

Final Reports should include a review of performance and activities covering the entire grant period.

PROJECT INFORMATION *(Please type directly on this form)*

1. Please summarize the expected outcomes for this project and to what extent they have been achieved.

2. What have been the principal accomplishments of the project to date and how have they been achieved?

3. The Foundation recognizes that circumstances can change, possibly affecting project implementation. What, if any, difficulties have you encountered; why did they occur; and what refinements or plans have been made to overcome them? Please indicate activities that are behind schedule or not yet begun, and any changes in project plans or personnel.

Revised 4/4/06

4. What have been the most challenging or surprising aspects of this project? Have there been any unexpected outcomes?

5. Based on your experience to date, what advice would you give to other organizations planning a similar program? What have been the strengths and limitations of the project? What would you do differently if you had the chance?

6. Please describe your post-grant plans for this project. How will it be financed?

ORGANIZATIONAL INFORMATION

It is very helpful to understand the organizational context in which your project is proceeding. Please take this opportunity to update us on any significant organizational changes, developments or challenges. How have these developments contributed to or impeded the success of the project? Additionally, are there any problems or issues confronting your organization that may require assistance? How might Foundation staff be helpful?

ATTACHMENTS (Optional)

Please attach two copies of any public recognition, awards, press releases or news articles pertinent to this project.

Revised 4/4/06

The Cleveland Foundation guidelines are particularly applicable if you have received special project support. Don't be concerned if your project does not lend itself to many of these questions. For instance, if you have received $15,000 to hire a tutor for your after-school program, some of the sections are probably not applicable. Others, like post-grant plans, should be addressed in some fashion in almost any report.

Even if you have received unrestricted, general-purpose support, funders want to know what overall goals you set for your agency for the year. Did you achieve them? What were some specific triumphs? What were some particular problems you faced, and how did you overcome them? Or, are you still dealing with the challenges? (Remember, being realistic is what counts, along with a sense of confidence that you are appropriately managing the grant.) What follows is a report using the format required by The Frances L. & Edwin L. Cummings Memorial Fund of its grantee, the Center for Alternative Sentencing and Employment Services.

I. General Information:

Interim Progress Report – August 15, 2006

Name of the Organization: Center for Alternative Sentencing and Employment Services (CASES)

Address: 346 Broadway, 3rd Floor West, New York, NY 10013

Contact Person: Joel Copperman
Employer ID#: 13-2668080
Amount of Grant: $50,000
Date of Award: January 25, 2006

II. Program Information:

Project Description:

CASES is deeply grateful to The Frances L. & Edwin L. Cummings Memorial Fund for its support of The Career Exploration Project (Career Ex) and pleased to submit an interim report on the project. Career Ex is a unique workforce development program that enables court-involved youth to obtain tangible job skills and employment experience by providing career guidance and training, challenging internships and a comprehensive system of support. Over the course of the intensive four-week preparatory program, participants learn résumé writing, job search, interviewing, team building and problem-solving skills. Following the preparatory program, participants interview for and select jobsites where they spend the remaining 10 weeks acquiring real work experience in the form of paid internships. The hourly stipends provided during the internship period, along with basic budgeting exercises, help participants learn to responsibly manage their earnings. With simultaneous career counseling, positive role model mentoring, and academic services, Career Ex positions its participants to continue their education and pursue their career goals.

Total Project Budget: $340,978

What were the expected results of the project as outlined in the proposal?

Program targets for the grant period were set as follows:

- Career Ex will serve an additional 30 youth, increasing in size from 90 to 120 participants served by conducting two additional program cycles and adding new staff.
- Approximately 75% of all participants will complete the four-week employment skills training, and 65% of those youth will go on to complete ten week internships.
- More than 80% of Career Ex graduates will continue their education.
- Approximately 65% of participants will find employment following graduation from CEP.
- 100% of Career Ex graduates will successfully complete CEP and fulfill their obligations to the court.
- Less than 5% of Career Ex graduates will be convicted of a new felony offense within two years of graduation.

What results have been achieved to date?

Midway into the grant period, Career Ex is on target to meet and exceed our goals for the year. In the first six months of the grant, between January and June 2006, Career Ex began four new cycles of the program, enrolling 62 participants. Also in the first half of 2006, four cycles of the program concluded, with 70% of participants completing the employment skills training, and 44% of these participants completing ten-week internships. Since January, 100% of Career Ex graduates have completed CEP, thus fulfilling their obligations to the court. Our post-program outcomes have also been exceptional. Of all graduates from 2003-2005, 86% continued their education and 63% secured employment. Ninety-four percent successfully completed CEP and less than 5% were convicted of a new felony offense within two years of graduation.

As part of ongoing innovations in education services provided in-house, we have further enhanced the educational programming available to Career Ex participants. Each participant is now given an educational assessment at intake. Those wishing to participate in our in-house classes are placed based on skill level: Basic Literacy (remedial), pre-GED (intermediate), and GED Preparation (advanced). These classes focus on addressing the skill deficiencies and gaps in previous education that prevent scholastic success. For those students currently enrolled in community schools, a Homework Help class is offered that directly connects their educational activities at CASES to their coursework. In addition to the college preparatory support received by Career Ex staff, the Educational Unit also assists participants with their college application process, through the new *Next Steps* class. *Next Steps* is offered to students who have already obtained their GED or high school diploma and focuses on academic skills, essay writing and research.

During this reporting period, guest speakers from a variety of professions were utilized to engage participants during the training period. For instance, an attorney from the EEOC with expertise in employment discrimination volunteered her time to speak to the participants on sexual harassment issues in the workplace, giving them a realistic understanding of appropriate and inappropriate behavior in a professional environment, and the consequences of this behavior. Susan Gottesfeld, of the Fortune Society, volunteered her time to speak to participants on making ethical and moral choices in the workplace. The Fortune Society, staffed primarily by former prisoners, is a not-for-profit community-based organization that dedicates its services to helping former prisoners and at-risk youth break the cycle of crime and incarceration. Nadia Jones, Esq., from the law firm Paul Weiss, volunteered to speak to Career Ex participants on the law and youthful offender status. Ms. Jones gave the participants direction on how to appropriately respond to the convicted/arrest question when searching for a job and participating in an interview.

During this period, Career Ex commenced the Issues Dinner, a new activity for participants. The project coordinator treated the participants to a formal dinner, and required each participant to bring up a current event topic to discuss during dinner. This activity provided an opportunity for participants to work on their communication skills and increase their knowledge, which resulted in them feeling competent and prepared for their interviews. Due to the success of this dinner, Career Ex will continue to offer this activity in future cycles.

During their internships, participants meet every Friday at CASES to discuss their experiences and concerns and to participate in career awareness activities such as job shadowing, worksite visits, and additional presentations by guest speakers. For example, during this reporting period, Career Ex took participants on four of the Friday classes to Eyebeam, a non-profit technology center in Chelsea that fosters and develops new media technologies through educational programs that identify and expand innovative technology. These activities offer youth the chance to learn about a particular industry, observe professionals at work, and pose questions to the professionals.

Also, during this period Career Ex initiated post-program/alumni group meetings held at the two- and four-week points after graduation and held regular meetings for all graduates. Meetings focused on assisting participants with the job search and college application process and provided an opportunity for our more experienced alumni to mentor recent graduates. These sessions included trips to nonprofits, banks and restaurants, as well as meetings at our offices. Also, during this grant period Career Ex invited a speaker from NPower into the program to conduct computer training for alumni as well as current participants. To support the increase in alumni services, we hired a part-time graduate assistant, Teury Martinez.

Have there been any obstacles which prevented you from achieving the goals of the project?

Career Ex has a long track record of success, dating from its inception nearly 10 years ago. Lessons learned and experiences gained through the years add to our effectiveness. One of the obstacles we have discovered is participant substance use. To address this issue, we are bolstering our efforts to provide access to coordinated substance abuse classes, counseling, and treatment for our clients through the hiring of an additional drug counselor for CEP.

Where applicable, indicate number of clients you expected to serve. Indicate actual number of clients served to date by project.

Career Ex added two additional cycles and staff and increased the annual goal for participants served from 90 to 120. Halfway through the grant period, Career Ex has served 62 participants.

What has been the cost per client served?

CASES will serve a total of approximately 120 youth in Career Ex with a budget of $340,978 over the course of the grant period, resulting in a cost per client served of $2,841.50.

Please note any changes that you are planning to make based on the project to date.

To more fully develop and coordinate workforce development and educational programming in CEP overall, CASES has created a new position: Director of Workforce Development and Educational Initiatives. We are currently recruiting and hope to fill this position within the next two months. The Director will oversee all workforce development and educational initiatives within CEP, including Career Ex. In addition to providing strategic direction and oversight for Career Ex, the new Director will develop alternative workforce development initiatives for CEP participants not yet ready for Career Ex. These activities may include group employment counseling, employment training, and/or job development curricula for our oldest participants. The Director will work with the substance abuse and mental health counseling staff to develop appropriate interventions that will increase self-awareness among prospective Career Ex participants to better prepare them to succeed in CEP.

CASES is additionally planning to hire a third drug counselor for CEP. This new addition will enable case coordinators to more efficiently address CEP participants' substance use and prepare them to successfully utilize more of the services offered at CASES, such as Career Ex.

Conclusion

CASES is deeply grateful for the support of The Frances L. & Edwin L. Cummings Memorial Fund during this critical period of expansion. Career Ex is on track to providing 120 court-involved youth each year with an effective program of employment readiness training, an opportunity to pursue a paid internship and a comprehensive set of supports.

These examples are presented as general models only. If a foundation supplies its own guidelines for reporting, then be sure to adhere to those instructions.

In sum, good practice when a grant has been awarded includes:

- saying thank you
- conveying excitement about your work and its success
- sending requested materials, such as a signed grant contract, to the donor
- knowing what you are obligated to do
- getting reports in on time
- communicating both positive and negative news to the grantmaker

Sometimes plans change, or unanticipated events occur. Here is an example of a request to the William Bingham Foundation to reallocate grant funds received.

July 23, 2001

Ms. Laura H. Gilbertson, Director
The William Bingham Foundation
20325 Center Ridge Road, Suite 629
Rocky River, Ohio 44116

Dear Ms. Gilbertson:

In 1999 the William Bingham Foundation granted Fieldstone Farm Therapeutic Riding Center (TRC) $20,000 toward a list of several site development projects. Since then we have had several other foundations review our site needs and they have also helped to fund these projects. However, several of these other foundations have restricted their funding to particular items on our list. We ask that the William Bingham Foundation consider allowing Fieldstone Farm TRC to use $14,747 of the granted $20,000 to complete the funding need for the farm's parking lot paving, which is a site development need that was not stated on the original proposal. Since your funding was restricted to capital projects, we hope this will fit in with your interests.

Please contact me with any questions. Fieldstone Farm TRC is very appreciative of the support that the William Bingham Foundation has given. Thank you for your time and consideration.

Sincerely,

Lynnette Stuart
Executive Director

Seeking a Renewal

In certain cases, you will want to request that the grant be renewed or that a follow-up project be supported. Some funders refuse to give renewed support because they do not want to encourage dependency or because they see their funding as providing "seed money."

Other funders require a certain period of time to elapse between the grant and the renewal request. For instance, the Hearst Foundations currently require three years between grants.

Even a grant that could be a candidate for renewal may be labeled a one-time gift. Ordinarily the phrase "one-time gift" means that the funder is making no commitment to future funding. It does not necessarily mean that no possibility for future support exists.

If you know that you will want to request renewed support, you should communicate this early on to the foundation in order to determine the best time to submit another request. Be careful not to wait too long before requesting a renewal. By the time the funder receives the request, all the foundation's funds may be committed for the following year.

You should also determine early on the format required by the funder for submitting a renewal request. Some foundations require a full proposal; others want just a letter. This is another illustration of the differences among funders. It reinforces the need to communicate with the grantmaker to determine its particular requirements.

A report on funds expended and results of the first grant is a particularly critical document if you are going to ask for renewed support. However, many funders want your request for renewal to be separate from the report on the grant. In larger foundations, the report and the request for renewal might be handled by different departments; therefore, if you submit your renewal request as part of the report on the first grant, it might not find its way into the proposal system.

Following Up on a Declination

The most important response to a rejection letter is not to take it personally. An old fundraising adage is, "Campaigns fail because people don't ask, not because they get rejected." If your proposal gets rejected, it means you are out there asking. You are doing what you should be doing. Hopefully, you have sent your proposal to a number of other appropriate funders and have not put all your eggs in one basket.

Some funders will talk with you about why the proposal was rejected, particularly if you had a meeting with the program staff at the granting institution prior to or at the time of submission. A phone call following a rejection letter can help you clarify the next step. Your request may have been of great interest to the foundation but was turned down in that funding cycle because the board had already committed all the funds set aside for projects in your subject or geographical area. For example, if your request was for an AIDS program in South Chicago, the foundation may have already committed its grants budget for that geographic area. A call to a foundation staff member might result in encouragement to reapply in a later funding cycle.

All funding representatives emphasize, however, the need to be courteous in the process of calling once you have received a rejection letter. It is never easy to say "no," and a program officer who fought hard for your proposal may feel almost as disappointed as you are that it was turned down. While foundation staff usually want to be helpful, it is important to recognize that it can often be difficult to tell someone why a proposal has been rejected.

Julie Farkas of Consumer Health Foundation says: "I will give feedback on why the request was turned down. It can be gratifying—a teachable moment. I will explain why the fit wasn't good, or if there were other concerns about the program plan or organization." And Rick Moyers of the Eugene and Agnes E. Meyer Foundation reminds us to be careful in the course of the conversation: "Grantees should understand that this is not the time to argue the program officer out of the decision. It is probably not possible to do that. What you do in that call sets the tone for the next interaction with that program officer, so you want it to be a positive conversation. Many grantees come back with better requests the next time."

It is important to take your cue from the funder, either from the rejection letter or from the follow-up call to staff. If you are not encouraged to resubmit, then you probably shouldn't.

There are times when a funder will encourage you to resubmit the same request at a particular time in the future. If you have been given this advice, then follow it. In your cover letter, be sure to refer to your conversation with the funding representative, remembering to restate, but not overstate, the earlier conversation.

Even if a foundation is not interested in funding the particular project you submitted, by keeping the lines of communication open and remaining respectful you will be nurturing the opportunity for future funding. David Grant of the

Geraldine R. Dodge Foundation says: "It's nice to hear from the organization. Say 'thanks, I'm disappointed but I understand what's going on. We will address that and come back to you.' If your request is appropriate, don't give up. Build the relationship with the grantmaker."

In summary, best practice, when your request has been rejected, includes:

- say thank you
- figure out with the grantmaker what your next step should be
- follow the grantmaker's suggestions
- refrain from arguing.

What follows is a simple thank you following a rejection, written by the executive director of Ali Forney Center.

June 26, 2006

Michael Fleming
Executive Director
David Bohnett Foundation
2049 Century Park East, Suite 2151
Los Angeles, CA 60067-3123

Dear Mr. Fleming:

I am writing in response to your recent correspondence regarding the Ali Forney Center's letter of inquiry.

Although we had hoped for better news, we understand that the David Bohnett Foundation cannot respond favorably to every organization's request.

We appreciate your consideration and hope that the future will allow the David Bohnett Foundation to partner with the Ali Forney Center in providing security, care and comfort to homeless LGBT youth.

Sincerely,

Carl Siciliano
Executive Director

Final Tips

What to do if you receive a grant:

- Send a personalized thank you.
- Keep the funder informed of your progress.
- Follow the funder's reporting requirements.

What to do if your request is turned down:

- Don't take it personally.
- Be sure you understand why.
- Find out if you can resubmit at a later date.

14

What the Funders Have to Say

In this chapter we will explore what the grantmakers who were interviewed for the *Guide* are saying collectively about the environment in which they are currently operating, about various aspects of the proposal submission and review process, and their respective grantmaking strategies. We begin with some overall observations on the current philanthropic landscape and some key trends in grants decision-making derived from the conversations we had with these funders. We then proceed to specific questions that were posed as part of the interview process and provide responses in their own words from the interviewees.

The 40 grants decision-makers who were interviewed for this edition of the *Guide* were extremely generous with their time, forthcoming with their thoughts and opinions, and concerned that these be expressed coherently and correctly. Their comments are remarkably frank and straightforward. What comes across unequivocally as you read their comments is not only a high level of dedication to their work but a true empathy with those who seek funds from their foundations. As will be evident from the responses below, a top priority for virtually everyone we interviewed is to do everything possible to help nonprofit grantseekers succeed. We noted a greater level of intensity about their work expressed by the interviewees than we have in the past. This may well be due to some of the conditions described here, including increased scrutiny by Congress, the media, and their own board members.

The funders whose comments are included in this chapter were selected for a variety of reasons. For consistency's sake and as a means of identifying trends, we sought to include as many as possible of the group that was interviewed for the prior edition. A number, however, have retired or otherwise moved on. We were successful in incorporating into the mix comments from several funders interviewed for the very first time, while at the same time maintaining a balance among type and size of grantmaker, geographical scope and areas of giving. Despite this broad diversity, a very clear consensus emerged on a number of issues. On some issues, on the other hand, there was quite a divergence of opinion in their responses, as will be noted below.

The Philanthropic Landscape

What is on the minds of funders today? One complex issue is best summarized as follows: There is a proliferation of nonprofit organizations occurring simultaneously with broad and deep cutbacks in government support. Nonprofits are being challenged to expand their donor bases while facing a range of challenges related to leadership transition in the offices of their executive directors. All of this pressure causes severe constraints for many agencies attempting to sustain financial stability and build good boards—two key indicators of effectiveness that grantmakers look for in awarding funds to nonprofits. While these problems are not unsolvable, they do require creative responses on the parts of grantmakers and other nonprofits.

Even worse than the growing number of nonprofits, from the grantmaker's perspective, is the apparent duplication of services in certain fields and communities. As Danah Craft of Sun Trust Bank, Atlanta Foundation said: "I remain concerned about the duplication of services and the amount of money being spent on overhead within the same community." In an era when there are not enough dollars to go around, grantmakers view this situation as particularly wasteful. It is frustrating for the program officer who is faced with deciding who gets funded and who does not, when several agencies appear to be nearly identical in their missions, audiences, and service delivery models. David Grant of the Geraldine R. Dodge Foundation notes that grantmakers and nonprofits alike seem to be talking a good deal about possible consolidation among nonprofits rather than proactively finding means to actually make it happen.

When asked what was on their minds, quite a few of the funders we interviewed expressed concern about the loss of government support across federal, state and local levels, and pointed out that these cutbacks further exacerbate the precarious situation of many nonprofits today. Bruce Esterline of the Meadows Foundation underscores the severity of the problem by reminding us that traditionally government support has represented a significant proportion of nonprofit income, whereas this is unlikely to be the case in the future. And Kathleen Cerveny of the Cleveland Foundation notes that government support is being withdrawn not just from peripheral activities, but from core services in the community that needy individuals have come to rely upon. A key question we found our funders asking themselves is: Who will make up the difference?

While nonprofits are pushing for alternative solutions to government support, the funders we interviewed acknowledge their inability to come up with ready answers. What is clear is that foundation funding will not be able to fill the potentially enormous void left by withdrawal of government support. These grantmakers expressed concern for the sustainability of the projects they have funded in the past or are presently supporting. Interestingly this dynamic may be engendering subtle changes in how grantmakers view their roles vis a vis their grantees. While traditionally some foundations have performed as catalysts to assist nonprofits in developing new ideas and approaches to addressing society's ills—solutions that once put forth would be supported on a long term basis by various government and other sources—in the future, this may no longer be the case. Severe reductions in government support of nonprofits alter the status quo and leave some in the foundation world feeling pressured to provide more by way of unrestricted support to their grantees in order to keep them afloat, something many foundations have eschewed up until now.

One suggestion that came up frequently among the grantmakers we talked to was for nonprofits to look beyond government, foundation and corporate support to strengthening their individual donor bases. This is not a particularly new suggestion, but one that makes sense in precarious fundraising times when it may be becoming harder to secure necessary financial support. For many nonprofits there is a potentially large pool of individual donors left untapped because they have not figured out how to access these donors. As David Ford of the Richard and Susan Smith Foundation indicates: "As it becomes more difficult to raise money, individuals are a prime target for support. Grantseekers are trying to figure out how to approach them." And Danah Craft adds that in her opinion, nonprofits cannot survive without a diversity of donors.

A possible solution put forth by a number of the grantmakers we interviewed is for nonprofits seriously to consider forming closer alliances and possibly even mergers moving forward. This would address the funding pressures they are facing as well as the gap in the availability of new nonprofit leaders. As Peter Bird of the Frist Foundation notes: "Financial pressures have forced nonprofits to look at mergers as a survival strategy." And David Egner of the Hudson-Webber Foundation says that nonprofits should consider "transformational collaborations" as a way to be ahead of the game and thinking about the future. Grantmakers recognize that for many nonprofits finding an appropriate merger partner and making that relationship work on a permanent basis will take a tremendous amount of effort and energy but is time well spent, if it leads to future stability. While nonprofit mergers reduce the number of nonprofits, help eliminate duplicate and overlapping services, and address redundancy in administrative expenses, this is often a painful step for a nonprofit's board to consider. Board and staff leadership of both organizations must be not only willing, but enthusiastic about such a merger in order to make it work. Some of the grantmakers we interviewed indicated an interest in helping facilitate the process among their grantees.

Another matter for concern touched upon by quite a few of the grantmakers we spoke with is the turnover occurring in the executive offices of many nonprofits. This current and anticipated significant leadership transition is due quite simply to the fact that many of today's nonprofit CEOs are baby boomers ready or nearly ready for retirement. And according to a recent report issued by CompassPoint Nonprofit Services and the Eugene and Agnes E. Meyer Foundation [*Daring to Lead 2006: A National Study of Nonprofit Executive Leadership*], a significant percentage of nonprofit leaders report an inclination to leave their current positions for two additional reasons as well: lack of board support and/or the pressure of building long-term financial resources for their organizations, as described above.

Vincent Stehle of Surdna Foundation commented that the availability of outstanding nonprofit leaders ultimately comes down to a question of supply and demand. Several of our interviewees expressed concern that nonprofits are not confronting this issue sufficiently in advance of the expected turnover. Matthew Klein of Blue Ridge Foundation New York suggests that nonprofits should create transition plans and engage in careful recruitment and development of new CEOs. David Grant reminds us that the occasion of succession in a nonprofit's founding leadership might also provide a "golden opportunity" to at least consider a graceful merger with another organization.

In discussing these and other challenges nonprofits face today, one theme that came across with great unanimity among the grantmakers we interviewed was every nonprofit's need for a strong board of directors. All agree that it takes time and energy to recruit, build and train board members effectively. William Engel of E. J. Grassman Trust tells us that in times like these, when nonprofit board activities are being held up to increasingly rigorous scrutiny, and when people have limited time to commit, it becomes more difficult to find good people willing to serve. At the same time Andrew Lark of the Frances L. & Edwin L. Cummings Memorial Fund reminds us how important it is to spend time on board development because ". . . a healthy board unquestionably leads to a better/healthier agency."

When asked about factors affecting their own grantmaking practices and operations, again there was a great deal of consensus among our interviewees. They pointed with consistency to a number of items on their collective minds. These include: increased and anticipated stringent government oversight of grantmaker operations and those of other nonprofits; staff transition similar to the nonprofit leadership transition already mentioned but in the grantmakers' own offices; and possible ongoing fluctuation in foundation assets, making it difficult to announce policies and to plan for the future.

In the period of time that has elapsed since the prior edition of the *Guide*, foundations and other nonprofits have found themselves coming under increasingly intense scrutiny from Washington. Much government attention has focused on such things as careful review of administrative expenses and overhead, the five percent payout requirement for foundations and who is and is not meeting it, executive salaries and trustee reimbursement, and even in some quarters the appropriateness of certain grants. Among the grantmakers we interviewed, reactions to increased government oversight ranged from welcoming the opportunity to demonstrate effective management to dismay at tactics that are viewed as intrusive and having a dampening effect on creative support for worthwhile causes. Here are two examples of similar but subtly divergent views on the matter. David Grant indicated: "I welcome the oversight from Washington. It minimizes abuses and urges you to do your best work." And Ruth Shack of Dade Community Foundation observed: "The attitude coming out of Washington is intimidating, but I understand that Congress is reacting to real or perceived abuses." Most of our funders feel that while increased government scrutiny has not really changed the ways in which they operate, it has indeed led to greater transparency. A few grantmakers expressed concern that dollars spent responding to this oversight might well reduce the amount of money that could be expended on core grantmaking activities. But most agree with Andrew Lark that "Self-policing is a good thing, if we all do it."

A number of the grantmakers interviewed referred to recent changes in staffing at their own foundations, following upon a time of relative stability, and they view this trend as traumatic. Christine Park of Lucent Technologies Foundation remarked that people who work for foundations do not appear to remain in their jobs as long as they used to. Several of our grantmakers mentioned a high burnout rate among foundation program officers. Many of our interviewees point out that a loss of grantmaker staff members often translates into a loss of knowledge and historical background information about a foundation's relations with its grantees. A few grantmakers observed a welcome trend among young people who are opting for philanthropy as a career and joining the staffs of foundations immediately after college. Others expressed concerned about a higher proportion of new staff members who are not seasoned, and who lack appropriate experience relevant to philanthropy.

Over the years, with earlier editions of the *Guide*, our conversations with grantmakers have taken place during stock market highs and lows. Those who seek funds from foundations often overlook the fact that the availability of grant money may be directly impacted by how well foundation investments have done in a prior period. At the time of the writing of this chapter, foundation assets do seem to be in recovery mode and possibly showing signs of growth, which should translate into more funders being positioned to give more away in future years. But given the extreme upheaval in the world today, many of our interviewees were very cautious in their predictions of future increases in giving and expressed concern that assets might well fluctuate downward again at any time.

As had been covered extensively in the media, the much heralded "generational transfer of wealth" may well be upon us. A substantial influx of funds into the nation's foundations is likely to affect family foundations in particular. Danah Craft reminds us that as younger family members become more involved in serving on foundation boards, they are changing the focus of what those foundations support. It's likely that concurrent with a period of greater affluence, the agendas for some family foundation giving may change as well.

Trends Impacting Proposal Submission and Review

You may be reading this chapter hoping to uncover the silver bullet that will ensure your next foundation or corporate grant. While this may be disappointing news for some, the grantmakers we talked to were quite consistent (as they have been in the past) in stating that in fact there is no one magic formula. Rather, they recommend a holistic approach to thinking and strategizing about the proposal-writing process. They agree that the most important steps to take are also the most obvious: Follow the funders' guidelines (often posted on the funders' web sites, if they have them) and continue to cultivate and reach out to those that support you and those that are not yet donors.

Advice shared almost universally by these grantsmakers is to do your research thoroughly prior to any contact with a funder. Your conversation with a funder will be more conclusive and lead to specific next steps if you have done the necessary homework in advance. Be persistent in cultivation of candidates that your research has uncovered who might support your organization. Don't take it personally if your proposal is declined the first or even second or third time you submit it. And, although this may seem obvious, be sure to include the amount you need in the cover letter. Also be sure to send a thank-you note when you receive a grant, and when you do not. Strive constantly to improve on your writing and view the process as a continuous learning experience. It is critical to always keep the lines of communication open with current and prospective funders on your list.

In general the foundation and corporate grantmaking representatives we spoke with are satisfied with the components of a grant proposal and elements of the proposal package as they are presented in this *Guide*. When asked specific questions about new aspects of grantmaker operations and what strategies today's funders are engaging in to improve the decision-making process, several themes arose with great regularity. These are: more collaboration and joint ventures among grantmakers, particularly those active in the same community or field of endeavor; an increase in targeted giving by foundation donors and/or boards; and the importance of formal evaluation of each funded project aimed at determining its success in meeting its stated objectives and in achieving measurable outcomes.

It has always been a fact of fundraising life that grantmakers talk to one another, most often quietly behind the scenes. And while grantseekers might worry about this, the truth is that they may well benefit from such conversations, as long as they do what they say they're going to do and run their organizations well. Indeed such conversations have sometimes resulted in two or more grantmakers joining forces to support a project that had too hefty a price tag for any one of them to take on on their own. The end result of such collaborations may actually have a very positive impact on the grantmaking process.

Grantmakers today are talking more openly about such collaborations and their potential impact. A number of our interviewees described conferring with their colleagues at other foundations about a particular grant applicant or project as standard operating procedure. When asked why this approach seems to be on the rise, they responded that they call upon their colleagues as a means to leverage funds, to broker resources, and because in general grants decision-makers are more comfortable with one another nowadays. This may be due to the intensified efforts of national organizations like the Council on Foundations and of grantmaker affinity groups and regional associations aimed at fostering better communication and convening funders around particular issues and shared concerns. The funders we spoke with acknowledge the impact of such partnerships, which is lowering some boundaries that may have existed among grantmakers in the past. Many of the funders we interviewed pointed to collaboration among themselves as a trend that grantseekers should expect to increase in the future.

In the first edition of the *Guide* and in each subsequent volume, we identified a trend among grantmakers toward accepting fewer proposals "over the transom". And this trend continues to intensify. More foundations these days are identifying problems that need addressing and even possible solutions to those problems and then issuing Requests For Proposals (RFPs) so that nonprofits can respond within given pre-set parameters. When asked about changes in grantmaker operations, Elizabeth Smith of the Hyams Foundation noted an increase in the number of grantmakers issuing RFPs. Some of our interviewees expressed concern, however, that foundations not overstep their prescribed roles. Leslie Silverman of the Bill & Melinda Gates Foundation described the grantmaker function as being a "shaper, not an implementer."

Simultaneously in an effort to be strategic about the awarding of highly sought after grant funds, there seems to be a narrowing of focus among some foundations and corporate givers. This may include more precisely defined subject areas and/or geographic guidelines. Often this comes about as the result of a strategic planning process on the part of a foundation and its board. These new directions may well lead to more professionally run grantmaking operations. But several funders we interviewed fear that as a result, fewer dollars may be available for general operating support of nonprofits. What this means for the grantseeker attempting to construct a compelling request for funding is that grantmakers are not going to react simply to an agency's critical need. As has been described elsewhere in this *Guide*, the grantseeker will be required to pay even greater attention to establishing a good "fit" with a potential funder. Researching prospective funders and developing the relationship will both be critical elements, as will proposal writers' learning to hone their skills at searching out and effectively responding to grantmaker-issued RFPs.

Consistently over the years, we have heard grants decision-makers discuss the importance of knowing what impact their support has on an organization and its constituency. In today's climate of uncertainty, with the entire nonprofit sector under scrutiny, the desire for detailed information on the outcomes of grant projects is stronger than ever. Nonprofit board members, including those who govern the nation's foundations, may now be held personally responsible for the operations of their organizations. The topic of evaluation came up frequently in our conversations with the funders we interviewed. And the discussion went beyond providing advice to the grantseeker about developing a successful evaluation component of a grant proposal. What's different today is that along with requiring evaluative reports from grantees on how well they met or did not meet the specific objectives of the funded project, grantmakers are also engaged in evaluating the impact of the grants they award and their own organizational effectiveness. Many foundation boards are requiring such self-assessment. While an increased emphasis on evaluation has become a fact of life for those on both sides of the funding equation, there is still much ongoing conversation about it.

Under the circumstances we have described, reporting back to one's funder about the success of one's grant project becomes ever more critical. The complaint about evaluation on the nonprofit side is that it can take nearly as much time and effort to report to the grantmaker on the results of the grant as it took to secure the funding and administer the project! Our grantmakers are sympathetic and very aware of this fact. Those we interviewed acknowledge that there is a growing interest in and need for detailed reports, however. Many are developing specific guidelines to assist their grantees in conducting effective evaluations of their projects and in reporting back with precisely the information the funder needs. Our interviewees acknowledge that these procedures are time consuming and occasionally onerous for their grantees and say that they want to strike a balance between what most nonprofit organizations are able to produce by way of evaluative grant reports and what today's funder requires to achieve its own level of comfort, often prescribed by its board of trustees.

Many of our grantmakers, in their "other" lives, sit on boards of a variety of nonprofit charities. They observe first hand the critical role that board members play in both governance and fundraising. Hence, virtually all of the funders we interviewed state that their foundations require as part of the application process that nonprofits provide information about the involvement of their board members, beyond a simple list of who they are. And many say that they expect financial support of the organization by each and every member of the board. During site visits that many of the funders we interviewed conduct as part of their due diligence process when considering a grant request, quite a number noted that it is advantageous for the nonprofit to include at least one board member as part of the team that meets with the funding executive. As noted previously, an active board can make quite a difference in ensuring a positive outcome for a grant request.

All told, this is an exciting though potentially anxiety-provoking time for those making grants to the nation's nonprofits. While many foundations have experienced a return to modest asset strength recently, there are no guarantees that the situation will remain so. Ingenuity will be required on both sides of the grantmaking equation to respond to the various circumstances that are making the effective awarding of grant funds ever more challenging. Grantseekers should take heart, however. The most clearly delineated trend that comes across as you read the commentary below is that funders really want to assist nonprofits in making their way successfully through the proposal application and review process. Those we interviewed are more willing than ever to be involved in a very direct way with those applying to them for funds. Victoria Kovar of the Cooper Foundation sums it up best. Her message to grantseekers is as follows: "Don't be afraid. It is not natural for most of us to ask for money. We need grantseekers to focus on what they need and what their program needs are in order to really make a difference."

What follows are selected responses to our questions, in the grantmakers' own words. Other responses to interview questions will be found throughout the *Guide* as quotations we've selected to exemplify key points being made.

Do you find that most grantseekers have done their homework before contacting you?

Yes:

Grantseekers today are generally well informed. We don't get many requests that don't fit our guidelines. Our web site delimits our program focus, and word of mouth also plays a part in that. (Robert Crane)

Far more grantseekers are doing research. The web site has provided them with more instantaneous information. The grantseeker is better educated, and we're finding that the quality of proposals is better. Some, who may have submitted proposals in past years when they did not fit our mission, are no longer doing so. We are saying "no" less often than we used to. (David O. Egner)

Many grantseekers are. This is a trend that has been improving. The message is getting out that it is a good idea to do research, and people are aware of the resources that they can go to. (William V. Engel)

We have seen a shift toward people doing better research, partly because we have made a conscious effort to improve our communication. Since we started accepting online applications, we have seen a higher percentage of applications that are closer to our guidelines. (John Goldberg)

Most of the grantseekers who come to us have done their homework. We have been around for a while, and because so much of our grantmaking is regional [focused on New Jersey], we are not getting too many things out of left field. (David Grant)

More than half are doing their homework. In the proposals that we review relative to the information that we ask for, seventy percent have done their homework. This has not changed significantly in the past few years. Most proposals reflect a conscientious review of what we do. (David Palenchar)

Of late, I have found that more organizations have done their homework. And I can credit the Internet with helping people know how to apply and what we fund. I can also credit those organizations that have attended grant writing workshops. (Karen Topakian)

No:

Some grantseekers are not doing their research; they seem to think that sending out a blind application is okay. (Rene Deida)

It is not possible to generalize, but far too often the case is that we receive phone calls from applicants that do not often reflect good research. (J. Andrew Lark)

Sometimes:

It goes in cycles. It's improving, but we do have cycles where we get a rash of phone calls or e-mails when they truly know nothing about us, and the nonprofit does not align with our strategic focus. We receive some calls from organizations that don't do their homework at all, and it is frustrating. Generally, the people who don't do their research are the smaller, start-up agencies with no experience in nonprofit work. (Julie Brooks)

Overall, grantseekers are doing their research better. However, we still do get requests that are not pertinent to us. (David Ford)

We get a lot of requests from out of state for things that don't qualify for funding, which come in more as a result of people selling lists. Otherwise we don't get too many requests from people who do not qualify. In general, people know what an appropriate request is. (Victoria Kovar)

Generally, grantseekers are doing their homework and seem to be more professional. We are getting fewer proposals that are totally off the mark. (Ilene Mack)

The first approach to our foundation is a letter of inquiry. In some grant rounds as many as fifty percent of the letters of inquiry fall outside of our funding priorities. For example, we only fund in DC, but in almost every round we get one or two letters of inquiry from out of state. I always encourage organizations new to our foundation to call me first and discuss their funding idea before they submit. (Bob Wittig)

What is the best initial approach to your foundation?

Telephone:

Most nonprofits call. They call with an idea. If the idea is appropriate, we hammer it out on the phone together. (Peter F. Bird, Jr.)

A call to me is fine. I help the applicant understand the Bank's priorities and what they should do to reach out. A "fishing expedition" is okay with me because I can provide feedback as to what will fit best. I can give the grantseeker specific information that our trustees will be looking for. (Danah Craft)

We always get calls. The vast majority are asking for specifics within our program mission. Also, a letter of intent is fine, but it should be as concise as possible. Grant applicants shouldn't spend time reinventing something for us. Sometimes I will ask the grantseeker to send a proposal that they sent to another foundation so that I can just read it and determine if it is a fit for us or not. (David O. Egner)

I am happy to have a five- to ten-minute phone call, if people have questions. The purpose is more for what I can tell them than for what I might learn. They want to know if their organization is a fit and if it is worth it to submit a full-blown proposal. (William V. Engel)

I am open to calls. This saves everyone time. (David Ford)

We want to be flexible and helpful. Speaking on the phone with the grantseeker is part of that objective. (Marilyn Gelber)

We get quite a few phone calls. We find that in the weeks leading up to a deadline, the amount of calls picks up considerably. We do our best to handle them and try to be responsive. (Robert Jaquay)

I will set up telephone appointments. I ask six journalistic questions—who, what, where, when, why, how, and how much—in determining if we can support the project. (David Odahowski)

Usually a phone call begins the process. (Michele Pritchard)

It is best if grantees do their research and then call. Then, staff is available by phone to answer unique questions. The grantseeker should send a letter of intent if they are unsure whether they fit our criteria. (Elizabeth B. Smith)

We strongly encourage people to call because the process is so competitive. We want people to put their best foot forward. Most of the pre-application conversations happen on the phone. (Lita Ugarte)

I would rather have a short phone conversation about the organization and their needs. If we are not the right place, I will do my best to direct the grantseeker to other funders. (Nancy Wiltsek)

Letter:

While a letter of intent is optional, we receive a great many of them and it works well as a first filter to ascertain our possible interest without a large time investment by the nonprofit. We're able to sort through and determine what is most appropriate to our initiatives. We do respond to all inquiries and will alert the organization if we are interested in considering their proposed program. (Carol Kurzig)

We want to save the nonprofit time. We try to be flexible; we don't want the nonprofit to put a lot of upfront time into the request. The initial step via the letter of intent is to find out if the work proposed fits our guidelines. (Maria Mottola)

Various means:

We get mostly phone calls, letters, and e-mails. We provide as much support as the grantseeker requests from us. I review draft applications and provide suggestions, and editing in some cases. (Victoria Kovar)

I will respond to questions by phone and via e-mail from people seeking general information. I receive a half dozen calls per day. This might be because our web site is so complete. (David Palenchar)

The best initial approach is to review our web site and the funding guidelines for different grantmaking areas (e.g. some grantmaking areas accept letters of intent, while others may conduct an RFP, and another area may have a policy of not accepting unsolicited proposals); so reading the web site carefully is advised. (Leslie Silverman)

Once a proposal is pending, is it acceptable for the grantseeker to call you to check on the status of the request or to share information? Is it okay to send additional materials?

It is fine for grantseekers to call to confirm that the application was received and that there are no missing documents. Other than that, there is no advantage to doing this. The grantseeker can call if he or she has new or updated information to share or they can just send it along. (Danah Craft)

Our staff has a lot of contact with grantseeking organizations. They should not have to check on the status of requests, since we inform them when their request is complete. If they haven't heard from us within a reasonable time, it is perfectly okay to check in. (Robert Crane)

Having updated information is helpful for when we begin reviewing the request. (David O. Egner)

We welcome this, especially via e-mail. But, if we are doing our job well, the program officer would be keeping applicants updated on their status. (Bruce Esterline)

We would appreciate hearing from grantseekers if they need to update us on changes in the organization or the proposal. We provide a date when the proposal will be considered. Checking in is okay, but is not very productive unless we are considering an invited proposal rather than a letter of inquiry. (Laura H. Gilbertson)

More often, we are communicating with grantseekers on questions about their proposal or to seek clarity on what they have said, and as part of that process they provide us with additional information. (Marilyn Hennessy)

It doesn't hurt. It helps to get more information. The grantseeker can call or send a letter. (A. Thomas Hildebrandt)

I am happy to receive whatever information comes along. I try to understand the anxiety and desire of the grantseeker to keep me informed. (Robert Jaquay)

Grantseekers should stay in touch, but do it in moderation. I believe strongly in open and honest communication. A grantseeker has the right to know where we are in the review process. (Ilene Mack)

If it enhances the proposal, let us know about it. But don't make yourself a "pest." (David Odahowski)

I absolutely encourage the sharing of information, especially if there are changes. I also encourage sending updates. (David Palenchar)

It usually is not an issue because our turnaround time is pretty quick (we are a small foundation). But I have no problem being contacted to check the application status. (Bob Wittig)

Yes, if there are significant changes relating to the project, such as a change in personnel or additional funding received. (Victoria Kovar, Carol Kurzig, Elizabeth B. Smith, and Lita Ugarte)

Once a proposal is pending, is it okay if one of the nonprofit's board members contacts one of your board members directly?

This does happen. It's not something that we encourage, but it's not something we can prevent either. It could backfire. While our board members understand that it is not their role to intercede or advocate for a specific proposal, some enjoy being engaged in those conversations or want to know more about our thinking on an issue. (Kathleen Cerveny)

If their board member knows our board member, then personal endorsement of the quality of the organization is certainly appropriate. If an organization has board members who don't know our board, then I would not recommend that they reach out to them. (Danah Craft)

I don't have a problem with this. My board will refer people directly to me. There is not really a conflict with my group, since our board realizes the difference between governance and management. (David O. Egner)

It is not necessary. In terms of endorsements, it doesn't make much of a difference. (William V. Engel)

This is how it often works out anyway because our board members are also our program officers. They are the ones who are in touch with the organizations in many cases. It is good to close the loop with staff, and I usually know about this contact. (Laura H. Gilbertson)

It is human nature to want to do this, and it doesn't bother me. It is fine if it is done sensitively, and not too intrusively. I can't cite a single example of an agency that lost a grant because of contacting someone on the board. (A. Thomas Hildebrandt)

People are free to speak to anyone. I don't know that this would affect our board's decision one way or another. We have an established conflict of interest policy. (Victoria Kovar)

Endorsements of any type are very helpful. But trying to advance a request by contacting multiple Avon Foundation or Avon Products, Inc. employees or board members is usually inefficient and not particularly productive. (Carol Kurzig)

I feel this is a "backdoor" approach, and it is not to be recommended. It puts board members on the spot and doesn't put the agency in a favorable light. It is a clear end-run attempt, which slows the process down. (J. Andrew Lark)

This is always a tricky issue. It is awkward if the organization is somewhat "iffy" and we are not sure we want to fund them, and they go to a board member. Yet, I am a realist. I don't get bent out of shape about it. Grantseekers should talk to me first; I don't like surprises. (Ilene Mack)

In our case, it doesn't help, since our board members generally respect the boundaries between board and staff roles. However, every foundation is different, and at foundations with limited staff, board members may function more like program officers. It's also a mistake to make the program officer feel that you've tried to go around her or over her head. Even if it produces a successful outcome once, it's not good long-term relationship building. (Rick Moyers)

Nonprofits have to be advocates for themselves. Part of advocating may mean reaching out to our board members who are also doing their job by being visible in the community. (David Odahowski)

We discourage this because it cuts out organizations that don't have social access. We try to make it as level a playing field as we can. (David Palenchar)

Knowing someone on our board typically does not make a significant difference, since our process is staff-driven. Sometimes a board member might ask questions or ask for additional review. (Lita Ugarte)

Following the rejection of a proposal, do you speak with the applicant about the reasons why, if they ask you to?

I will give them my best assessment of why the request didn't make it.
(David Ford)

If they follow-up and ask us for an explanation, then we will have a conversation with them and try to provide helpful ideas—such as proposal presentation, things that were missing, or questions that were raised that could not be answered—which would help them in a future submission. Often the proposal is well done. The funding decision reflects the values of the trustees, the decision makers. When we have a limited amount of money, we can only fund so many requests. Limited resources require difficult decisions, and these reflect values. (Marilyn Hennessy)

Often, the call is a thinly veiled appeal for reconsideration. Without disclosing inordinate amounts of information or the rationale for the trustees' decisions, I will try my best to give a sense of where our priorities lie, where our money is going, and the tough choices we need to make. (Robert Jaquay)

We call all applicants to inform them of our board's decisions, funded or declined. If the applicant asks, we will discuss the proposal and offer guidance about next steps. (Victoria Kovar)

We are happy to talk to grantseekers and have a policy to be as responsive as possible. If a grantseeker takes the initiative to contact us, we will try to put our decision in perspective for them. (Carol Kurzig)

I'd advise grant applicants to call the foundation and politely probe. Find out if there is something they might have done to make the proposal stronger. Ask if it would be appropriate to reapply for that same program or whether it would be better to approach us with something different. We will provide guidance as to what concerns need to be addressed, and next steps. We don't want to waste people's time going forward. (J. Andrew Lark)

If there is some issue that caused the proposal not to be funded, we will convey that information. In most cases there was nothing wrong with the request. There is just not enough money and too many applications. For fundraising projects that I am engaged with, I take turndowns very badly myself. (David Palenchar)

These are very difficult conversations to have. We give very serious consideration to all proposals and do not turn things down randomly; the process is highly competitive. One project may look like another, but not have all the elements we are looking for. If there are two projects, and we can only fund one, we're going to select the stronger one. If it is just a matter of tweaking the proposal, this is an easier discussion to have. However, it is usually not so much about the proposal as about the project itself. (Karen Rosa)

We want to remain friends with nonprofit grant applicants. We want to keep a relationship going, and we want them to understand what our priorities are, the project's shortcomings, or how the proposal just didn't fit in. Often they come back with a stronger proposal. (Ruth Shack)

Following the rejection of a proposal, what is the best thing an organization can do?

The best thing is to call and ask why you were turned down. Don't be discouraged. When you are asking for money, you have to take a sales approach. You can learn from every situation. (Peter F. Bird, Jr.)

Listen and learn. Don't take the turndown personally because it is truly a business decision. The program officer feels just as badly as you do. It is so much more rewarding to say "yes." Don't take the "no" as the end of the relationship. Rather, keep the door open and be professional about handling the declination.
(Julie Brooks)

Send an acknowledgement or thank-you letter for considering your request. Call and ask for a phone or face-to-face appointment to talk about how you might improve your request for the next time. (Danah Craft)

If an organization is declined because it does not fit the guidelines, it is best to move on. Recalibrating a proposal to fit the foundation's guidelines generally does not work. (Robert Crane)

Before making the call to ask questions, the grantseeker should go back to the foundation's guidelines and read their proposal as if they are reading it for the first time. That way they can see what might not have been in sync with the guidelines. The time that has gone by between writing the proposal and receiving a decline provides an opportunity for a fresh perspective on the part of the grant writer. This should facilitate an honest dialogue with the grantmaker. (David O. Egner)

I admire people who call. They can learn from the turndown, move on, or come back to us later. (David Ford)

The best thing is to find out why you were turned down and see if there is anything that might be done differently, but we always let you know if there is a specific reason. But don't complain about it. Rather, see if it would be appropriate for your organization to apply again. (Laura H. Gilbertson)

Seek any information to improve the proposal or probability of funding and ask for suggestions of other funding sources. (Marilyn Hennessy)

Learn to take "no" for an answer. This is an art. (A. Thomas Hildebrandt)

Press us for reasons and advice on what can be done to strengthen the application. Ask about adjustments that might make the proposal fit the funding interests of other foundations. Follow that advice and tailor your application to other funders. Meanwhile, stay in touch through newsletters and announcements. (Matthew Klein)

Don't be afraid to ask questions. Sometimes a miscommunication or lack of communication can cause bad feelings, and that is certainly not our intent. One decline does not mean that an agency will always be declined; so keeping the lines of communication open is important. (Victoria Kovar)

Express an open willingness to hear whatever constructive criticisms that the foundation may have to offer, and don't be defensive about it. (J. Andrew Lark)

Show evidence in your next application that you listened to the feedback from the grantmaker. Find out how to cultivate the grantmaker. Cultivating people who have said "no" is just as important as cultivating the people who said "yes." (Rick Moyers)

Say thank-you for considering it and suggest that you will be back if there seems to be a possibility for funding at a future date. Try to find out where your organization was off the mark. Finding grantmakers that are more on the mark is a better use of time. If a funder invites you to come back in the future, be sure to do it. (Christine Park)

If an organization doesn't feel that they know why they were rejected, they should contact the program officer and find out why. This will tell them whether or not to reapply. Knowing whether they are a good fit will save them time in the future. Sometimes proposals are rejected because the foundation is not focused on that issue at that time, but might be in the future. Ask if you should re-apply, and if the answer is no, move on. But please don't argue with the program officer. It probably wasn't their decision to reject you. And, it's unprofessional.
(Karen Topakian)

Following the rejection of a proposal, what is the worst thing an organization can do?

Never ask the foundation again. The grantseeker's first encounter with a grantmaker often ends in a decline, but that does not mean that there is no hope for a future relationship. (Peter F. Bird, Jr.)

Try to go over the program officer's head and use influence with executive staff or the board. This sours the relationship with program staff, and it is hard to mend once this happens. (Julie Brooks)

Call a trustee and ask for reconsideration. This puts the trustee in a difficult position, especially since the decision was made by the group. The turndown does not necessarily mean that there is something wrong with the organization or objectionable about the proposal. It could simply be, and usually is, that we just ran out of money. (Danah Craft)

Send a letter to the president of the foundation or to the chair of the corporation and express your disappointment. (Rene Deida)

Call my board members and complain. (David O. Egner)

Call up and start being accusative or impugning us with bad motives. If you are not acting professionally and positively with us, this will be remembered for the future. (William V. Engel)

Become belligerent toward the grantmaker, such as sending off angry e-mails when you are upset. Better to call or e-mail and simply ask for feedback. (Julie Farkas)

Express disappointment too strongly or continue to submit requests after you have been informed that it is unlikely that you will be funded. We try to let people know if it would be best to direct their efforts elsewhere. (Laura H. Gilbertson)

Not count to ten before you pick up the phone to call us. Making the call, having the conversation or writing the letter without thinking first is a mistake. (J. Andrew Lark)

Attempting to talk the grantmaker out of that decision is a mistake. (Rick Moyers)

Acting as if there is an expectation that because this organization is a nonprofit and seeking funding, it is our obligation to support it. (David Palenchar)

It is a mistake to be angry. Such anger is misplaced in this situation, since I am only the messenger at that point. The grantseeker should keep the relationship professional and civil, because we will probably run into each other again, and there may be opportunities for future funding. (Nancy Wiltsek)

If the request does not meet our funding priorities, it is a mistake to keep applying over and over again, expecting a different result the next time. (Bob Wittig)

If a grant is awarded, what is the best thing an organization can do?

Send multiple "thank-yous." Let the donor know that you think of them as an investor, not just a benefactor, and treat them that way. Let us know what is happening with the money and the organization. (Peter F. Bird, Jr.)

Stay on top of paperwork and reporting requirements. Do a periodic check of anticipated outcomes. Call us if there are issues or problems. Our program officers want to know about any changes or issues the grantee is having early on, not during a yearly progress report or at the end of the grant. (Julie Brooks)

Keep us informed along the way. Invite us to activities. Tell us about staff changes. If there is a problem, tell us. If things are going well, let us know that too. (Rene Deida)

Cash the check! Occasionally, we have to remind the grantee to do this. It makes you wonder if they really need the money. (William V. Engel)

First, say thank-you to everyone involved. A phone call or note to the program officer would be nice. Second, complete the required reports on time and accurately. Take the offer of a partnership seriously to keep the foundation appraised of your progress, both good and bad. Third, do the best job you can. Be a success so that everyone wins and you are encouraged to return for another grant. (Bruce Esterline)

Stay in touch. Send newsletters and e-mails. Let us know about upcoming events, and invite us to things. Consider us part of the family. Let us know what is happening. Don't forget about your connection to us. We are building communication with you. We encourage people to stay in touch beyond reporting requirements. (Marilyn Gelber)

A quick and personal and excited thank-you is really nice. (David Grant)

Get your signed grant letter back to us quickly so that we can issue the check. If this fails to happen promptly, we begin to wonder whether you really need the money. And we take this as an indication of possible poor future execution of your project. (Robert Jaquay)

Develop a trusting relationship with the funders. Don't hesitate to contact your program officer to ask for advice or introductions to other funders who could be interested in your work. (Matthew Klein)

Fulfill the terms of the grant efficiently, effectively and economically and report on progress as requested. Because we are affiliated with a public company, recognition of our support is always appreciated and helpful. (Carol Kurzig)

The foundation needs to feel good about its work. Send us things such as press clippings. Use the grant from us to leverage other support. Make contact with the program staff and invite them to visit. (Marvin McKinney)

Go from promise to performance. This relationship is about delivering what was promised. (David Odahowski)

Send a thank-you letter that states the amount and the purpose of the grant. This may seem too basic to mention, but our auditors look for such a letter and we need it for the files. Communicate with us, but don't over-communicate. We want to know what is going on, but don't need to know what is happening every week. Challenges are just as important to us as successes, because funders do not want to find out at the end of a grant cycle that something has gone wrong when we thought the grant project was moving along smoothly. So keep us posted. We are not here to be punitive; we are here to help the nonprofits that we have funded do the best possible job they can. We can't help you if you don't let us know there is an issue. (Karen Rosa)

Produce a splendid program. We are made good by their doing good. They demonstrate impact in the community and attract other funders to the work. (Ruth Shack)

Send an acknowledgement of the grant. Say that you are looking forward to working with the foundation and keeping us up-to-date. (Elizabeth B. Smith)

Communicate without being excessive. I love it when people invite me to see the results of our investment. Let us know about your successes. (Lita Ugarte)

If a grant is awarded, what is the worst thing an organization can do?

Spend the money on something else without permission. (Peter F. Bird, Jr.)

Not doing what you said you would do. Not submitting your reports on time. When the project is done, we'll have no clue whether it met its goals or not. (Kathleen Cerveny)

Complain that it wasn't the right amount. (Danah Craft)

Misuse the funds or use the money for another purpose. This breaks the trust and creates a problem for everyone. (Bruce Esterline)

Fail to be in contact with the foundation about significant delays in implementation of the program. We are more than happy to grant extensions, but we need to know there is a problem in getting the program off the ground. (Julie Farkas)

Lose their enthusiasm about what they are doing. (David Ford)

It disturbs me if there are major changes in the organization, and I hear about it from somebody else. I want to hear about it, even if the message is hard to deliver. Forgetting to give us credit is also a mistake. (Marilyn Gelber)

Use the grant money for other than the requested purpose without communicating with us first to seek our approval. This happened once and we asked for the grant money back. (Jane Hardesty)

Never send us a report on what happened as a result of the grant. This is a mistake, particularly if you are going to come back to us in the future. If we don't know what happened the first time, we may not be inclined to fund again. (Marilyn Hennessy)

Not acknowledge the grant and simply cash the check. (A. Thomas Hildebrandt)

Not be accountable for the use of the money. You should use the money as you represented you would. We can tolerate failure if it was a good faith effort. (Robert Jaquay)

Not fulfill the terms of the grant agreement or report back to us when they encounter problems in developing or completing the project as represented in their grant request. Lack of recognition is also problematic for us, because as a public charity we also raise funds from the public, and we want our donors to see the good use to which their support is put. (Carol Kurzig)

I think the worst thing would be not sending an acknowledgement and thank-you letter. Also if there is to be some publicity about the grant, announcing the grant without talking to us first is not really acceptable. (Ilene Mack)

There are several things including disappearing until you need money again, or making radical changes in the project without consulting the grantmaker. (Rick Moyers)

Complain that you didn't get all that you asked for. This is an ongoing problem, which may be due to the focus and intensity that people have on their own efforts. There needs to be a realization that the funder's priorities may not be aligned 100% with your priorities. (David Palenchar)

Not tell us about serious problems you encounter. We don't want to find out about it in the newspaper. (Karen Rosa)

Besides not honoring the terms of the grant, losing the check. (Nancy Wiltsek)

Let us hear from you only at the next grant renewal cycle. (Bob Wittig)

What role does reporting play in your grantmaking process?

For large grants, I will call the nonprofit and ask how things are going. I want to know if the grant has changed things or crystallized matters for the organization. If it is relatively risky, I will flag it for follow-up. (Peter F. Bird, Jr.)

In part, because of the scrutiny foundations are undergoing at a level that perhaps wasn't so in the past, we are paying a lot more attention than we ever did before to making sure that reports are completed and are on time. We now track reports electronically. If a report is overdue, we send the organization a letter. Also as a funder, we are trying to evaluate the effectiveness of our own grantmaking, and the reporting process is a very important piece of that. (Kathleen Cerveny)

When you have to prioritize grant projects, it has become more important to ask the question: what impact is this project going to have in the community? The report helps us learn about the impact. (Danah Craft)

It plays a significant role, since we are very interested in following the progress of the grants we make. Our grant letter lays out clear reporting requirements, including what is to be covered in the report and the dates that reports are due. We remind grantees if we don't get reports on time. (Robert Crane)

We look for very straightforward reports. We are anxious to know what you have learned thus far and how that will inform what you propose to do in the future. (Julie Farkas)

We have a lot of interaction with grantees to ensure that we receive well-executed reports. Most nonprofits are doing a good job with reports, but some have a hard time meeting the reporting schedule. We use the information from the reports in an internal document (grant brief) that goes to the board and staff. A final assessment form allows the program officers to determine the degree to which the nonprofit's goals were achieved. We always respond to the final report. We send an acknowledgement letter that comments on the report and may ask additional follow-up questions. The reports inform us about how the money is spent and provide learning for our future grantmaking. (Marilyn Hennessy)

We very rarely ask for reports. Because of the nature of the projects we are funding, we will know whether the work happened. A way to say thanks is to write and tell us "here's what we did with your money." It is appreciated but not required. (A. Thomas Hildebrandt)

What did you learn? What will you be doing differently? Be forthcoming. For financial reporting, I like to see actual income and expenses expressed in a way that is consistent with the original budget, which makes it easy to compare. (Victoria Kovar)

We want to know how things are going. Were there any surprises? Not everything works exactly as planned. Often there are constructive changes that can be made to the project. If there is a glitch, let us know. We can help rethink the project. As your funding partner, we want to see the project succeed as much as you do. (J. Andrew Lark)

At our foundation a six-month interim report triggers the next payment on the grant. Then, there is a ten-month report which is sent to us before the year is over and prior to the nonprofit seeking a renewal. There will be a site visit in between the six- and ten-month reports. Late reports can be a big problem for us because it can delay payment of the grant. (Maria Mottola)

We use reports to generate ideas for our web site, feature grantees in our annual report, and inform ourselves as we talk to other funders and our board. We don't declare victory in every instance: we don't expect final reports to gloss over the difficulties. Grantees should not be afraid to share the good and the bad with the grantmaker. We're your partner, and you can help us become smarter by means of the report. (Rick Moyers)

We look for two reports: one at midpoint and one at completion. The midpoint report may be a one-page letter to tell us how the project is progressing. The final report contains the most information about how funds were expended and what the results were. (Michele Pritchard)

We only require one final report. We don't require interim reports, although we do value being kept informed. The end-of-grant report, however, is very important. We review the organization's progress in light of the expectations and outcomes outlined in the original proposal and in our grant transmittal letter. Further funding, whether for that particular project or for future work, depends on that progress. (Karen Rosa)

We use a form that reflects the application information. We don't want to catch people off-guard. Some people forget about the deadline and have to be reminded. When reports don't come in, it is viewed somewhat negatively. For applicants to be able to apply in the future, they have to have completed their reports. (Lita Ugarte)

We send a report form with the grant agreement letter, so the organization knows from the start what we expect and when we expect it. Reports are not about jumping through hoops. They are more about the learning process. We try to create an opportunity for reflection so that people are thinking about what they have done. (Nancy Wiltsek)

What specifically are you looking for in a grant report?

Reports vary by grant type and institution, based on the nature of the work we are funding and the duration of the project. Most of our work is advocacy and policy related. We ask grantees to provide specific information on: 1) the work carried out to meet the goals and objectives of the grant, including any changes in objectives or strategy as presented in the original proposal; 2) tangible momentum building or institutional policy results, if applicable; 3) unforeseen objectives or opportunities and how they were handled; 4) a description of their outlook going forward with the work; 5) an accounting of how the money was used; 6) materials or publications produced; and 7) audited financials. (Robert Crane)

Much of the work we do is anything but simple. There are two types of reports we ask for. When it's not a "program" grant we want to know how the funds were spent and how things turned out. For program grants, we will prepare specific questions we would like answered at the end of the grant period. It's really a matter of being concise and boiling it down to real outcomes and real next steps. I want to know what didn't work and what we should do to fix it. (David O. Egner)

A grant report should tie the project to previously identified measurable outcomes, and it should be precise and to the point. We want to know if the grant made a difference. (Bruce Esterline)

We look at both process (or outputs) and outcomes. Have you hired the person you said you would? Have you started the program? How many clients have you served? Down the road, we hope to get information on two or three outcomes, not ten. (Julie Farkas)

We ask three central questions: 1) What are the goals for the project? 2) What actions will the nonprofit take to achieve those goals? 3) What indicators measure success? We want an update on these central questions and an accounting of how funds were used. (John Goldberg)

We look for a timely report on activity and outcomes of the project. It does not have to be formal, but should be complete and address all of the goals described in the proposal and grant agreement. (Carol Kurzig)

We are looking to see if the program unfolded as it was designed. If not, why not? (J. Andrew Lark)

We require a very simple report on what you did with our money, how it was spent, and how effective the outcomes were. Did it meet your expectations? We are actually reworking our reporting guidelines to make it simpler for the grantee to give us the exact information we want. (Ilene Mack)

From the reports we hope to learn the following: 1) If the nonprofit is carrying out the proposal as written; 2) How the program is integrated into the agency; 3) How the nonprofit leveraged Kellogg's money; and 4) What else is going on in conjunction with this grant in terms of informing policy, practices or other programs. (Marvin McKinney)

We are looking for a reasonable narrative on what happened with the project and an accounting of how the money was spent. (Rick Moyers)

We have four or five questions that the recipient receives in advance. We want to know what didn't work and why, and if it is possible to make interim changes. (David Odahowski)

We are looking to see how consistent the application of the funding was relative to the proposal: is there an alignment between what was proposed and what actually happened? We don't want a fifty-page report. (David Palenchar)

We want to know about lessons learned. What transpired that was educational and how is the project being altered to accommodate these learnings? It's about constant course correction. All too often grantees are afraid to admit to anything outside of what they think the funder wants to hear. (Christine Park)

Reporting should not cause the organization to incur additional cost and should not take much staff time. (Michele Pritchard)

We use a very simple form whereby the grantee reports against what was planned with actual activities and outcomes. This report vehicle gets mixed reviews. Some like it because it is concrete. Others find it limits them too much or loses the nuances of what they do. They feel we are not asking for enough narrative and that the report is too numbers oriented. But it is always possible to provide additional narrative. (Elizabeth B. Smith)

Beyond the basic information, what else should the proposal contain?

We look for detail on sustainability and risks to implementing the project. We want the grantseeker to be honest and not put an unrealistic positive spin on the program or project. Our foundation is not afraid to take on risk. (Julie Brooks)

We want to see an articulation of the long-term systemic social change being sought by the organization, as well as strategies and the timetable for implementation of the work. (Robert Crane)

The nonprofit should be very clear about the dollars they need from us, the purpose for which funds are needed, and the time period in which the funds will be used. (David O. Egner)

Who you are and what you are asking for is paramount. It is discouraging to go through a proposal and not be able to figure out what the grantseeker wants. We also like to know that the nonprofit's board is supporting this project both financially and managerially. (William V. Engel)

The proposal should include a compelling need statement for your particular community. It should talk about the target population. And it should be direct, clear, and realistic. (Julie Farkas)

It should help me to visualize what I would see if I were to walk in the agency's door. (Laura H. Gilbertson)

The proposal should be a succinct statement of what you need in one or two pages. (A. Thomas Hildebrandt)

The proposal should state the need upfront: "We're requesting X amount for this project that will do Y." This puts it in context right away. Often we ask the grantseeker to shorten the proposal and present complex information in a way that is visually appealing. This could be done by means of bullets or charts. We ask that applicants not use jargon. (Victoria Kovar)

Tell us what success looks like for this project and for your agency. Describe what you do. The program must be strong and have a strong organization behind it. (Karen Rosa)

The document should be fully integrated without separate chunks. Some proposals read as if five different people wrote the proposal, which may be the reality, but it needs to all pull together. (Leslie Silverman)

We need to know what organizational resources are available to meet the need—that includes staff, facilities, and finances. We also like to see evidence of local support. (E. Belvin Williams)

Tell your story and back it up with data. I want the proposal to be personalized, but brief. (Nancy Wiltsek)

What makes a proposal document stand out?

Getting it in in advance of the deadline helps. Grantseekers need to put themselves in our position and think a little bit about what we are trying to do. We have one staff member who is logging in all these proposals. There's only so much one person can do. If a request comes in the last day or two before the deadline, it really slows our process down, and it means that the proposal may not receive as thorough a consideration as it should. If it weren't for this deluge on the last day or two, we would have had all the proposals logged in and it would give us more time to read them thoroughly, at a leisurely pace, and allow us to really think about the proposal. (William V. Engel)

A compelling need statement followed by a clear program response with measurable outputs and outcomes. And the proposal writer should tie the process directly to the outcomes. (Julie Farkas)

Clarity is very important and helps the reader to visualize the program. Proposal writers should avoid "fluff," repeatedly stating in general terms how important the program is without providing details to back up the claim. (Laura H. Gilbertson)

Clarity—the proposal should explain what difference the project will make and to whom. What will be different at the end of the grant period, what will the money be used for, and what is the relationship between the budget and the activities described? (Marilyn Hennessy)

We like to see how broad the applied benefit of the grant project is. The ability to describe both immediate and ripple effects is very important. (A. Thomas Hildebrandt)

My advice is to emphasize substance over form. (Robert Jaquay)

The best proposals describe a very specific problem as well as a solution that is uniquely tailored to address the particular elements of that problem. The reader should get the sense that if the grantseeker does what they describe, they are likely to have an impact. Many proposals make the mistake of being too general in describing the issues they are confronting, and as a result their proposed solutions are less plausible. (Matthew Klein)

Clarity and brevity. Use simple language that is easy to understand. The proposal writer would be well advised to take out extra words. (Victoria Kovar)

The proposal should be concisely written—most are too long and include too much peripheral information. And it should include a solid budget that clearly ties to the narrative. The writers should use testimonials well, but selectively. We do not need exhaustive detail or extensive history on the organization. (Carol Kurzig)

A proposal should be short, concise, and clear. Format is not as important as content. (Maria Mottola)

Give us information both from the financial perspective and from your heart. (David Palenchar)

We require no bells or whistles, no elegant binding, and no pictures. We don't want videos; no one is going to watch them. We don't want to give grants to people who know how to compile fancy grant proposals. We want to give grants to people who are doing what the community needs and deserves. We want the grantseeker to tell us why their program makes Miami-Dade a better place, how it is going to strengthen the community, and how it will make it easier for us to survive and flourish. (Ruth Shack)

If the proposal is well written, it is much more engaging to read and it will rise to the top. It will get noticed. The layout often pulls me through, but the proposal has to make sense. We don't want to read it and wonder what the nonprofit does. The proposal should state the program goals and objectives clearly. Stories and examples make the proposal compelling. They underscore that people give to people. (Bob Wittig)

Do you have any other advice to help the proposal writer succeed?

Send in the proposal early, to be sure that your application is complete. Don't wait until the last minute. (Kathleen Cerveny)

Evidence of an effective program, and a well-managed, effective organization make a proposal stand out. (Rene Deida)

Don't go on and on about how critical the need is and how important your work is. (William V. Engel)

Use your proposal as a vehicle to tell your story concisely and compellingly. (Julie Farkas)

Clarity, clarity, clarity—crispness, crispness, crispness. Get to the point. Avoid too much verbiage. Be persuasive, show your character. We ask people to express in very few words the facts about what they are doing, what they want to do, and the emotions behind it. Develop that sense of electricity. (David Ford)

Pay attention to detail. Proofread your proposal. Double-check the math on the budget. Sometimes we get the impression that a nonprofit has backed into a project budget based on the amount they are requesting rather than what the project will actually cost. Spell the name of the grantmaker correctly. (Laura H. Gilbertson)

When you write, the first paragraph should state what you are asking for. Sometimes the writer gets caught up in the text and forgets what the point was. Consider who the audience is. You are not writing only for us, but also for our board members who may not be professionals in your field. Eliminate jargon. (John Goldberg)

Help us to understand the landscape you are operating in by describing other approaches that complement your own. As a very practical, mundane piece of advice: format the proposal with section titles that help the reader follow the flow of your presentation. (Matthew Klein)

We have to be able to read quickly and explain your project to our colleagues succinctly. And we have to be ready to go to bat for the proposal. Anything that makes it hard for me to serve as an advocate for the project should be avoided. Fancy binders and glossy annual reports can work against you. (Maria Mottola)

Be sure to articulate early in the proposal what the need is and what you are asking for. Don't bury it on page 10. Make sure the proposal is user-friendly. It is helpful for corporations if the nonprofit can articulate any connectedness to the company. Explain how content area, volunteers, and geography connect to the company. (Christine Park)

Sometimes grantseekers assume that the proposal reviewer knows certain things. That can be a mistake, even if it is a past donor. Tell us how your program operates, who is involved, and what the numbers are. Answer the funder's questions clearly and honestly. (Elizabeth B. Smith)

We ask the grantseeker to tell us what management challenges the organization faces and how these are being addressed. We hope that the nonprofit will be open and honest with us about this issue. It helps to build trust between grantseeker and funder. (Nancy Wiltsek)

Some applications are literally squeezed onto each page; this makes it very difficult to read. Be sure to use margins and white space to help facilitate the reading of a proposal. Also, we do not penalize an organization if they do not use all of the pages allotted to the narrative. Sometimes less is more! (Bob Wittig)

Beyond the basic information, should the appendix contain any other materials?

We would like to know if the board has provided financial support for the project. And what percentage of the total is that giving? We want to see their strategic plan. This helps us see how their proposal fits into their plan for growth and expansion. (Danah Craft)

We'd like to know the five largest funders for the past five years and their cumulative support. (Robert Crane)

We would like to see the following documents: 1) organizational chart; 2) table of contents from the board manual; and 3) summary of the organization's strategic plan. I also like to see newspaper clippings. Sometimes they provide a different view of the organization than the proposal does. (Laura H. Gilbertson)

The board list is important to us. We look to see whom we know on the board. (A. Thomas Hildebrandt)

We expect that we will not be your only funder and that you will go to many grantmakers at once. Applicants should supply a list of other funding prospects and their current status. (J. Andrew Lark)

We need one-paragraph résumés of your key staff. Also, videos and DVDs are hard for us to manage and they don't help; so don't include those. (Maria Mottola)

A copy of their Florida State Registration must be included. (Ruth Shack)

Could you say how your web site fits in with your grantmaking procedures?

It's amazing! We get 16,000 hits versus 600 inquiries in prior years.
(David O. Egner)

We have had our web site for about ten years, and it has resulted in a massive, positive change for us. By now, most nonprofit agencies have and use Internet capability, and they can quickly and easily find information about us. It is obvious from the proposals we now receive that almost everyone follows our grant application guidelines, which they can obtain from the web site. (Bruce Esterline)

Our web site is the place for us to communicate. It is very helpful. If you read it carefully, you will understand what we are looking for. (David Ford)

We are working on developing a web site. We recognize the value of having one and we are trying to be thoughtful about it. (Jane Hardesty)

We do not have a web site. The next generation of our board can take this on. (A. Thomas Hildebrandt)

Our web site is transparent in content to provide a listing of approved grants and funding guidelines for interested grantseekers. (Leslie Silverman)

We have had a web site for several years, but it was redesigned a few years ago. And since then, I've found that people are visiting it and using it more often. We are receiving more proposals that are appropriate to us. Before that, we were getting a higher percentage of proposals that were inappropriate because people didn't know what we funded or how to apply. And now with access to the Internet, there's less of an excuse not to know. (Karen Topakian)

Our goal is to be thorough and share information about who we are and what we are interested in. We do this via our web site. (Lita Ugarte)

Having a web site has greatly reduced the number of applications that don't fit our guidelines. Yet we are getting 88,000 hits! (Nancy Wiltsek)

Does your foundation/corporation accept items related to the grant application process electronically?

We do not accept letters of intent or proposals electronically in order to protect sensitive information about the nonprofits who reach out to us. (Robert Crane)

We can edit documents jointly with the grantseeker by e-mail. We still ask for the hard copy of attachments to the proposal. (David O. Egner)

Electronic submissions are best for letters of intent, but the online format does not work as well for developing a comprehensive proposal. It is deficient in several ways: 1) There are formatting problems, often making the document hard to decipher. 2) People write an online proposal cryptically as if it were an e-mail. 3) Often, it ends up taking more time to review an online submission because we have to go back and ask for a lot of the information that was not included in the original. (Bruce Esterline)

We are not there yet. At this point, we would have to print everything out on our end in order to create a paper file. (Julie Farkas)

We accept letters of intent and proposals electronically, and it is working well! (Marilyn Gelber)

We need the final document and attachments in hard copy. We cannot distribute proposals electronically to the board, since some use electronic media more than others. Most board members like to see requests on paper. (Laura H. Gilbertson)

We have begun the transition and give groups the option of applying online. I think we are a couple of years away from accepting everything electronically. Meanwhile, we are trying to adjust our own habits; most of our program directors still like to have the hard copy in hand. (David Grant)

We require multiple copies of the proposals, audits, and financial and other documents and do not accept them electronically. If additional information is sent while the proposal is under consideration, we accept these materials electronically. (Marilyn Hennessy)

We accept everything electronically. We use an Excel tracking sheet. The electronic copies make it easy to keep track of all the materials. (Matthew Klein)

Much of our "pre-work" is by e-mail: the draft application, and proposal edits. The official submission still comes by mail. (Victoria Kovar)

Yes, absolutely. We have seen an increase in the number of electronic submissions we receive. However, most submissions are still sent by mail because we support many small organizations, and we also appreciate receiving multiple copies. Ideally, we get an electronic version and multiple hard copies. (Carol Kurzig)

We don't need the proposal so quickly. We can wait for the hard copy. Once the request is here and information seems to be missing, that can be sent electronically. We prefer not to receive requests via e-mail or fax. (Ilene Mack)

Electronic submissions are both good and bad. E-mail creates a pressure to respond in a way that paper doesn't. E-mail has an urgency requiring not as much reflection but a faster answer. I have a love-hate relationship with e-mail. (Christine Park)

I am ambivalent about moving to electronic submissions. After the hurricane in 1992, we received proposals written on notebook paper in pencil. We accepted and funded them. (Ruth Shack)

We are working toward this. In the past, we didn't think our own technology was reliable enough. Also, we were concerned about the digital divide, which is diminishing as time goes on, but we want to be conscious of potential differences in access to technology. When proposals are fully electronic, it will be easier to share them with the board. That having been said, we would always accept proposals by mail, just to keep it fair for everyone. (Karen Topakian)

Yes, once a proposal has been accepted for board review. With respect to the initial proposal, I like to see what an organization sends me. That way I get a feel for who they are and how they operate. Hard copy helps portray the qualitative nature of the organization. (Nancy Wiltsek)

Do you use e-mail to communicate with grantseekers?

Since 90% of our grantees are technologically up-to-date, e-mail makes a big difference. (Peter F. Bird, Jr.)

Yes, e-mail allows for quick response. However, the danger of using e-mail and responding quickly is that e-mails are often not crafted with care. The same level of precision should be used in preparing an e-mail as in writing a letter. (Robert Crane)

We are doing more and more via e-mail. I like to know ahead of time that a document is coming via e-mail. (David O. Egner)

We get quite a few e-mail inquiries—maybe about the same number as phone calls. We have some stock e-mail responses. (Laura H. Gilbertson)

Nonprofits can send their letter of intent as an e-mail attachment. This is an informal part of our process. We want to save the applicant time in preparing the complete proposal. We do that via the letter of intent. After seeing it, we can discourage those who don't fit and provide guidance to those who do. Our ultimate goal is to get a good proposal, sufficiently detailed, with a good chance of being funded. (Marilyn Hennessy)

It is making life easier. (Ilene Mack)

I'm afraid it is another distraction. It gets overwhelming. (Maria Mottola)

We use e-mail for information like change of address, phone number or staff, and also for directions for site visits. (Michele Pritchard)

I use e-mail to let the applicant know that their proposal is being reviewed, to get additional information, questions and answers, and for sharing information. (Lita Ugarte)

What do you look for in your review of grant proposals?

We look at how the project lines up against ten indicators: 1) Does the project align with foundation's interests? Examples of previous grants can be found in our annual report and on our web site. 2) Is the project viable? Is it a duplicate of another funded project? 3) Is the project something that could increase the impact of another grant we made? 4) Is there any earned income in relation to the project? 5) Is there a need for communication outlets, such as web sites or media? 6) Is there a need for technical assistance? 7) Is an evaluation component built in? 8) Is there evidence of collaboration? 9) How will the grant impact the community? 10) What percentage of the project are we being asked to fund? Are we the largest, the only, equal to another grantor, or one of many? (Julie Brooks)

We want to be part of projects that fit our grantmaking focus, are making a difference in the community, and are also good for the nonprofit organization. (Danah Craft)

We analyze the program strategies and an organization's track record very carefully and spend considerable time on budgets. Too often an organization's budget has little relationship to the work described in the narrative. Budgets often can tell you much more about an organization's priorities that its narrative proposal. (Robert Crane)

We have boiled down a lot of our decision making to six risk areas. If the initial three factors are present, there is a 75% chance that the grant will be successful. If one of these is missing, the odds drop to 33%. 1) Is there a champion for the project? In some cases, there is an internal and an external champion. 2) What is the relationship to the foundation? Do we have an honest, brokered relationship? Do we know the executive director and/or members of the board? Could we help connect the dots on activities so that we can suggest who else they can talk to on those issues? 3) Is there an exit strategy for the foundation? Since we can't fund anything in perpetuity is there an immediate way out or one that we know is going to take a decade? 4) What is the financial strength of the institution? Do they have the capacity to run the programs? 5) What is the overall soundness of the program idea? Does it make sense? 6) What is the overall risk rating? We use a "red, yellow, green" system on all of our recommendations to the board. Green is a go. Yellow is a caution. Red means there is reason to stop and talk further about this. (David O. Egner)

We focus on the project. Is it well planned? Does it make sense? Does it hold up under critical analysis? Does the agency have the capacity to carry out the plan? Does the organization have the necessary financial resources to begin and sustain the project? Where will the dollars come from? Who will support the project over time? (Bruce Esterline)

I look to see that the organization's mission is in alignment with the Smith family's interests. Is there outstanding leadership? Are they social entrepreneurs? Is there excitement behind what the group does? I know it when I see it. (David Ford)

What is key to me is that the organization is passionate about its work. I want to see more of a history of success than failure. We can help them in making sure that happens. (David Odahowski)

I look for consistency with the policies, goals, and direction of the foundation. Applicants that do good work but are not in line with what the foundation does might not get past this first screening. I look at their track record, impact, and duplication of services. I look more closely at new organizations. Statistically, fewer than 50% of requests make it to our trustees. Of those, 60-70% have been funded before. Then there is the financial review. I look at the type of organization and how their administrative costs relate to their service costs and program costs. I look at fund balances and balance sheets. Are assets growing or decreasing? We ask for three years of financial information for that specific purpose. I also look for a breakdown of funding sources. Finally, I ask two questions: 1) Would you as an individual sit down and write this organization a check? 2) If this organization closed its doors, would anybody care? (David Palenchar)

We are looking for an opportunity to further our mission by supporting good work. It is really important that the program/project be strong and that there be a strong organizational structure behind it. (Karen Rosa)

How does it fit into our overall mission? How healthy is the agency? What is the prognosis for the future of the agency? I look at the board members and the finances. (Ruth Shack)

Is there alignment with the foundation's strategy, including any targeted geographic areas specified on the web site? Who are the key partners dedicating resources, time, or expertise to the project? We also assess the capacity of the grantee to carry out the project, especially with the larger grants. Do they have sufficient and competent staff to manage the funds? (Leslie Silverman)

After an initial screening indicates that the proposal meets our guidelines, we look more deeply into the quality of the organization and program: how is it structured; who is involved; and what results is it having? What about the governance of the organization? How is the board functioning? What about board and staff diversity as it impacts the effectiveness of the organization and reflects the communities being served? What is the financial situation of the organization and its need for resources? What role does the organization play in its community? (Elizabeth B. Smith)

First, I have to make sure that they fit our guidelines for the applicant organization's age and budget. Then I look at the issue that they are addressing. Is it really about social change? Is this something that we think is important? What are they doing and how, and is it reasonable that this group of people could accomplish this? I also look for writing that is free of jargon that only an insider would understand or know. And I can't say enough about presentation: please limit the use of bold text, underlining, and bullet points, and keep the font to 11 point or larger. Next, I look at the budget. And there, always, is the most telling information. That's where we look to see if the program discussion matches the budgeted amounts. (Karen Topakian)

Five things are important to us: 1) The financial capacity to carry out the proposed project. Do the numbers add up; is the budget appropriate? Does the organization have: a fundraising plan, sustainability plan, other funders? 2) Expertise and knowledge to carry out the proposal. Are people qualified? 3) Outcomes. 4) The program fits within our priorities. 5) Clarity of the proposal. Is it well written? Did the organization answer all of our questions? (Lita Ugarte)

What else is part of your "due diligence" process?

Speaking to other funders

If the donor has been cited by the organization as a past supporter, we want to know what their experience was like. If a donor is noted as a prospective supporter, we may ask them to tell us where the request is in their review process and what is the likelihood of it receiving their support. (Bruce Esterline)

Especially if the applicant is new to us, we always ask who the other funders are. (Marilyn Gelber)

In addition to looking at financials and audits along with the request, we speak to other donors to get their point of view on a particular organization. And of course, we make site visits to all our grantees. (Ilene Mack)

We will sometimes speak with other donors. It depends on what the request is for. This happens more often when I have a question about a pending application with another donor. (Lita Ugarte)

I will compare notes and weigh the risk. I will speak to individual donors as well. (E. Belvin Williams)

If the grantseeker is new to us, I will speak with other funders. I want to see what other program officers think. I will do this after I have reviewed the proposal and done the site visit. (Bob Wittig)

Speaking to other knowledgeable nonprofits

I will speak with other nonprofits on occasion. If there is an issue I am curious about, I will talk with someone I trust. (David Ford)

I will speak to people with whom I have had long-time relationships. (Karen Rosa)

We ask for references. (Elizabeth B. Smith)

We do this to gauge reputation and competence. (Vincent Stehle)

I speak with other nonprofits, especially if they are working with the applicant. I will do a "curiosity check," e.g. why the state discontinued support. (E. Belvin Williams)

Other

Buzz in the community is something we are sensitive to. (Marilyn Gelber)

I frequently find relevant information on an agency's web site that is not in its proposal. (Laura H. Gilbertson)

In addition to site visits and meetings, web sites are a great source of background and detail. They give a very good sense of how the organization likes to present itself, as well as providing a great deal of information. We also check with colleagues in the field for more insights. (Carol Kurzig)

I often will do a Google search before a site visit to find out what information is out there about the agency. (J. Andrew Lark)

The first thing we do is an internal search. Have we ever funded this organization? Did they submit timely reports? Did they run a good program? Did the project inform policy? What kind of evaluation was performed? Was public will impacted? What were the lessons learned? (Marvin McKinney)

I will use the Better Business Bureau questionnaire, and refer to BBB standards. (Karen Rosa)

We read local papers that might cover our grantees. (Elizabeth B. Smith)

What is the role of your board in the proposal review process?

The board sees a summary that the staff writes for them. It can be as short as one page or as long as six pages, depending on the complexity of the request. That write-up includes: 1) enough background on the organization so that the board member understands what the agency does; 2) a little bit of information about our relationship with the organization; 3) background on the issue or challenge in the community that this project addresses (the need); 4) a brief explanation of what the project is and what we are being asked to fund; 5) our evaluation of the proposal and the arguments leading to that recommendation. (Kathleen Cerveny)

The board sees a summary of each proposal, plus an executive summary. The summary is a two-page analysis of every decision and the details of every discussion. (David O. Egner)

The board reviews summaries of all proposals, even if they are likely to be turned down. Board members can review any full proposal they want. (William V. Engel)

The board gets a two- to three-page write-up and a budget summary. The write-up includes details of the proposed project and measurable outcomes for the grant. Program officers serve as advocates for the applicant and answer board members' questions. (Bruce Esterline)

Our board reviews the staff write-ups of the proposals, which can sometimes be almost as long as the proposals themselves. However, they can review the proposal itself if they ask for it. The board makes the ultimate decisions on grant requests. (Julie Farkas)

For major, multiyear grants, we will invite the executive director, board chair or a board member if the board chair is not available, and a client of the program for a one-hour visit with our trustees. There are very brief opening remarks from the agency. Then our board members start asking questions. There is usually a rollicking exchange. (David Ford)

We are a bit different from many foundations in that each of our trustees acts as the program officer for the applicants from their geographic area. For decisions, all of the trustees receive a summary along with the actual proposal and attachments. I don't prepare a recommendation. If trustees have questions, they will either ask me or the trustee who knows the organization best. We have a very collaborative process. (Laura H. Gilbertson)

Our board members are actively involved in joining our executive director in meetings with prospective grantees. In preparation for board meetings, the board receives the applications as well as attachments and notes from the meeting. If the request is complex, they will be given additional information. (Jane Hardesty)

The board makes all grant decisions. Six weeks before the board meeting, board trustees receive proposal summaries (usually ten or twelve at a time and each eight to 20 pages in length) accompanied by a ballot describing the proposal and the staff's recommendations. The trustee has four options: 1) approve; 2) decline; 3) ask for a consultant review; 4) discuss. Ballots are mailed back to the office in advance of the meeting so that we have a summary of the proposal votes by the time of the meeting. Probably one-third are unanimous decisions and two-thirds are subject to discussion (no unanimous vote). This ballot process is a way to structure our grant agenda. The trustees get a list of those proposals that are outside of our guidelines; these are called "staff declines," and these actions are ratified by the board. (Marilyn Hennessy)

Our board is directed by John Griffin, the founder of the Foundation. He runs a hedge fund and makes good judgments quickly. He also asks solid questions. He takes a hands-off approach to the day-to-day activities, but gets involved in the major funding decisions. Our grants are made on a rolling basis, so we don't have a scheduled board-review process. (Matthew Klein)

Board members get materials a week to ten days before the board meeting. There will be a consent agenda for smaller grants or recommended turndowns. Board members spend most of the discussion time on the larger grants. They will see a summary of the proposal with the full narrative. For grants over $100,000 we may ask one or two people from the organization to come in and sit down with us to answer questions. (David Palenchar)

After the staff has eliminated the proposals that don't fit our guidelines, the board begins its review process: first, by reading the entire proposal and completing the evaluation sheet that is also available to the grantseekers; then by discussing each proposal with the other board members. Through consensus, they decide which groups should be invited to make a presentation at the granting session. The groups are also invited to listen to the other presenters, as well. I cannot do nearly as effective a job presenting an organization's work as the person who wrote the proposal or a representative of that organization can do. I can put it in context, but there's no way I can do it justice. That is the grantseeker's job.

This process is important because our foundation does not conduct site visits. What we hope to accomplish by having grant applicants come in and make a presentation to the board is to be able to see if they are able to answer questions that we may have about their project and to elaborate further on things that they did not have the space to include in their proposal or tell us about changes that have happened since writing the proposal. We also want to meet the people behind the organization. This is a way to build community between the board of trustees and the presenters. Finally, they are also invited to witness the board's deliberations at the end of the day. Here is where they can see and hear for themselves why they were funded or why they were not. The last agenda item of the day is the evaluation of the entire session in which all presenters are invited to participate. This transparent and open process is part of our practice of nonviolence. We really do believe in breaking down the walls between the grantmaking community and the grantseeking one. (Karen Topakian)

Do you meet with prospective grantees, and if so why?

Yes. The visit helps clarify ideas about the project, the operation, and the nonprofit's board. (Peter F. Bird, Jr.)

This has always been tremendously important to us. For prospective grantees, we always visit them at their site in the community because the leadership, staff and location are all critical to our decision-making process and, ultimately, the program's success or failure. (Julie Farkas)

The relationship starts with what is on paper, but we have to get to know the grantseeking organization. The visit occurs after the full proposal has been submitted. (Marilyn Gelber)

We often meet with organizations that are new to us, when there is a new director, or new staff, or a new program. We also may request a meeting if a program or proposal is especially complex. (Victoria Kovar)

We find that visits with prospective grantees enable us to come away with a clear view of the organization. We are able to better learn the merits of the project this way. (J. Andrew Lark)

What do you look for in the course of a site visit?

I have to say that I look for a sense of energy and excitement about the work being done at the site. For example, I like to see clients being treated with respect and kindness, and staff operating with a sense of purpose and an ability to solve problems. If I visit an early childhood center, I want to see that the place is clean and spacious enough for the children. If I tour a center that is providing job skills to low-income individuals, I like to step inside a classroom for a few minutes. I'm not going to move through anyone's facilities or offices wearing a white glove to test for dust, but I can get a better sense of whether the applicant can and will do what they are committing to in the project by scheduling a visit. I never drop in; I would feel as though I were being inconsiderate if I did that. A site visit can sometimes tell you just how enthused the executive director and staff are about the project—is it just a way to get more money to keep the doors open, or does it represent a passion for this work? (Anne Corriston)

We want to see the program in action and understand what it is they are trying to do. (David O. Egner)

The executive director will decide what they think is important for us to see. We want to observe programs in action, and get a sense of the climate of the organization. We want to see classes in session, that people are motivated to be there, and whether the place has a vibrancy to it. Figuring this out is more of an art than a science. (David Ford)

For large grants, we usually do a site visit. It gives us a general sense of the organization and those running it. We look at the environment and attempt to get to know more of the key people involved with the organization and the program. We are very interested in the quality of the staff and in meeting key volunteers, as appropriate. We also get a sense of the organization's capacity to manage the proposed project. (Carol Kurzig)

The site visit is really important. We can tell if a program is "gussied-up" for the occasion. We learn things you can't from the written proposal. We get a sense of the atmosphere beyond the written page. The best proposal will not tell you the staff is unhappy. But if you are a good judge of people, you can get that from the site visit. The site visit gives us a direct look at the agency. (Ilene Mack)

We get a sense of the work environment. If clients are there we get to see who's there, how busy it is, and who is being served. It is helpful to acquire a hands-on feel for the work. We get a flavor of what the organization really does. (Rick Moyers)

We want to see that what is written in the proposal matches up with the activities actually taking place on site. (David Odahowski)

Whom do you want to meet with representing the grantseeking organization?

Typically I meet with the executive director because he or she usually has the most complete information about a proposed project, outcomes, budget, partner relationships, and other important details. If the executive director is too busy to meet with me or to return my call, it is usually an indicator that the grant project is not all that important or that there are other internal issues that need to be resolved. I am always glad to meet with other staff or a board member, but I do want to make sure the executive director is in the loop. (Anne Corriston)

There is no formula. As a rule of thumb we want to meet the people actually doing the work. Sometimes it is useful to meet with board members as well. Development people are surely welcome as part of a group visit, but not in the leading role. (Robert Crane)

I want to see the principal managers: executive director, project director, and a board member. The board representative is important because the board has final responsibility for a grant. It speaks volumes if the board member is aware of the request, can talk about what is being done, and supports the staff. (Bruce Esterline)

I prefer to have the program leadership and staff present at the meeting. Volunteers who are important to the delivery of the service should also be present. And graduates of the program are the best sales people; so organizations should try to include them. (Julie Farkas)

We ask the agency to bring no more than three people, representing both board and staff. We want to know about the direction of the agency and its leadership. (Jane Hardesty)

It depends on the nature of the proposal. The project director and staff can describe the bigger picture and where the work is going. Whether we want to talk to a representative of the board depends on the size of the organization. It is nice to know that the board is supportive and involved. Professional fundraisers seem to get in the way during these meetings. (Robert Jaquay)

It is up to the organization whom they bring to the meeting, but we are interested in the leadership team, mainly management staff. We want to meet the founder, key staff, and board members. (Matthew Klein)

The executive director gives us the overall view of how things are going with the agency, tells us what issues they are facing, and about funding challenges. That is,—he or she provides a "macro" picture. We may ask the executive director questions about the agency's audit. It is also helpful to talk to a board member about the frequency of board meetings and what the board's role is at the agency. We will ask them questions about their strategic planning efforts. It is helpful to see how committed they are to learning about the agency from a board member's perspective. We are looking for a connected, energized, knowledgeable board. Those are the kinds of groups we want to partner with. If there is a specific program the agency is seeking to fund, we look for the program person to be in the meeting as well. This is the individual who has charge of the day-to-day operations of the program. We can gauge whether or not he or she is committed and capable of running the program. Sometimes we sense a disconnect between the program person and the executive director as to how the program might optimally be designed or operated. (J. Andrew Lark)

I leave it to the discretion of the agency. (David Palenchar)

On a site visit, I want to see clients, patients, students, or whoever else relies on the organization's services. It is to the nonprofit's advantage to set up the visit for a day when people will be there, yet this doesn't always happen. (Karen Rosa)

I usually try to meet with the key people for the project to be funded. This could be the project director along with the executive director. Having a board member present can be helpful in order to judge how well the board and executive director are in sync regarding the strategic goals for the agency. I try to avoid meeting with development directors, since they are not as knowledgeable about the agency as are the executive and/or project directors. (John Williams)

Do you have any tips for nonprofits preparing for a meeting with your foundation?

Approach the meeting with the assumption that the grantmaker has read the proposal. Don't go through the information in detail. Rather, spend time building on the information in the proposal. Expect hard questions, especially about strategic planning decisions. (Danah Craft)

Become familiar with the foundation: our guidelines, what we fund; look at the most similar grant recipients. Talk to other grantees that have worked with the foundation. Treat the meeting like a job interview. Show how your proposal fits within the foundation's interests. Try to promote a good exchange of views and ideas. Be able to answer all kinds of questions about your agency and the proposed project. Finish by identifying the next steps in the application process. (Bruce Esterline)

The visit is not intended to be social. Don't waste time getting coffee and donuts. The meeting is essentially about the program. Be prepared to have a serious discussion on why and how you will measure effectiveness. We want to see your program in operation, and gain a better understanding of what you do. (Marilyn Gelber)

Good advice is to ask the grantmaker what to prepare for the meeting, and don't do it at the last minute. The best prepared people simply show us that they go about everything they do with high standards for themselves. We want to see not only the work being considered for funding, but also evidence that the agency is a high-functioning organization. (David Grant)

To make the most out of the meeting, call and ask the grantmaker who should be there. Find out the agenda in advance. This is a clarifying process and provides context for the meeting so that it doesn't become just a "pro forma" exercise. (Robert Jaquay)

Give us details on the program model: what challenges do you anticipate, what advantages do you foresee? What is your relationship with others in the field? Discuss the organization's strengths and be open about its weaknesses or uncertainties. (Matthew Klein)

Bring materials to move the conversation forward. If appropriate, bring financial information. Be prepared to discuss and answer questions about the proposal. (Victoria Kovar)

With web sites so informative today, we do find that grantseekers come to meet us with a much greater knowledge and understanding of the Avon Foundation than five years ago. We have come to expect that groups we meet with will be well informed about our funding interests, priorities and procedures. It's important to have the right people at any meeting. The senior manager in charge of the program under consideration is key. And we like to meet leadership volunteers, as well as clients who can personally describe what the organization has meant to them. Ideally, they should put together a proposed agenda for the meeting and share it with us in advance so that we are all focused on the same meeting objectives and have realistic timeframes and goals in mind that are already agreed upon. (Carol Kurzig)

The site visit should be viewed as a constructive give-and-take discussion. The nonprofit's representatives should not feel defensive about the program. We ask programmatic questions to try to gauge how the project might unfold. We may make a suggestion such as, "have you considered this aspect?" Along with a constructive dialogue with the funder, it's important to be responsive. Send a letter following the site visit. The site visit should occur on a typical day when normal activities take place. The grantmaker should be flexible when scheduling the site visit in order to see clients and meet the people who will run the program. (J. Andrew Lark)

Be prepared and be professional. Let us know what to anticipate beforehand. Make sure there is an agreed-upon agenda prior to the visit. Make sure that all the people who said they will be there are there, if at all possible. I try to set the tone—very informal—so that the conversation is not stiff and awkward. It doesn't help to be nervous. I don't want people to feel that they are being tested. (Ilene Mack)

The grantseekers should assume that the program officer has read the materials and is going to have specific questions related to the proposal. Often grantseekers launch into their standard speech, which is sometimes lengthy, without giving me a chance to ask any questions. I will probably come to the meeting with three or four things I want to ask about. In the best meetings, the grantseeker asks at the beginning of the meeting how we should spend the time. It's also best not to distribute large packets of materials. Offer to provide copies if the person shows interest or requests a document, but every program officer won't need a complete packet of organizational information for every meeting. (Rick Moyers)

Be prepared but not overly so. It's good to go with the flow. Both parties learn from the meeting and become aware of new information. The best such meetings result in an "A-ha!" moment. (David Odahowski)

The organization has to be prepared overall to answer questions about what it put in the proposal. Organizations often call in advance to find out what the grantmaker is going to ask. (Elizabeth B. Smith)

What trends are you seeing?

Government Oversight of Foundations and Other Nonprofits

There is anxiety over what is happening in Washington. We're all wondering if there are going to be additional requirements for private foundations. (Peter F. Bird, Jr.)

I am concerned about oversight and scrutiny from Washington, but I don't know that it has changed the way we operate. We did a thorough governance and management review in December 2003. We looked at every policy and procedure. We added a few things such as a whistleblower's policy and a principles statement. In terms of our grantmaking process, we were already very rigorous. There is such a fine balance between making sure you've dotted the i's and crossed the t's on the letter of the law while still giving the grantee the flexibility within their program mission to do things creatively. (David O. Egner)

We have always been transparent in our processes and strive to be extremely accountable to our community. (Julie Farkas)

There is a movement for more transparency and for more honest communication and partnership with grantees. (Victoria Kovar)

There is a need for greater transparency. Everybody needs to keep administrative overhead within reasonable means. Self-policing is a good thing, if we all do it. (J. Andrew Lark)

The scrutiny from Washington has not translated into changes in grant giving. (Rick Moyers)

I am concerned about corruption. There is a heightened awareness leading to transparency. Sarbanes-Oxley has led to more accountability. (David Odahowski)

The oversight from Washington has led to more accountability. (Leslie Silverman)

Leadership Transition in the Sector

I am very concerned about staff burnout. When you lose staff, you lose very important historical information. Training new staff takes time and resources. If you don't train staff adequately, you are setting them up to fail. (Julie Brooks)

Some people stay in their jobs too long since there is not a lot of opportunity to move around. (Robert Crane)

We need to begin to focus on transition, especially with regard to retirements. We need to bring the next generation along, especially on the board. (William V. Engel)

The succession of founders is a golden opportunity to gracefully merge organizations. A part of good succession planning is to raise that question. (David Grant)

In foundations where trustees are connected to the founder, trustees are the decision makers. The next generation of trustees may have a different perception of their role. In foundations with a long history and less direct connection to the founder, my sense is that the staff is the driver and has a stronger decision-making role. (Marilyn Hennessy)

There is a lack of talent. Executive directors tend to burn out. There needs to be leadership development, recruitment, and transition plans. (Matthew Klein)

It's a generational thing. People of differing ages obviously bring their respective experiences. Some of the younger people coming into grantmaking have an array of technical expertise but may lack extensive practical experience. At the same time there is burnout phenomenon among veteran foundation people because the outside demand coupled with the high level of responsibility results in a pressure-producing situation. How can we attract younger generations and honor their work in the nonprofit sector? There needs to be an examination of the core values that are expected of them and more training to offset burnout. (Marvin McKinney)

I am concerned about the stability of leadership above anything else. (Rick Moyers)

Baby boomers are getting ready to retire. Often there is no number two in place and no transition plan. (David Odahowski)

People don't stay in these jobs as long as they used to. There is turnover with no succession planning. Younger people are not getting involved or willing to work for nonprofit salaries. (Christine Park)

More people are coming into the industry right out of college. They are choosing philanthropy as a career. (Michele Pritchard)

There is a leadership crisis. It's a simple question of supply and demand. (Vincent Stehle)

Nonprofits are trying to get people with more competence and credentials to work for them. (E. Belvin Williams)

Leadership transition is a huge issue for the field. (Nancy Wiltsek)

There is increasing "buzz" around succession planning. Nonprofits must demonstrate that they are able to address it. (Bob Wittig)

Asset Fluctuation

With regard to family giving, the generational transfer of wealth is taking place. Younger family members are more involved in their foundations and are changing the focus of what they give to. Older generations are having to learn to let go. All of this causes competition on boards. (Danah Craft)

There is more money in the foundation world today, and grants are substantially bigger. That trend has led to more rigorous analysis of the work and greater accountability requirements for grantees. (Robert Crane)

Foundation endowments are still recovering from the bad hit the stock market took in 2001-2002. (Maria Mottola)

There is uncertainty in the life of some foundations. Corporate mergers cause a shrinking of donor bases and put pressure on everyone. (Rick Moyers)

Some funders are paying off long-term commitments and staying away from making them in the future. They are focused on their ability to make grants in the current year. (David Palenchar)

Some funders will have more resources in the future. Assets are getting stronger, and endowments are growing. (Elizabeth B. Smith)

One caution: not all endowments have come back. (E. Belvin Williams)

Collaboration among Funders

We partner with other grantmakers to leverage funds. We ask ourselves how we can make a difference and get to the "tipping point" of greater impact. (Julie Brooks)

Strategic partnering among grantmakers goes on informally all the time. (David Ford)

There are increased partnerships among grantmakers, because the problems and challenges we wish to address are too big and complex for any single organization to handle. These partnerships are not exclusively public or private. Although some grantmakers still like to keep their prerogatives close to the chest, I think the majority are beginning to work together. (David Grant)

There is a lot more collaboration among grantmakers, which I think is a good thing. We all have something to learn from one another. (Ilene Mack)

We are brokering a variety of resources such as other funders, technical assistance and knowledge sharing. (Leslie Silverman)

Grantmakers are forming partnerships with other foundations and corporations for projects that are worth doing. (Vincent Stehle)

Targeted Giving

Grantmakers increasingly are looking to make grants that have some measurable impact in areas they care about. They are making more grants for special projects and grantmaking initiatives, and moving away from general support. (Kathleen Cerveny)

Corporations are more focused in their giving. (Danah Craft)

There is a more narrowly targeted approach to grantmaking in the community. (Marilyn Gelber)

Grantmakers are more strategic and proactive in making grants. They desire to make a difference in a directive way. At a recent retreat, we focused on where we are as a grantmaker and how to balance this with being responsive to an agency's needs. (Jane Hardesty)

There seems to be a trend among foundations to define the problem and the solution and to have fewer and fewer dollars for support of ideas generated by nonprofits. (Marilyn Hennessy)

There seems to be a move away from supporting intermediary organizations and giving instead for those providing direct service. (Ilene Mack)

Fewer foundations are accepting unsolicited proposals. This means foundations are not as accessible to grantseekers. (Maria Mottola)

Grantmakers need to narrow their focus areas in order to be more strategic in terms of business interests. This moves a number of funders away from "general societal needs." (Christine Park)

We are shapers, not implementers. This requires that funder and grantee have a clear understanding of expectations. Fewer grantmakers are making grants for general operating support. Grantmakers are engaged as partners with nonprofits on certain projects while helping grantees define benchmarks. (Leslie Silverman)

I wish more grantmakers would provide general operating support. (Lita Ugarte)

Grantmakers are cutting back on their geographical coverage and focusing their area(s) of interest more narrowly. (E. Belvin Williams)

Evaluation of Grantmaking Effectiveness

How do we measure effectiveness? We ask the applicant to tell us how they will measure their own effectiveness. Sometimes we have to prod them to be more deliberate and precise about what they are going to evaluate. But ultimately, our grants are only as good as the people we fund. (Bruce Esterline)

There is increased interest in program evaluation. Well-run nonprofits are getting more sophisticated about doing this. (David Ford)

Grantmakers and grantseekers can get so deep into evaluation that it causes resources to be pulled away from basic services. (Robert Jaquay)

Grantmakers should measure their own performance and be more accountable. (Matthew Klein)

I see increased accountability around grantmaking; are we making a difference? (Elizabeth B. Smith)

Funders are realizing the importance of evaluations and outcomes. They actually expect to hear something back from their grantees regarding the impact of their grants. I notice that nonprofits are stepping up in this area. (Lita Ugarte)

Proliferation of Nonprofits

Financial pressures have forced nonprofits to look at mergers as a survival strategy. It is an example of taking the high road for nonprofit boards to do this. How does this affect grantmaking? This requires sophistication on the part of the grantmaker. Grantmakers can facilitate mergers, but they have to look at the viability of a combined organization. (Peter F. Bird, Jr.)

The proliferation of nonprofits is really becoming burdensome, and it is a huge waste of money. Grantseekers should sublimate their egos and work together. (Kathleen Cerveny)

Even before 9/11, there was a proliferation of nonprofits. Many were duplicating services in the community, competing for a finite set of dollars. I remain concerned about the duplication of services and the amount of money being spent on overhead within the same community. Organizations are merging to create efficiencies, but some are disappearing. They can't survive without a diversity of donors. (Danah Craft)

Nonprofits have to consider mergers and "transformational" collaborations. How do you operate differently in this changed environment of funding? You've got to be ahead of the game and think about the future. Innovation is going to be key to this sector in the next decade. (David O. Egner)

There is increased competition for dollars among nonprofits. There are so many good agencies and not enough money. (William V. Engel)

The number of nonprofits competing for limited dollars has led to conversation about mergers and consolidation. It is hard to keep going the way we are. The current trend is toward talking about merging, though, not doing it. (David Grant)

There is a proliferation of nonprofits, but many of them are critical and are doing good work. (Maria Mottola)

We don't need more nonprofits. (David Palenchar)

Withdrawal of Government Support for Nonprofits

I am concerned about government cuts. Nonprofits are expected to pick up the demand for services previously provided by the government. (Julie Brooks)

Federal and state support has been withdrawn from core services in the community. This has put a lot of pressure on the nonprofit service provider. (Kathleen Cerveny)

There has been continuous refocusing of government priorities and funds. Many nonprofits receive a significant percentage of their support from government sources. So the loss of one or two public funding streams can be disastrous. Privatization of so many government programs, which is increasingly being used across our system, has often resulted in shredding the safety net, and it takes a long time to repair it. (Bruce Esterline)

Nonprofits are seeking alternative solutions due to the change in government support. Unfortunately, foundations and individuals in the community can rarely fully replace government funding or sustain organizations in the long-term. (Julie Farkas)

There has been a serious reduction in government dollars available to the civic sector. Nonprofits and government expect that private funders will pick up the slack, but the nonprofit sector lacks the taxing authority. That is why those who are most vulnerable look to their government for recourse. A frightening development is the conscious effort not to fund health or human services. The privatization movement is equally frightening. (Ruth Shack)

There are increased financial pressures due to the loss of government funding. Nonprofit organizations are undercapitalized, and many have cash-flow problems. (Elizabeth B. Smith)

With regard to the cuts in government support, nonprofits have to be more creative and strategic to piece together funding streams that are sustainable. (Bob Wittig)

Need to Expand Donor Bases

Since funding is so limited, more agencies are fighting for the same dollars. (Julie Brooks)

Nonprofits should strive for greater diversity in their funding streams so they can survive changes in their donor base. (Danah Craft)

Nonprofits have to rely more on the individual donors. (William V. Engel)

With shrinking government grants, for many nonprofits, it is becoming harder and harder to secure long-term, sustainable funding. When considering huge expansions or capital campaigns, it is critical for nonprofits to be realistic in terms of the availability of sufficient funding for both the expansion and the sustainability of the organization. Most nonprofits are looking in the right places—foundations, corporations, congregations, individuals—but the funds are highly competitive and limited. (Julie Farkas)

So many nonprofits are seeking money that funders can't keep up with the demand. It is getting harder and harder to raise money. (Marilyn Hennessy)

Money is tight for all nonprofits. (Victoria Kovar)

Building communication and fundraising capacities have received too little attention in the nonprofit sector. I notice this every day. Nonprofits need to find a way to hold on to fundraising professionals. (Rick Moyers)

Nonprofits are being more creative about how they fundraise and capture different types of support. One example is in-kind support. (Lita Ugarte)

Importance of Strong Nonprofit Boards

The role of an effective board cannot be underscored. It is evidence of the leadership capacity of the organization. (Rene Deida)

It is harder to find good board members. And there is more demand for committed board members than there used to be. At the same time people are saying they can't serve on the board due to time constraints, especially if they have young children. (William V. Engel)

We hear more and more from our grantees that they understand the impact of a well-functioning board, but are having trouble finding the people willing and able to put in the time required to address the needs of the organization as a whole. (David Grant)

I am seeing better prepared executive directors and board members, but there is still a great need for enhanced board member development and training. (Ilene Mack)

I have noticed a lack of people of color on governing boards. Nonprofit boards need to be more diverse. (Marvin McKinney)

Good boards are important, and organizations should not undersell the role of the board member. More is being demanded of board members these days. They cannot perform this function casually. (Nancy Wiltsek)

Other Commentary

There has been increased discussion about philanthropy: Is it a business or is it not a business? Should it come from the head or come from the heart? I would hope that we don't forget the service aspect of what we do. Foundations are working as hard as they can to try to be conscientious with the resources that are available to them. (David Palenchar)

There has been an increase in the number of grantmakers issuing RFPs. There need to be clear sets of guidelines for these. There is limited capacity to review everything that comes in. (Elizabeth B. Smith)

There is a communication overload. Even though technology has helped with proposals, it has streamlined only part of the process. There is a crush of e-mail, voicemail, and snail mail. The expectation that grantmakers can be responsive to all of it is overwhelming. (Vincent Stehle)

Would you share some final words of advice with grantseekers?

It is critical to develop a relationship with the grantmaker. (Peter F. Bird, Jr.)

Innovation is going to be key to this sector in the next decade. Grantseekers need to be ahead of the game and think about the future. (David O. Egner)

It's important to listen for the "no." Know when to stop and read the tea leaves. Respect what people are saying to you. (A. Thomas Hildebrandt)

Remember that program officers are human beings. People like to be liked. They like their own ideas better than other people's ideas. They want to have a good reputation in their professional field. At the same time they don't want to be bored. They want to work on innovative projects. All of these things have implications for how you will interact with a funder and what the program officer is thinking about. (Matthew Klein)

Since it is our job to give away the money, we want an agency to come with the best idea for the community, and we want to put them at ease. Nonprofits should be confident about their program. Keep in mind that we want to be partners with you. (Victoria Kovar)

Be aware of your public image. Good program work and a credible reputation in the community are more important than any written proposal. Be sure your web site and materials reflect who you are. (Maria Mottola)

Fundraising should be confined to the work environment. Approaching grantmakers in the grocery store puts them in an uncomfortable position. They have to react off-the-cuff. (Christine Park)

It makes our job easier if grantseekers do the following: 1) fill out the application form; 2) provide current information on the form and in the proposal; 3) be sure the web site address works; and 4) give us current information on people, such as telephone numbers and extensions. (Michele Pritchard)

We really want to be open to all comers. We find that we get fresh ideas this way. (Vincent Stehle)

Appendix A: Sample Proposal

Comprehensive Youth and Family Services

Proposal Submitted to

THE EARLY RISER FUND

By

William Sullivan, President and CEO
Ronald McDonald House of New York City
405 East 73rd Street
New York, NY 10021
Tel: 212-639-0500
Fax: 212-744-8922
Email: wsullivan@rmdh.org

Executive Summary

Research demonstrates that keeping children and their families together during cancer therapy alleviates physical and emotional stress, thus increasing the rate of successful treatment and recovery. The Ronald McDonald House of New York (RMH) House offers a compassionate and supportive environment where families can remain together during a child's cancer treatment and maintain their unity and stability during a period of profound crisis.

Occupancy at the House—85 rooms—is limited to families who cannot afford the high cost of prolonged hotel stays and who are referred to us via social workers at one of the 12 oncology centers with which we partner. In 2005:

- 1,271 patients stayed at the Ronald McDonald House of New York City
- 635 siblings stayed at the House—an average of 1 per family
- 1/3 of patient stays were for a period of one year; another third for several weeks.

Our RMH staff and volunteer team provide fun, enriching and cultural activities that provide a much needed break from the exhausting days of cancer treatment. Further, we provide educational services such as arts and crafts, homework help, music lessons, a recreational teen program, and a computer technology program to the youth in the house. To further support these children and their families, RMH offers mental health counseling services, stress reduction classes, and maintains a Chaplain on staff to provide spritual and emotional support while organizing various activities.

Our professional team has identified additoinal opportunities to strengthen our programs and services so they are responsive to the more complex needs of our guests:

- Hiring a Child Life Specialist to oversee playroom youth activities and professionalize our staff's ability to interact with and respond to the children;
- Offering new educational and tutorial services for both young cancer patients and their siblings; and
- Providing new and better support services such as workshops and informational materials for both incoming and longstanding guests at RMH to help them to deal with the many issues associated with childhood cancer and its treatment.

It is our hope that The Early Riser Fund will consider a grant of $50,000 in support of our new Comprehensive Youth and Family Services. Thanks to your generous partnership, this initiative will greatly expand and enhance our ability to respond to the needs of an entire family—including parents and siblings—living at RMH while a youngster receives life-saving cancer treatment.

Need For Comprehensive Youth And Family Services

RMH is fundamentally designed, both in its physical structure and through its mission, to provide affordable shelter and physical resources for cancer patients and their families during treatment in New York. Over time, we have developed a number of recreational, educational, mental, and emotional support services in order to make our families' time here more comforting and more supportive.

Patient stays at the House have increased over the past decade, thanks in part to new drugs and therapies that can prolong a child's life. While lengthier stays are contributing to an improving cure rate, we are seeing some new challenges.

First, because families are choosing to remain together during stays that can last as long as a year or more, financial, psychological and educational burdens are increasing. According to parent surveys some of the key concerns for caregivers staying at the House are:

- Breaking a family up; deciding who stays behind and who travels to New York
- Financial burdens including lost wages, travel and living expenses

- Uncertainty or lack of confidence about who is handling household affairs at home
- The need of a patient's sibling(s) for attention and support

Second are siblings who are accompanying children and parents or caregivers for stays at RMH. Often referred to as "the forgotten population" at the House, the siblings of cancer patients have also been uprooted from their homes, friends, and schools, and spend much of their time either at RMH or at the hospital. In some cases cancer patients have become so immunodeficient that their sibling cannot attend school for fear that he or she will contract bacteria or viruses there. Because families' resources are so devoted to the child with cancer and the treatment itself, oftentimes the siblings feel forgotten and neglected. Many siblings exhibit negative behavior both at school and at the House; their grades may slip and their behavior become antisocial.

Parents themselves are underserved as well. Many parents, due to language barriers or improper education on the subject, are not aware of the variety of resources available to support them through their child's cancer treatment. Parents come to rely on hospital staff and social workers who they do not necessarily see every day, and certainly not 24/7, to identify their needs and steer them in the direction of resources and support. Furthermore, parents are so focused on the health of their sick child, that they are not able to take care of themselves emotionally and physically so that they can best care for their families.

RMH's guests already have relationships with social workers, doctors, and teachers, so it is not RMH's intent to duplicate these services. However, RMH is a place where many issues surface in part because it is a place where families can relax and let their guard down. The need to stabilize and preserve the family is always a priority for RMH as new programming is being developed and longstanding programs are being improved upon. Ensuring that families are able to communicate and support each other while receiving the outside support they need during this critical time is critical to the emotional well-being of the patients, their siblings, and their parents as well as to the success of the treatment. While undergoing life saving cancer treatment, it is important to do so under the best possible circumstances. RMH tries to create as comfortable, supportive, and productive environment as possible for its guests by making certain that family units remain intact while away from home.

Project Description: Comprehensive Youth And Family Support Services

The Comprehensive Youth and Family Support Services currently in development at the House form a three-pronged approach to providing for our families. These services will:

1) Provide new tutorial and educational support services specifically geared towards the siblings of cancer patients who are currently housed at RMH, while simultaneously making available extra educational support for patients;

2) Professionalize our staff through the addition of a Child Life Specialist, who will have the background and certification to properly identify and respond to the varied social and emotional issues our guests exhibit; and

3) Offer new programs for parents and families that will provide helpful literature and better education in how to cope with cancer treatment, while at the same time helping families to form closer bonds and better support each other.

It is especially important that our new Comprehensive Youth and Family Support Services remain flexible because it is so hard to anticipate how many children, parents, and siblings will require these services at any given time. The reality at RMH is that our population is itself flexible: roughly 1/3 of our families stay with us for only a few weeks, whereas 1/3 remain for months and 1/3 reside at RMH for a year or longer. Therefore, it is important that we have programs in place designed to respond to needs as they arise and on a case-by-case basis.

These programs will ideally begin with the calendar school year and continue year-round. The tutoring and educational programming, in particular, will be maintained year round to accommodate students who may fall behind during the regular school year and need to use the summer months to catch up on their studies.

OUR NEW COMPREHENSIVE YOUTH AND FAMILY SUPPORT SERVICES WILL INCLUDE:

Tutoring and Education for Siblings and Youngsters:

Ronald McDonald House of New York City refers siblings of patients who remain at the House for an extended stay to nearby P.S. 158, Wagner Junior High School or Eleanor Roosevelt High School. RMH plans to offer tutoring and educational services on a regular basis during non-school hours geared specifically towards the siblings of cancer patients. Not only will this help siblings to remain current on their schoolwork, and help them to continue to progress academically despite their difficult circumstances, but will be instrumental in communicating to the siblings that they are not neglected, forgotten, or secondary. Based on the ever-changing number of guests, tutorial services will be designed to accommodate different sized populations. The goal is to have tutors available who can help siblings on a case-by-case basis, with a focus on the critical shortage areas of Math and Science and on enhancing students' test scores. The tutors will also focus on the areas that have been identified as specifically needing attention amongst the RMH population, such as: Reading & Reading Comprehension, Language Arts, Science, English, and English as a Second Language. The curriculum for these subjects will be prescribed by the School Board so that the work the RMH children are doing parallels that of their peers. While these services will be designed with the siblings of cancer patients in mind, they will also be able to accommodate young patients who are well enough not to require constant hospitalization and need extra help with their schoolwork.

Students will be directed to our tutorial service both upon arrival and as need arises during their stay. Upon arrival, each parent and child is given information regarding the educational services available to the student by their appointed Social Worker. Each child is then given a proficiency test in Math, Science, and English. If the child does not score well enough on this test, they will be referred to a tutor. Tutoring is provided on a one-to-one basis.

RMH will seek tutors with NYC teaching certificates as well as an additional reading specialist. Once tutors are hired with sufficient experience and credentials, they will participate in Board of Education seminars specifically designed to equip educators with the necessary skills to deal with the needs of terminally ill patients. Once the tutors have completed these seminars, they are not only prepared to tutor in the structured program RMH is developing, but they will be certified to teach Home Instruction for the students who are more critically ill than others.

In addition to funds needed for these tutors' salaries, this program will require funding for space and equipment, as RMH does not currently have an area designated for educational purposes. The tutors will need a base of operations to store supplies and books, and the children will benefit greatly from the atmosphere a separate, quiet, official educational space will provide. RMH has recently completed renovations to its facility and two libraries have been incorporated into the new design with these new tutorial services in mind. The addition of two libraries will give the students a quiet, structure place to study and learn while also allowing RMH staff to keep different age groups separate when necessary.

Addition of a Child Life Specialist:

The addition of Child Life specialist to RMH staff will create a more collaborative effort between families, health care providers, and RMH.

Child Life specialists do not operate independently, but rather work with parents and health care professionals to ensure that all of the developmental, educational, and therapeutic needs of patients and their families are being met. Frequently, Child Life Specialists employ techniques such as art and play therapy to help young children express their emotions and deal with frustrations in a healthy and productive way. The goal of all of the services a Child Life specialist provides is fourfold: 1) to increase understanding of the stress and unfamiliarity of a hospital and treatment experience; 2) to recognize and nurture the bonds and strengths within each family unit; 3) to provide emotional support; and 4) to promote normal growth and development of all members of each family as well as the family as a whole.

The addition of a Child Life Specialist to our staff will mean that RMH will be a place where families not only live, but where they can rest assured that there is a capable professional who can address the needs of families and refer them to the appropriate support. The Child Life Specialist will also refer residents to RMH's counselor, Dr. Mark Roberts, or our Chaplain, Cherilyn Frei, dependent upon whether their problem may need clinical or spiritual attention. Additionally, the Child Life Specialist will help ensure that hospitals and schools are aware of the needs of RMH's families.

Parent and Family Programs:

RMH plans to improve its ability to foster bonds within families so that parents and children can help each other through this difficult time. As a facility, RMH exists so that families can remain intact during cancer treatment away from home, as research has shown that keeping children and their families together during cancer therapy alleviates physical and emotional stress, thus increasing the rate of successful treatment and recovery.

It is not enough simply for RMH to provide a space for families to live during cancer treatment. Many families arrive at RMH and are never properly made aware of the options and resources available in support of their struggle with cancer. Foreign families, especially, are not familiar with the recreational, educational, and emotional resources the hospitals and schools have to offer.

- Welcome Packets: It is important to us that each family' transition to RMH is as seamless, comfortable, and supportive as possible. In the next year, RMH plans to develop a comprehensive welcoming packet for the incoming guests. These packets will include various educational materials, early intervention materials, and information on the various services available at RMH such as information on the libraries and the computer programs. The Direct of Human Services at RMH will conduct orientation programs about the House for the parents, which will take them through these packets, the facility, and will outline the support services available to them and their children.

- Cancer Care Workshops: Additionally, RMH plans to reinstate and expand upon its ongoing, regular "Cancer Care" workshops faciliated by New York City-based Cancer Care Inc. and are designed to help parents and entire families understand and deal with the complex psychosocial aspects of dealing with cancer. Families need support in coping and identifying the foreign emotions and emotional responses associated with dealing with life-threatening illness. These workshops will help families understand that their responses to stress are normal and that there are many resources available to help them cope. Furthermore, this setting will provide opportunity for families to interact with people sharing similar experiences, giving them the opportunity to form beneficial and lasting bonds with other guests. These workshops cover topics such as "Medical Update on Childhood Cancers", "Childhood Cancers and Family Dynamics", and "Cancer, Loss, and Grief". RMH hopes to reinstate such workshops on a quarterly basis to provide our families with a supportive setting in which they may educate themselves about cancer on a regular basis. Workshops are lead by certified counselors and social workers from the organization "Cancer Care" as well as a Nurse Practitioner from one of the area's medical facilities.

STAFFING

Supervision of workshops and tutorial services and development of materials will be the responsibility of our Director of Volunteers and Services, Ralph Vogel. Mr. Vogel has been employed by the Ronald McDonald House of New York City since 1996, serving during his tenure in a senior supervisory staff capacity. Mr. Vogel is currently responsible for the planning and provision of all direct services to families.

The Child Life Specialist will provide all services described above. The successful candidate will hold a Bachelor's or Masters Degree as well as a certification in Child Life or a degree in Psychology. This educational background and certification allow them to assess the psychological, emotional, and developmental progress and status of each child and prescribe the appropriate therapeutic response as problems arise.

All services will be supervised by William Sullivan, President and CEO of the Ronald McDonald House of New York City since May 2005. Previously, Mr.

Sullivan served as Assistant Scout Executive and Chief Operating Officer of the Boy Scouts of America, where he was responsible for both the Finance Division and Field Services to a membership of over 120,000 youth in the five boroughs.

EVALUATION

The Ronald McDonald House programs are evaluated by the feedback received from the children and families who stay at the House. House meetings are held throughout the year where families can discuss topics that relate to daily life. Topics include: youth and family programs, special events, volunteer and staff involvement, and implementation of new activities.

Volunteer Feedback: We encourage feedback from our volunteers. This past year, RMH compiled feedback from our volunteer survey. From the surveys turned in, we found that:

- 50% of volunteers have been volunteering at RMH for 5 years or more — an especially high rate of retention for volunteers;
- Half of our volunteers also volunteer at another non-profit agency; most of them finding RMH to be the most rewarding experience;
- When asked how satisfied they were in being a volunteer at RMH and how rewarding of an experience it has been for our volunteers, the average response was between 4.5 and 4.7 out of a possible 5.0.

Family Feedback: Our ability to offer affordable accomodations for our families is one of our greatest successes. Much of our positive feedback can not be quantified. Anecdotal feedback from our families, the frequency with which we observe them attending our special events and taking advantage of the programs we offer, and the lasting relationships that we maintain with them even after they have left the House and treatment has ended are some of the ways we see results and know that we are achieving our goals. However, with regards to our educational and tutorial programming, RMH will be able to measure effectiveness and results based on individual student internal progress reports as well as reports and tests generated by the Board of Education.

SUSTAINABILITY

The Ronald McDonald House of New York City raises approximately $5 million annually, with one-third of its support donated by independent owner-operators of McDonald's Restaurants in the Tri-State Area; the agency receives no financial support from McDonald Corporation itself. The remaining two-thirds is secured through fundraising acvitities including:

- Annual Board Campaign, through which the agency secures 100% participation of individual directors;
- Fundraising Events, including an Annual Dinner, Skate-With-The-Greats in partnership with the NY Rangers and a Golf Outing;
- Direct mail and major individual gifts;
- The Early Riser Fund and corporate grants in support of general operations as well as special projects.

Our goal is to secure $173,250 in restricted contributions from The Early Riser Fund and corporte grants to underwrite the first year of the Comprehensive Youth and Family Services Program. Beginning next year, we will begin to cover program expenses through 1) sustaining grants and 2) allocated income from the aforementioned annual fundraising activities.

BUDGET

Satff

President and CEO	5% Supervisory	$ 7,500.00
Director of Volunteer Services	20% Direct Service	20,000.00
Child Life Specialist	100% Direct Service	75,000.00
Tutors	Part-Time ($35/hour)	35,000.00
Fringe Benefits	30% FTE	30,750.00
Total: Staff		**$168,250.00**

Other Than Personnel Services

Training for Tutors	$ 5,000.00
Welcome Packet (design/printing)	15,000.00
Copying	2,500.00
Postage	2,500.00
Workshops/Events	5,000.00
Total: Other Than Personnel Services	**$30,000.00**

Total Expenses	**$173,250.00**

Organizational Information

In 1978, the Ronald McDonald House of New York (RMH) doors opened to families with children undergoing cancer therapy in New York City. Families come to stay at the House after their child is diagnosed with cancer and is referred to a New York City medical center for last resort treatment. In 1993, due to an ever increasing demand for our services, which always exceeded available space, the House moved to a new location; housing 83 families per night, our facility makes us the largest pediatric oncology facility of this kind in the World.

Our mission is to keep each child's life outside the hospital as normal as possible by providing the comforts of home and interaction with others who are in a similar situation. Throughout its history, RMH has provided a compassionate and caring "home away from home" for over 50,000 families dealing with childhood cancer. Our staff includes 22 full-time employees and 12 part-time staff members. In addition, 105 weekly volunteers work in different capacities within the House. Additionally, many volunteers are fluent in foreign languages such as Russian, Korean, Spanish, and Greek, a vital resource for our international guests, who often have a difficult time communicating in English. The volunteers come from all walks of life, and are of great assistance to the families as they go through a difficult time.

The Ronald McDonald House of New York maintains partnerships with a number of health, religious and educational organizations across New York City. Our visitors receive treatment at a 12 medical centers located in New York including, Memorial Sloan-Kettering Cancer Center, The Mount Sinai Medical Center, and New York Hospital-Cornell Medical Center, all of which have been designated as "comprehensive cancer treatment centers" by the U.S. Department of Health and Human Services.

Conclusion

The Ronald McDonald House of New York City is a resource of first choice for its partnering oncology treatment centers who must find affordable housing and a supportive, enriching environment for their young patients and their families. For nearly 30 years, the House has provided a level of comfort, care and compassion second to none. Recognizing changing needs and emerging challenges, we too recognize the opportunity to better both our services and care. We welcome the support of The Early Riser Fund as we look to become a stronger partner and resource for our guests and contribute to the quality of life for youngsters living with cancer.

Appendix B:
Selected Resources on
Proposal Development

Anderson, Cynthia. *Write Grants, Get Money*. Worthington, OH: Linworth
Publishing, 2001.
> This is a proposal-writing guidebook for school media specialists and other
> K–12 librarians who wish to improve library programs and facilities. Written
> for novice as well as veteran proposal writers, the book covers all stages of the
> proposal-writing process. Appendix includes samples and a glossary.

Barbato, Joseph and Danielle S. Furlich. *Writing for a Good Cause: The Complete
Guide to Crafting Proposals and Other Persuasive Pieces for Nonprofits*. New York,
NY: Simon & Schuster, 2000.
> The authors share practical instructions about the art and craft of writing
> related to fundraising proposals, as well as case statements, newsletters, and
> other communications devices used by a typical development office. Includes
> glossary.

Barber, Daniel M. *Finding Funding: The Comprehensive Guide to Grant Writing*.
2nd ed. Long Beach, CA: Bond Street Publishers, 2002.
> This handbook provides advice for writers of proposals to government
> agencies, foundations, and corporations. The book includes a section on
> responding to a request for proposals and instructions for creating a letter
> proposal. Includes glossary.

Burke, Jim and Carol Ann Prater. *I'll Grant You That: A Step-by-Step Guide to Finding Funds, Designing Winning Projects, and Writing Powerful Grant Proposals.* Portsmouth, NH: Heinemann, 2000.
> The main part of the book is organized according to the sections of a proposal and covers project planning as well as proposal development. The book also explains how to write a letter of inquiry. Each chapter concludes with a checklist. The appendices contain a glossary and sample proposals.

Carlson, Mim. *Winning Grants Step by Step: The Complete Workbook for Planning, Developing and Writing Successful Proposals.* 2nd ed. San Francisco, CA: Jossey-Bass Publishers, 2002.
> This workbook contains instructions and exercises designed to help with proposal planning and writing and to meet the requirements of both government agencies and private funders. Provides a special resource section that includes how to research funders, how to evaluate a proposal through the funder's eyes, and a bibliography.

Chapin, Paul G. *Research Projects and Research Proposals: A Guide for Scientists Seeking Funding.* New York, NY: Cambridge University Press, 2004.
> Directed to scientists who wish to design and write proposals to funding agencies. Includes project planning, information about specific government funders (as well as more general recommendations about researching private foundations), and grants management. Includes glossary and index.

Clarke, Cheryl A. *Storytelling for Grantseekers: The Guide to Creative Nonprofit Fundraising.* San Francisco, CA: Jossey-Bass Publishers, 2001.
> Clarke puts forward the notion that proposals share much with great stories: characters, setting, and plot. She shows proposal writers how to craft documents that include elements of drama. The book also covers the research process and cultivation. Includes a sample letter of inquiry and sample budgets, as well as information on packaging the proposal.

Collins, Sarah, ed. *The Foundation Center's Guide to Winning Proposals.* New York, NY: The Foundation Center, 2003.
> The guide reprints in their original form 20 proposals and four letters of inquiry that succeeded in securing foundation support. Each proposal is accompanied by commentary by the funder who awarded the grant and proposal writing advice.

Margolin, Judith B. and Gail T. Lubin, eds. *The Foundation Center's Guide to Winning Proposals II*. New York, NY: The Foundation Center, 2005.
> A companion to the *Guide to Winning Proposals*, volume II includes more than 30 new proposals from some of the nation's most influential funders. Each proposal, reprinted in its entirety, includes a critique by the decision-maker who approved the grant. In addition to cover letters and budgets, volume II includes winning proposals for general operating support, special projects, seed money, evaluation, capacity building and other needs.

Geever, Jane C., Liliana Castro Trujillo (trans.), and Marco A. Mojica (trans.). *Guía para escribir propuestas*. New York, NY: The Foundation Center, 2003.
> A Spanish translation of *The Foundation Center's Guide to Proposal Writing*, 3rd ed. Includes an appendix of technical assistance providers who will assist Hispanic nonprofits.

The Gill Foundation (http://www.gillfoundation.org/usr_doc/NashvilleCARES2.pdf) has a proposal submitted by Nashville CARES available in PDF format. The sample grant is punctuated throughout with useful comments by the Gill Foundation, pointing out what the grant decision-makers liked about this "clear, concise, and simple" proposal.

Hall, Mary Stewart and Susan Howlett. *Getting Funded: The Complete Guide to Writing Grant Proposals*. 4th ed. Portland, OR: Portland State University, 2003.
> Hall explains the components of a standard proposal, with advice about project development and researching funders. This edition includes a recommended syllabus for those who teach proposal writing.

The Idea Bank (http://theideabank.com/onlinecourse/samplegrant.html) has a number of proposals available online for fire and safety organizations (indicating which ones have been successfully funded).

Miner, Jeremy T. and Lynn E. Miner. *Models of Proposals Planning & Writing*. Westport, CT: Praeger, 2005.
> Provides a step-by-step strategy for creating proposals and other documents for applying to both private funders and government agencies. The models that are reprinted include a letter of intent and a complete proposal to private foundations, as well as a preliminary and final application to the U.S. Department of Education. The book also explains how grantseekers can assess a request for proposals.

New, Cheryl Carter and James Aaron Quick. *How to Write a Grant Proposal.* Hoboken, NJ: John Wiley & Sons, 2003.
> The authors cover the key elements of standard proposal formats, including the executive summary, need statement, project description, evaluation, and budget. Each chapter contains examples and checklists.

Nonprofit Guides (http://npguides.org) has sample proposals, a proposal cover letter, cover sheet, letter of inquiry and budget, and other useful items.

Orlich, Donald C. *Designing Successful Grant Proposals.* Alexandria, VA: Association for Supervision and Curriculum Development, 1996.
> The author presents the standard elements of proposal writing, with checklists at the end of each section. Includes a copy of a funded proposal and a reading list.

Quick, James Aaron and Cheryl Carter New. *Grant Seeker's Budget Toolkit.* Hoboken, NJ: John Wiley & Sons, 2001.
> In this guidebook on project budgets, the authors explain the calculation of direct costs, with chapters specifically describing personnel and travel costs. The book also discusses the estimation of overhead and indirect costs and elaborates on the entire budgeting process, including writing the budget narrative. Sample budget worksheets are included.

Robinson, Andy. *Grassroots Grants: An Activist's Guide to Proposal Writing.* 2nd ed. San Francisco, CA: Jossey-Bass Publishers, 2004.
> The writer provides step-by-step guidance on how to create successful proposals, design projects, and manage grants. Several sample proposals are included.

School Grants (http://www.k12grants.org/samples) offers a number of education-focused, successful, sample proposals. Most are directed to corporate or government funding sources and are downloadable in PDF format.

Wason, Sara Deming *Webster's New World Grant Writing Handbook.* Hoboken, NJ: John Wiley & Sons, 2004.
> Covers project planning, funding research, proposal development, and writing. A sample proposal is included. Includes glossary and index.

Wells, Michael K. *Proven Strategies Professionals Use to Make Their Proposals Work.* (Grantwriting Beyond the Basics Series). Portland, OR: Portland State University, 2005.
> Provides a treatment of specialized concerns related to the proposal, such as evaluation methods, project development, researching the need section, and effective use of attachments. Includes one sample proposal, bibliographical references, and index.

W. K. Kellogg Foundation. *Evaluation Handbook.* Battle Creek, MI: W. K. Kellogg Foundation, 1998. (http://www.wkkf.org/Pubs/Tools/Evaluation/Pub770.pdf)
> Part one outlines the W. K. Kellogg Foundation's expectations for evaluations by grantees, and part two delineates the steps in project evaluations.

Wholey, Joseph S, Harry P. Hatry, and Kathryn E. Newcomer, eds. *Handbook of Practical Program Evaluation.* San Francisco, CA: Jossey-Bass Publishers, 2004.
> Each chapter is contributed by a specialist. The book is divided into sections on evaluation design, practical data collection procedures, data analysis, and planning and managing for maximum effectiveness. Indexed by name and by subject.

York, Peter. *A Funder's Guide to Evaluation: Leveraging Evaluation to Improve Nonprofit Effectiveness.* St. Paul, MN: Fieldstone Alliance, 2005.
> Evaluation is one capacity-building tool that funders can put into practice, and the book explains how the process can be implemented. Noting that both nonprofits and foundations benefit from this management tool, York provides step-by-step methods and many sample worksheets for assessing grantees. Includes bibliographic references and index.

Appendix C:
Resources of
The Foundation Center

From searchable online directories of funding sources to grantseeker training courses to research reports on the philanthropic and nonprofit sectors, the Center provides a full spectrum of fundraising and educational resources.

The Foundation Center's award-winning web site, foundationcenter.org, is the leading online information tool for grantseekers, grantmakers, researchers, the press, and the general public. Registered visitors gain access to a world of valuable information geared to their region and fields of interest. In addition, the Center's web site features *Philanthropy News Digest* (PND), the daily source for the latest philanthropic news, reviews, requests for proposals, and job openings.

Please note: you may order any of the Foundation Center's publications and subscription services at foundationcenter.org/marketplace, or by calling (800) 424-9836. For the most current details on any Foundation Center resource, please visit our web site, foundationcenter.org. These are some of the highlights.

Online Directories

FOUNDATION DIRECTORY ONLINE
Updated weekly, *Foundation Directory Online* is the nation's premier grantseeking database.

For top-tier intelligence, *Foundation Directory Online Professional* provides four searchable databases: Grantmakers, Companies, Grants, and IRS 990s. It includes detailed profiles of U.S. foundations, grantmaking public charities, and corporate donors, as well as hundreds of thousands of recently awarded grants, and key contact names. Each Professional database includes up to 19 indexed search fields plus keyword search capability.
$179.95/MONTH; $1,295/YEAR

To meet the needs of grantseekers at every level, *Foundation Directory Online* offers multiple subscription plans.

Platinum—complete profiles of all U.S. foundations, grantmaking public charities, and corporate giving programs; recent grants; trustee, officer, and donor names.
$149.95/MONTH; $995/YEAR

Premium—complete profiles of the top 20,000 U.S. foundations; recent grants; trustee, officer, and donor names.
$59.95/MONTH; $595/YEAR

Plus—complete profiles of the top 10,000 U.S. foundations plus recent grants; trustee, officer, and donor names.
$29.95/MONTH; $295/YEAR

Basic—complete profiles of the top 10,000 U.S. foundations; trustee, officer, and donor names.
$19.95/MONTH; $195/YEAR

All plans of service are available with monthly, annual, and two-year subscription options. Every plan includes links to foundation web sites and IRS returns, flexible search options, customer support, and direct access to the subscribers' electronic message board. Annual and two-year subscribers receive substantial discounts on Foundation Center publications. For complete details and to subscribe, visit fconline.foundationcenter.org

CORPORATE GIVING ONLINE
This directory, updated weekly, provides the fastest, most accurate path to America's corporate funders. It includes detailed company profiles, descriptions of company-sponsored foundations, key facts on direct corporate giving programs, and summaries of recently awarded grants. With three databases, subscribers to

Corporate Giving Online can search companies, grantmakers, and grants.
$59.95/month; $595/year
TO SUBSCRIBE, VISIT CGONLINE.FOUNDATIONCENTER.ORG.

FOUNDATION GRANTS TO INDIVIDUALS ONLINE
This unique directory, updated quarterly, is focused on foundations that provide
support to students, artists, researchers, and other individuals. Updated quarterly,
it includes nine search fields. Foundation profiles include name, address, and
contact information, fields of interest, types of support, and application
information. One-month, three-month, and annual subscriptions are available.
One month: $9.95.
TO SUBSCRIBE, VISIT GTIONLINE.FOUNDATIONCENTER.ORG.

Annual CD-ROM Directories

FC SEARCH
The Foundation Center's Database on CD-ROM contains in-depth profiles of U.S.
foundations, grantmaking public charities, and corporate donors. *FC Search*
includes detailed funder profiles, descriptions of recently awarded grants, key
contact names and addresses, and links to current IRS 990-PF returns. It's the first
choice for grantseekers who appreciate CD-ROM convenience.
SINGLE USER LICENSE: $1,195, INCLUDING UPDATE DISK.

GUIDE TO OHIO GRANTMAKERS ON CD-ROM
Profiles of thousands of grantmakers who support nonprofits in the state. Includes
grants awarded to Ohio nonprofits or from Ohio-based funders. Single-user: $125

GUIDE TO GREATER WASHINGTON, DC GRANTMAKERS ON CD-ROM
Details on grantmakers focused on supporting nonprofits within greater
Washington, DC. Includes grants awarded to nonprofits in the Washington, DC
area or from funders in the region. Single-user: $75

DIRECTORY OF GEORGIA GRANTMAKERS ON CD-ROM
Details on grantmakers focused on supporting nonprofits in the state. Includes
grants awarded to nonprofits in Georgia or from funders within the state.
Single-user: $75

DIRECTORY OF MISSOURI GRANTMAKERS ON CD-ROM
Profiles of grantmakers in the state or with an interest in supporting Missouri
nonprofits. Includes descriptions of recently awarded grants. Single-user: $75

Annual Print Directories

THE FOUNDATION DIRECTORY
This classic directory profiles the 10,000 largest U.S. foundations. Key facts include fields of interest, contact information, financials, names of decision-makers, and thousands of sample grants. Indexes help you quickly locate your best leads. $215.

THE FOUNDATION DIRECTORY PART 2
Broaden your funding base with details on the next 10,000 largest foundations. Each year, up to 2,000 new entries are added to this annual directory. Includes thousands of sample grants. $185.

THE FOUNDATION DIRECTORY SUPPLEMENT
This volume provides updates for hundreds of foundations included in the *Directory* and *Directory Part 2.* New entries include changes in financial data, contact information, and giving interests. $125.

GUIDE TO U.S. FOUNDATIONS: THEIR TRUSTEES, OFFICERS, AND DONORS
This three-volume set features detailed information on key decision-makers, including their affiliations. Each entry includes foundation assets, total giving, and geographic limitations. $395.

NATIONAL DIRECTORY OF CORPORATE GIVING
The most comprehensive information available in print on America's corporate donors. Complete profiles feature giving priorities and background on each company. $195.

FOUNDATION GRANTS TO INDIVIDUALS
The only directory devoted entirely to foundation grant opportunities for qualified individual applicants. Includes contact information, giving limitations, and application guidelines. $65.

GRANT GUIDE SERIES
Twelve subject-specific directories of grants awarded to organizations in particular fields of interest. Each *Grant Guide* includes Subject, Geographic, and Recipient indexes. $75 each.

Fundraising Guides

FOUNDATION FUNDAMENTALS
A popular textbook for nonprofit management courses, this volume provides beginners with a thorough overview of the funding research process. Includes a concise explanation of U.S. foundations and their role in the funding community. $24.95

THE FOUNDATION CENTER'S GUIDE TO PROPOSAL WRITING
Our best-selling Guide includes comprehensive instructions on crafting breakthrough grant proposals. Includes interviews with funders, revealing the latest trends among decision-makers in evaluating proposals. Available in print and audio CD. $34.95

GÚIA PARA ESCRIBIR PROPUESTAS
The Spanish-language translation of *The Foundation Center's Guide to Proposal Writing.* $34.95

THE FOUNDATION CENTER'S GUIDE TO WINNING PROPOSALS
Twenty actual proposals that were approved and funded by leading grantmakers. $34.95

THE FOUNDATION CENTER'S GUIDE TO WINNING PROPOSALS II
This Guide features 31 actual examples, reprinted in their entirety. Each proposal includes a critique by the decision-maker who approved the grant. $34.95

Nonprofit Management Guides

WISE DECISION-MAKING IN UNCERTAIN TIMES
Edited by Dr. Dennis R. Young, this book provides practical guidelines for nonprofits coping with escalating demand for services, economic downturns, and reduced government funding. $34.95

EFFECTIVE ECONOMIC DECISION-MAKING BY NONPROFIT ORGANIZATIONS
Practical guidelines to advance your mission while balancing the interests of funders, trustees, government, and staff. Edited by Dr. Dennis R. Young. $34.95

INVESTING IN CAPACITY BUILDING

Author Barbara Blumenthal shows nonprofit managers how to get more effective support, and helps grantmakers and consultants design better methods to help nonprofits. $34.95

THE BOARD MEMBER'S BOOK

Author Brian O'Connell shows how to find and develop the best board members and executive director, with strategies for fundraising and financial planning. $29.95

PHILANTHROPY'S CHALLENGE

Author Paul Firstenberg explores the roles of grantmaker and grantee within various models of social venture grantmaking. $39.95, hardcover; $29.95, softcover

SECURING YOUR ORGANIZATION'S FUTURE

Author Michael Seltzer explains how to strengthen your nonprofit's capacity to raise funds and achieve long-term financial stability. $34.95

AMERICA'S NONPROFIT SECTOR

Author Lester Salamon defines the scope, structure, and operation of the sector, and examines its relation to government and the business community. $14.95

BEST PRACTICES OF EFFECTIVE NONPROFIT ORGANIZATIONS

Author Philip Bernstein focuses on procedures that help practitioners define goals, adhere to mission, and respond to change by adjusting operations and services. $29.95

Research Reports

FOUNDATIONS TODAY SERIES

Published annually. The series includes:

- ***Foundation Giving Trends:*** *Update on Funding Priorities*—Examines grantmaking patterns of a sample of more than 1,000 large U.S. foundations and compares current giving priorities with previous trends. February, $45

- ***Foundation Growth and Giving Estimates:*** *Current Outlook*—Provides estimates of foundation giving for the past year, and final statistics on actual giving and assets for the previous year. Presents new top 100 foundation lists. April, $20

- ***Foundation Yearbook:*** *Facts and Figures on Private and Community Foundations*—Documents the growth in number, giving amounts, and assets of all active U.S. foundations since 1975. June, $45

COMPLETE SERIES AVAILABLE FOR $95 WITH FREE SHIPPING.

THE PRI DIRECTORY: CHARITABLE LOANS AND OTHER PROGRAM-RELATED INVESTMENTS BY FOUNDATIONS

This indexed directory lists leading providers and includes tips on how to seek out and manage PRIs. $75

SOCIAL JUSTICE GRANTMAKING

Providing quantitative benchmarks of grantmaking priorities, geographic distribution of funds, and giving by foundation type, this report includes grants awarded for civil rights, educational reform, and community development. $24.95

CALIFORNIA FOUNDATIONS

A Profile of the State's Grantmaking Community

Based on a Foundation Center survey, this report covers the latest foundation trends in California. It illuminates critical issues facing the state's funders, and includes an essay on the overall health of California philanthropy. $24.95

On-call Research Assistance

ASSOCIATES PROGRAM

Our members-only service for fundraisers. To find the best funding prospects and develop the most compelling proposals, let our research staff do the legwork for you. They have access to the full spectrum of Foundation Center databases, biographical information, studies, and reports on the field. For more information, call (800) 634-2953.

EDUCATIONAL SERVICES

Full-day training courses—The Foundation Center takes an interactive approach to sharing its wealth of information in classrooms coast-to-coast, fostering team-building through small group exercises and topical discussions. As a participant, you will learn the latest strategies to address the challenges facing grantseekers, and share your experiences with other nonprofit professionals from your region. Course topics: Fundraising Fundamentals, Proposal Writing, Nonprofit Management.

Online training courses—Designed for any nonprofit professional who wants to become a more effective grantseeker, our online courses provide self-paced lessons, interactive exercises and assignments, case studies, and a final exam. Course topics: Grantseeking Basics, Proposal Writing.

Contract training—Schedule as many full-day classroom training courses as your team needs, and the Foundation Center's experts will present in the location you prefer. This special service includes course materials and publications.

Free basic training—If you want a brief overview of some of the most popular topics for grantseekers, introductory courses—from 60 to 90 minutes—are presented at no cost in each of our regional centers, listed below.

REGIONAL CENTERS

For current information on foundations and corporate donors—with expert library assistance-visit one of our five regional centers in New York, Washington, DC, Atlanta, Cleveland, and San Francisco. Our extensive network of Cooperating Collections provides free access to the Center's online and print directories, fundraising guides, nonprofit management books, periodicals, and research findings on U.S. philanthropy.

To view the complete list of Cooperating Collections in all 50 states and Puerto Rico, visit foundationcenter.org/collections/

LOG ON TO FOUNDATIONCENTER.ORG

Continuously updated and expanded, the Foundation Center's web site is visited daily by tens of thousands of grantseekers, grantmakers, researchers, and others who are interested in the world of philanthropy. Find answers to your questions about seeking funds, nonprofit management, and how to start a nonprofit organization. Search recent IRS 990s at no cost. Check statistics on U.S. foundations, their assets, distribution of their grant dollars, and the top recipients of their gifts. Search the Catalog of Nonprofit Literature, our comprehensive bibliographic database, or look up a foundation-sponsored report on a topic of interest in PubHub.

The Foundation Center provides a host of free and affordable services and information resources—all focused on strengthening the nonprofit sector's ability to serve its constituents. Take a moment to register at our site, foundationcenter.org. It's free—and each time you log on, you'll find information tailored to your interests and geographic region.

You may order any of the Foundation Center's publications and register for training courses at foundationcenter.org/marketplace, or by calling (800) 424-9836. For the most current details on any Foundation Center resource, please visit our web site, foundationcenter.org.

About the Author

Jane C. Geever is chairman of the development consulting firm, J. C. Geever, Inc. The firm, founded by Ms. Geever in 1975, was the first woman-led fundraising company admitted into membership in the American Association of Fund Raising Counsel (AAFRC).

Among her achievements, she assisted in the creation of the certificate program in fund raising at New York University, spearheaded the first jobs bank at the National Society of Fund Raising Executives' (NSFRE) International Conference and New York NSFRE's Fundraising Day, and was appointed to the Independent Sector's ad hoc committee on Values and Ethics. Ms. Geever is a member of the advisory council for the national project *Funding Fundraising* at Baruch College and is active in Independent Sector's *Give Five* program in New York. She has been a member of the board and officer of the NSFRE Institute and of the AAFRC. Ms. Geever is also an instructor at Columbia University's Master of Science Program in fundraising management.

Ms. Geever holds a master's degree from the New School for Social Research, and she has done post-graduate study in business management at Stanford University. She delivered the May 1989 commencement address at the 71st commencement of her alma mater, Seton Hill College in Greensburg, Pennsylvania, at which time she received an honorary Doctor of Humane Letters degree.

Ms. Geever is a nationally recognized author and lecturer. She teaches seminars in association with the Foundation Center on proposal writing and approaching foundations and corporate funders.